maruhari (arrae-er) 9-22-04

Approaches
to Asian Civilizations

Approaches
to Asian Civilizations

Edited by

Wm. Theodore de Bary
and
Ainslie T. Embree

Columbia University Press
New York and London 1964

About the Editors:
Wm. Theodore de Bary is Professor of Chinese and Japanese and chairman of the Committee of Oriental Studies at Columbia University. He is the editor of *Approaches to Oriental Classics, Sources of Chinese Tradition, Sources of Indian Tradition,* and *Sources of Japanese Tradition.*

Ainslie T. Embree is Assistant Professor of History and executive officer of the Committee of Oriental Studies at Columbia University. He is the author of *Charles Grant and British Rule in India.*

The editors of this volume are also editors of *A Guide to Oriental Classics.*

Preface

Probably few persons who take up this book will need to be persuaded of the importance of Asian studies in college education. Since World War II, they will have witnessed the rising importance of Asia in world politics and recognized the need of our educated citizens for a better grasp of the forces involved. Or they will at least have felt discomfort in classroom or parlor conversation when it touched on areas of Asian experience, unfamiliar to them, which have suddenly become common points of reference in such fields as economic development, psychoanalysis, the study of religion, literature, and so on. Indeed, so rapidly has our consciousness developed of the need for greater understanding of Asia, and so widespread the effort to meet it—through all levels of education, through state and federal programs, through international exchange, through the intense competition among publishers for Asian materials—that the problem is no longer how to stimulate action in favor of Asian studies, but rather how to guide these burgeoning efforts in the right direction.

The papers contained here, and presented earlier to a conference at Columbia University of two hundred American college teachers, represent the thinking on this question both of Asian specialists and of scholars eminent in various disciplines (but not "area" specialists) who appreciate the significance of Asia to their own discipline. They have been asked to explain that significance particularly in terms of education in the liberal arts for undergraduates who may not take up Asian studies as a career, and yet should acquire, before they leave college, some basic familiarity with how Asian peoples have lived and what they have lived for.

The underlying assumption of such a discussion is that Asia, once a specialized subject of "area study," has now entered the sphere of general education. To some persons, this latter term may suggest catch-all courses and an almost unlimited license to teach, preach, or philosophize about human life. To us, however, the requirements of general education are certainly no less strict than other forms of instruction or learning. In fact, to distill what is most essential in human terms from the mass of accumulated knowledge of Asia imposes heavy limitations and a severe discipline on the instructor. To help him in this demanding task of selection and evaluation, the judgment of specialists responsive to this great challenge to contemporary education can be invaluable.

Another condition which we have had to accept for purposes of this discussion is the impracticability of agreeing in advance on the precise terms of the topic. What exactly does "Asia" represent? How does one define "civilization"? These questions were necessarily left open for exploration. One might accept the definition of civilization offered herein by Professor Wittfogel as referring to "the totality of the cultural conditions (ideas and beliefs) of a given country," which for his own purposes he distinguishes from "society": "the totality of its institutional conditions." Or one might follow the view of Professor Berry that a civilization represents a "dynamic equilibrium of many forces that are constantly interacting upon one another" and that "we have no adequate way of describing the unity that is observable in this process of change." In either case, one must admit the inexhaustible complexity both of "civilization" itself and of the methods by which we must seek to understand it. Hence the need to approach the subject from as many vantage points as our various scholarly disciplines afford and to proceed inductively toward a conception of what civilization represents. Each of the papers presented here is meant to enlarge our own understanding of the problem, without presuming to settle it for all time.

For purposes of our discussion, diverse conceptions of Asia had also to be considered. It has become almost anathema to speak of Asia as a unity, so conscious are scholars of the distinctiveness of its various civilizations and the superficiality of most generalizations applied to Asia as a whole. Moreover, given the impossibility of presenting or comprehending all of Asia in a single course, what one chooses to include in one's definition of Asia will vary with one's conception of civilization, and what one selects of the areas and aspects to be dealt with will reflect a diversity of approaches to the problem as well as the inherent diversity of the subject.

Allowing for this, however, our contributors seem to agree that there is a significant interlocking among the major civilizations of Asia, distinct though they may be from one another, and that there is a value in treating several of these together. This is true, substantively speaking, in terms of the common factors affecting the rise of these civilizations and their historical interactions. It is also true, pedagogically speaking, in terms of providing the Western student with a basis of comparison that is not purely Western. Thus, the geographer will show that important "continental" factors such as climate, mountain and river systems, and communications conditioned the development of these civilizations in a similar way; the anthropologist, that there are common features in the prehistoric racial and cultural substrata of Asian civilizations; the historian of religion, that pilgrims and missionaries moving across Asia established important transcultural links among these countries; and so forth. At the same time, even where there is no such historical link and the paths of Asian peoples diverge most widely, the very contrast among them forces us to seek deeper reasons for apparent peculiarities than lie on the surface of native tradition alone, or than would appear from direct comparison with the West.

But it is especially when we consider the Asia of today that we see its traditional diversity yielding to a new unity. As Professor Lerner expresses it with regard to the emerging modern civilization of the Near and Middle East, "The unifying element in the Middle East is not its past but its future. The historic 'sharing' of Muslim learning, Shariya law, Arabic language has shown itself to be a weak link. Far more compelling is the challenge brought home to every Middle Eastern country by the challenge of modernization." In his view, our understanding of this modernization process "goes far beyond the Middle East to include each and all of the great and small Oriental civilizations. It is this understanding that seems worth conveying to an undergraduate who will not be a specialist, for we are concerned with a historic process whose personal consequences are being felt acutely by many hundreds of millions of people outside of the diminutive Western world and will continue to be felt by their children."

Nor is this unity wholly of the future, but also of the present. Already this feeling of common aspiration has produced in Asians a sense of identity strangely in contrast to their past disparity. One recalls the upsurge of "Asian" sentiment at the dawn of the century when Japan's defeat of Russia evoked a passionate response from young Jawaharlal Nehru, "who dreamed of fighting, sword in hand, for 'Asiatic freedom from the thralldom of Europe'"[1] and from the Arab at Suez of whom Sun Yat-sen reported: "The joy of this Arab, as a member of the great Asiatic race, seemed to know no bounds."[2] True, such sentiments have not made of Nehru so much of an Asian that he is kept from looking to the West as well as to the East. Yet their appeal is felt even by the strongly Western-oriented Filipinos, drawing them to the East as well as to the West and, as recent developments in their foreign relations show, prompting them to seek a place for themselves within a specifically Asian framework.

It is probably safe to say that most students today, despite the growing appreciation of Oriental art and their curiosity about Oriental religion, develop an interest in Asia most directly from their concern with the contemporary scene. It is the newspaper

[1] Jawaharlal Nehru, *Toward Freedom* (New York, John Day, 1941), p. 29.
[2] Marius B. Jensen, *The Japanese and Sun Yat-sen* (Cambridge, Mass., Harvard University Press, 1954), p. 117.

headlines that stir them to learn more, and it is a political context into which they most often try to fit their first knowledge of Asia. From my own experience of teaching and lecturing to different audiences, Americans "come alive" in grasping Asian problems the closer one comes to the present and to Western involvement in the picture. This is natural, and most teachers responsible for introductory courses on Asia must inevitably try to satisfy this curiosity at the same time that they seek to go beyond it. No such course can fulfill the purposes of general education if it does not illumine both the present and the past. We must recognize the natural and legitimate interest in current affairs on the one hand; on the other, we must guard against the tendency to think of Asian peoples too much in terms of their direct effect upon our own lives. This was the great error of the pre-World War II period, which proved self-defeating insofar as it was preoccupied with surface phenomena and was unprepared to gauge the real depth and complexity of Asian reactions to the West.

The purposes of a truly liberal or humanistic education will be served only if we accept the peoples and civilizations of Asia, not as factors in the cold war or as means to some immediate practical end but because their experience in living together, what they have learned about life and what they have come to understand about the universe, is now seen as part of the common human heritage. They are to be studied, therefore, as people who can teach us much about ourselves, whose past can give us a new perspective on our own history, and whose way of looking at things challenges us to reexamine our own attitudes.

If this is so, then a course in "world politics" or "international relations of the Far East," whatever its value to specialists, would not meet the need. Something else is necessary to bring the traditional civilization of Asia into significant relation both with the modern world and with the modern student as an individual in a formative stage of his own thinking. But what is it to be? In general, the answer has been of two kinds: one is the establishment of introductory survey courses covering anything from a single Asian civilization to all of Asia; the other is the incorporation of some Asian materials in existing survey courses, converting them ostensibly from Western civilization, history, or literature courses to "world history" or "world literature" courses.

Both of these approaches have been tried and each has its own effectiveness, depending on the circumstances. To choose between them may be a gratuitous exercise. Given the limitations on curriculum and staff at many institutions and the difficulty of adding new courses, it may be argued that any opening for the inclusion of Asian materials in existing courses should be exploited. Such exigency may indeed be seen as a virtue by those who believe that to set up separate Asian courses is only to perpetuate a false dichotomy between East and West. All subjects should be taught on a universal basis, they argue, and there should be none peculiarly "Asian."

There is, however, a considerable gap between the actuality and the ideal here, between the tentative piecemeal inclusion of Asian materials in existing surveys and the full scale assimilation of them that would be required to put our learning and teaching on a truly universal basis. As an ideal to be striven for the latter is perhaps unexceptionable, but as a basis for our present efforts it involves serious difficulties. One of the most fundamental is that even on the most advanced theoretical level our scholarly disciplines are still far from achieving such an assimilation. We have no convenient and accepted framework in which to present world civilization as a whole. Indeed, even the monumental efforts of a few venturesome minds toward working out such a conceptual or theoretical framework have tended to be viewed with skepticism by specialists in each area as failing by far to take into account the complexities and intricacies of the Asian reality. And it is worth noting in this connection that the more advanced Asian nations themselves have not solved this problem in their own educational systems.[3]

[3] Cf. G. D. Parikh, *General Education and Indian Universities* (Bombay, 1959). pp. 132, 188.

Of the practical difficulties confronting the attainment of this ideal in education, certainly the most formidable is the undergraduate's ignorance of Asia and the need for Asia to make a massive intrusion into his mind before he can appreciate how stupendous is his lack. The piecemeal approach may add dashes of color to his intellectual landscape; it cannot truly enlarge his horizons. Only a stay of some length in this new territory will enable him to advance from mere tourism to genuine understanding—so inescapable are the differences in names and terms and the whole orientation of life and thought. Even granting that much more can be done to provide in secondary education the kind of factual information on Asia that is basic to further learning, it may still be questioned whether we can expect that the Western student's preparation for Asia will ever be brought to the level of his knowledge concerning the West. Certainly, few would claim that our students' acquaintance with the Western tradition is already more than sufficient on the high school level, and, therefore, that Asia could take a much larger place without crowding the basic curriculum.

As a sidelight on this question, one should consider the parallel developments in certain Asian countries, notably India and Japan, where educators of a humanistic persuasion have recently deplored the excessively "Western" emphasis in college education. They, too, have come to believe in the need for courses in the Oriental humanities, which would reacquaint students with their own classical traditions. A major infusion, not occasional mention, is their remedy for this deplorable neglect.[4]

A further point of fundamental importance is raised by Herbert Feis when he urges, movingly and cogently, that the student of Oriental civilizations should impose upon himself the requirement of learning a great deal about American civilization as well. "This is not needed by those who study the Orient as a whim or out of

[4] Cf. Yoshikawa Kojirō, *Nihon bummei ni okeru juyō to nōdō* (Receptivity and Activity in Japanese Civilization) (Tokyo, Shinchosha, 1959), chapter 1; "Report of the University Education Committee" (chairman, Dr. S. Radhakrishnan) (Government of India, 1950), pp. 55–63, 66.

intermittent curiosity, or as a collector of art objects and books. Nor by those who intend to remain observers of our relations with the Orient. . . . But a comprehensive and vibrant knowledge of American civilization is vital for anyone who takes an active part in the course or conduct of American relations with the Orient." Thus the knowledge of Asia which Mr. Feis seeks is one based on self-knowledge, and cannot be gained at the expense of education in one's own tradition, by which one becomes truly aware of its strengths and weaknesses. Asian studies, in this view, are not merely a supplement to Western learning but a vital extension of that learning, in its most dispassionate, self-conscious and yet also selfless form. To proceed without this grounding is to risk losing one's way altogether.

One sometimes hears from enthusiastic proponents of Asian studies as an "antidote to Western parochialism" that the proper place for a course on Asia is the freshman year in college. In this way, they contend, one catches the student while he is still "fresh" and unprejudiced by intense exposure to a traditional Western point of view. Actually, nothing could be further from sound educational procedure. Whatever the timing and sequence of undergraduate courses (which may be governed by other practical considerations, extraneous to the issue here), still it is profitless to assume that general education in the Western tradition must be prejudicial to a true understanding of the East. On the contrary, experience shows that a genuine appreciation of one is the best qualification for the other. These two basic needs—an adequate grounding in the major contributions to the development of Western civilization and a substantial exposure to the contributions of Asian civilizations—should be seen, not as incompatible or antagonistic but as complementary and mutually indispensable.

It need not be argued, in favor of such a program, that it satisfies completely the requirements of general education. Europe and Asia do not exhaust the possibilities. Other areas, too, have made their contribution in different ways, and eventually the educated man must learn of them too. But the embracing of all such areas in a single course under the heading perhaps of "Non-Western Civilization" has definite disadvantages. "Non-Western" is essentially a negative concept, suggesting that the primary significance of civilizations outside Europe and North America lies in their difference from the West. Indeed, the seeming impartiality with which so many civilizations are thus equated (actually negated) tends to obscure the true proportions of their respective contributions. The positive significance of Asia in particular tends to be obscured when it is simply lumped together with other areas equally different from the modern West, which by implication becomes the norm for all.

If it seems undemocratic and discriminatory to assign a higher priority (though certainly not an exclusive claim) to the major Asian civilizations, this is nevertheless justified by the greater richness and depth of their traditions, by the historical contributions to and influence upon other peoples beyond their own borders, and by the impressive continuity and stability of their traditional institutions down through the ages. It is little wonder that the natural interest of Westerners today should spontaneously incline them to learn about Asia, for here are the peoples whose technological "underdevelopment" can never be mistaken for immaturity of culture or society. Their social experience—their population problems, their political institutions, their economic dilemmas—in many ways anticipate those of the modern West. Their arts, literature, philosophy and religion in some respects achieved a refinement surpassing our own.

To focus, then, on Asian civilizations in a general education program is only to signify that there is more than enough matter here worthy of the student's attention and reflection, on a level with and as challenging for him as that which he encounters in Western civilization. Global scope—with Russia, Africa, South America, and what not thrown in—need not be the criterion, when to discover any one of the major Asian civilizations is virtually to discover a whole new world, and two or three of them a new universe.

This is most true, however, in approaching the traditional civilizations of Asia, and has less force when it comes to discussion of
contemporary problems. These the Asian nations, new and old,
share with other areas of the world caught up in the process of
modernization and industrialization. To the extent that the contemporary or current-affairs aspect is emphasized in such a survey
course, and especially if one can assume a prior acquaintance with
the traditional civilization involved in the modern transformation, it
is wholly appropriate to view this problem in the context of world-
wide experience with a common trend or process. Even then, however, unless the problem of modernization is examined in the light
of certain specific disciplines, which limit the field of investigation
to manageable proportions by isolating it from other aspects of
civilization, it seems only prudent to focus the discussion on a well-
defined geographic area and thus give greater point to generalizations derived from the wider field.

For purposes of our conference and the proceedings which follow,
Asia has been considered to represent four main centers of civilization: Islamic, Indian, Chinese, and Japanese, and by extension those
regions strongly influenced by each of these civilizations. It was not
our intention thereby to define the components or units of a course
in Asian civilizations, but simply to illustrate in different contexts
the problems involved in such study. In actual practice the possible
combinations of areas are not unlimited. Most colleges with well-
established programs on Asia for undergraduates recognize these as
the major areas, whether they attempt to cover them all in a single
course, separate courses for each area, or some combination such as
the inclusion of China and Japan in the Far Eastern area. The
relative advantages and disadvantages of any such arrangement have
been dealt with elsewhere [5] and were not a topic for discussion at
this conference. Our approach to the subject has been through the

[5] See Eugene P. Boardman (ed.) *Asian Studies in Liberal Education* (Washington,
D.C., 1959); Ward Morehouse (ed.) *Asian Studies in Liberal Arts Colleges* (Washington, D.C., 1961).

various disciplines pertaining to the study of these areas, whether
singly or in combination, hoping that the results might be relevant
to any scheme of organization adopted according to local needs
and capabilities.

Nevertheless, if we have taken the major civilizations of Asia
together, rather than individually, as the scope of our discussion, it
is because they represent a sufficient degree both of unity and
diversity to illumine one another. In these relatively well-defined
areas we may examine the pervasive problems of the ancient agrarian
civilizations, the economic relationships, social arrangements and
political institutions which contributed to the stability and dura-
bility of the most mature Oriental civilizations, and then see these
alongside the comparatively younger, more dynamic and less stable
society of Japan. We have an opportunity also to study the historical
role of the major religious and philosophical traditions—Hindu,
Buddhist, Islamic and Confucianist—as well as those lesser ones—
Jain, Taoist, Shintoist, for instance—which help to underline the
complexity of national traditions and the richness of Oriental
thought in general. This choice of areas has the advantage, too, of
presenting the historical confrontation of these systems with one
another on common ground—in India, Buddhism and Hinduism,
Islam and Hinduism; in China, Buddhism and Confucianism; in
Japan, both of these with each other and with Shinto. Similarly the
adaptations and permutations of a single tradition as it develops in
different historical circumstances may be considered, as for instance
the Confucian tradition in close association with the dominant civil
bureaucratic elite of China, on the one hand, and with the dominant
military aristocracy of Tokugawa Japan on the other. Even the total
absence of something like Confucianism in India acquires unex-
pected significance, when one considers that, lacking it, India was
unable to maintain the bureaucratic continuity and dynastic control
characteristic of China.

In any introduction to Asia, such comparative questions as these
must be considered as suggestive only; they cannot be pursued ex-

haustively for their own sake.[6] Where elements of similarity and difference are seen bound up together, the differences assume greater significance than they would as discrete facts. New meaning attaches to historical or social data that in isolation seem of no importance. And yet this same awareness tells us that thorough-going comparison would lead further and deeper into the labyrinth of each civilization than it is feasible for the nonspecialist to follow. (There is a question, indeed, whether it is feasible even for the specialist, given the present state of our knowledge). Therefore it seems prudent to avoid involvement in any overall comparison of civilizations, and to put primary emphasis on the articulation of each civilization within itself, while yet placing it side-by-side with others and compelling the student to develop a perspective which embraces both.

A proper introduction thus serves the purposes of liberal education in two ways. It broadens the horizons of the mind and liberates it from preoccupation with the immediate. At the same time it opens up new vistas, not in the sense of attaining the heights of knowledge and surveying in lordly fashion a vast domain, but rather in the sense of coming to a new realization of how much there is to be known. One thus appreciates the significance of specialized study for what it can contribute to our overall knowledge and for what painstaking labor is involved in making it available to others. Such an introduction should, then, leave the student eager to know more

[6] Since my views on this question are discussed later by Prof. Hsu, some further clarification is needed. To the making of comparisons I am not in general opposed. These must, however, remain implicit or suggestive only, unless, the comparison, as I have stated elsewhere, "deals with specific features or concepts in each work for which the grounds of comparability are well established and explicitly defined. Comparisons of whole traditions or religions are almost always out of place and have nothing essentially to do with general education." (See my preface to *A Guide to Oriental Classics*). Prof. Hsu's criteria for explicit comparison seem wholly appropriate to me, but time and circumstances do not often allow for such thorough-going analysis in class, and it seems best not to indulge in comparison as a regular practice if these criteria cannot be fully observed. Students are all too prone to glib comparison and it is my experience as a teacher in survey courses (which are particularly beset by this vice) that the instructor as often finds it necessary to restrain or question such judgments as to suggest or stimulate them.

about each of the civilizations he has encountered, rather than feeling that this survey has sized them up for him and he need go no further.

The essays that follow are meant to illustrate both aspects of the study of Asian civilizations referred to above. Some, usually historians or anthropologists, attempt to see each civilization essentially from within, emphasizing growth and development within a single pattern, but making specific comparisons to other civilizations where they shed light on their own. Others, usually representing the social sciences studying the contemporary world, stress general problems or trends that cut across national or historical boundaries. Both of these approaches are combined in the actual teaching of Asian civilizations in America today. There is frequent discussion as to the respective advantages of the historical and topical methods of presenting Asian civilization. In fact both approaches serve a purpose and neither can be dispensed with. A purely historical presentation is almost inconceivable if justice is to be done to the many-sidedness of a civilization. The complexities of social organization, economic problems, political institutions, thought, and religion—to say nothing of literature and the arts—must somehow be compressed into summary form, into generalizations that can serve as footholds for further study. The survey that undertakes an historical account of each such topic will have difficulty getting past 1 A.D. On the other hand, some general historical outline or chronological order of presentation is necessary if the misleading impression of a static civilization is not to be given, if the dynamic interaction of its parts is to be understood. There is the further, quite realistic consideration for most teachers that a chronological order is the simplest common denominator among civilizations and the most reliable framework for the student to hang onto when more complicated structures fail.

In most cases a compromise is worked out whereby either the subject matter is organized in topics presented in some general chronological order, or else major periods or events in the history of a country are used to exemplify characteristic features of the civilization at a formative stage. The precise combination will vary according to the disciplinary qualifications and outlook of the instructor in charge, the availability of specialists to supplement his efforts in presenting certain topics, and—always—the time at his disposal. There is no exact recipe for the combination of ingredients, and the papers here prescribe none. But it is remarkable how much convergence there is in independent judgments of the key topics to be covered in respect to a given civilization. Take, for example, China. Professor Wright has identified what he calls nine "nodal points" or "formative experiences" in the history of China which "encompass the total formative experiences that make a people what they are and not otherwise." There are, as he says, "developments on the economic, political, intellectual and other planes of history which permit each historian to emphasize what he knows best and finds most interesting." Thus the significance of each such stage may be variously interpreted by the individual teacher, but if we may judge from the textbooks or course syllabi used around the country, there is little dispute that one way or another these same key points in Chinese history must be treated in any introductory survey. This is true also, I believe, of the topics singled out by Professor Crane in respect to India and by Professor Craig in respect to Japan. For those charged with planning such courses for the first time in a liberal arts curriculum, it should be reassuring that there is such a concensus to serve as a guide.

A much broader topic of discussion, dealt with most fully by Professor Crane but a recurrent theme in other papers as well, is the distinction between traditional and modern civilization. Here again definitions vary widely among historians like Professor Crane, sociologists like Professor Lerner, and economists like Professors Lockwood and Issawi. Moreover definitions which fit the facts of one civilization such as India may fit very imperfectly in the case, say, of Japan. These discrepancies do not, however, detract from the usefulness of such categories of analysis in provoking the student to think more deeply and to consider on the basis of his total survey the applicability of such definitions to the manifold reality he is studying. For most students, it is the problem of the Asian countries' "coming of age" which serves as the point of their initial interest, and a course which undertakes to discuss the Asian civilizations in these terms will evoke a ready response.

For this reason, at Columbia (and I believe it is broadly true elsewhere), the basic divisions of our Oriental civilizations course are between the traditional civilizations in the first semester and the modernization process in the second semester. In the former we take up the traditional civilizations of India, China and Japan in that order. (For practical reasons Islamic civilization is treated in a separate course, with the same traditional-modern division between semesters). In the second semester the order is not quite so neat. Modern India is presented first, since Western power and influence were exerted there first and most fully. But then Meiji Japan is taken up, as the first example of resurgent nationalism and modernization in Asia, before examining the long process of disintegration in the Manchu empire and the unsuccessful efforts to reconstitute a stable social and political order before the outbreak of full hostilities between China and Japan in 1937. At this point we turn back to Japan, to the struggle between divergent forces in Japanese national life from the first world war to the present. Finally we take up the collapse of Nationalist China and Chinese communism.

We do not feel strongly attached or committed to this particular sequence of chronological periods, and our source readings, which are bound in separate volumes for India, China and Japan, would be adaptable to other schemes of presentation. The important thing for us is that within a general chronological sequence we be able to take up broad movements or broad topics of significance to the development of the civilization as a whole rather than feel obliged to study every aspect of every period.

Parallel with this broad chronological development, which emphasizes institutional and intellectual history, we present at appropriate junctures supplementary materials for discussion and audio-visual illustration. The arts, crafts, architecture and music of Asia may thus be introduced to enliven the proceedings. Special reports may also be assigned to suggest new dimensions of study which the use of standard textbooks might otherwise preclude. Thus, for instance, we have prepared supplementary readings on special "Problems in Asian Civilizations" through which a diversity of views and researches on a single historical or social problem might be examined. In this way the student is made aware of the range of scholarly debate and research which comes into play if, departing briefly from the broad survey method, we pause to examine the microcosm. From this in turn the student may gain insight into the relevancy, depth or superficiality of the survey itself.

At the other pole are writers who deal with Asian civilizations on a macrocosmic scale, such as Toynbee, Wittfogel, Northrop, or even less academically, Koestler ("The Lotus and the Robot"). To introduce these at the beginning, as if to suggest a range of methodological approaches, might well prejudice or distort the picture. There is danger of the student's becoming entranced or entangled in theoretical constructs before he has been exposed to any of the facts. To bring such writers in at the end of a survey, however, gives the student an opportunity to test their constructs against his own new store of knowledge and impressions, to weigh their plausibility in accounting for all the facts, or to gauge the extent of their applicability to certain aspects of Oriental civilizations but not to others. At the same time, of course, in the encounter with such writers he becomes aware of alternative schemes for organizing the information crowded into his survey, and gains some perspective on the original choices made by his instructors in the planning of the course.

For the instructor, however, these choices are not made once and for all at the inception of the course. They must be reviewed constantly in the light of new knowledge in the field and of experience in teaching (experience which more often indicates how much needs to be cut out than what should be added). In a field as underdeveloped and rapidly growing as Asian studies, new knowledge and interpretations compel us regularly to revise the generalizations which are essential to any introductory survey. In this respect all teachers of Asian civilizations face a similar problem of trying to keep abreast of developments in widely varied fields, though no doubt the problem is most acute in smaller colleges where the number of specialists to be consulted is quite limited. It is to meet this never-ending need, that the discoveries of eminent specialists and the views of experienced teachers have been brought together in this volume.

WM. THEODORE DE BARY

Contents

Preface by Wm. Theodore de Bary   v

PART ONE.   HISTORY

Chinese History for the Undergraduate, *Arthur F. Wright*   3
Comment: The Japanese Perspective, *Albert Craig*   14

Indian History for the Undergraduate, *Robert I. Crane*   21
Comment: The Chinese Perspective, *James T. C. Liu*   52

Reflections on the Study of Oriental Civilizations,
    Charles Issawi   57
Comment: Traditional Methods and Modern Needs,
    Hellmut Wilhelm   69

The Spiritual Form of the Oriental Civilizations,
    Thomas Berry, C. P.   73

Ideas and the Power Structure, *Karl A. Wittfogel*   86
Comment: General Theories and General Education,
    Ainslie T. Embree   98
Comment: Generalizations and Chinese History,
    Charles O. Hucker   102

PART TWO.   POLITICS

The Modern Far East and the Undergraduate, *Herbert Feis*   107

Asia in the Study of World Politics, *Harold D. Lasswell*   122

Contents

Comment: World Politics in the Study of the Middle East,
J. C. Hurewitz 134

PART THREE. ECONOMICS

Economic Forces and Social Change in Asia,
William W. Lockwood 145
Comment: The Humanistic Uses of Asian Economic History,
Stephen N. Hay 161

Some Basic Geographical Factors in the Study of Asian Civili-
zations, *Theodore Herman* 170
Comment: Geography and General Education,
John E. Brush 180

PART FOUR. ANTHROPOLOGY AND SOCIOLOGY

Asia via Japan: An Anthropologist's Attempts,
Douglas G. Haring 185
Comment: On Behalf of Comparative Civilizations Through
Intellectual Cooperation Between Disciplines,
Francis L. K. Hsu 208

Basic Problems in the Contemporary Transformation of Tradi-
tional Societies, *Daniel Lerner* 219
Comment: Comparativists and Uniquists,
Richard D. Lambert 240
Comment: Choosing a Position, *Richard K. Beardsley* 246

PART FIVE. GENERAL

The Integration of Asian Studies into the American Undergraduate Curriculum, *Meribeth Cameron* 253

Soviet Approaches to Oriental Civilizations,
George A. Lensen 262

Asian Studies in a Canadian Undergraduate Program,
W. A. C. H. Dobson 266

Contents XXV

PART SIX.   COMMENTS: THE ORGANIZATION OF COURSES

The Self-Image Approach, *Karl Potter* 273

Specialization for Teacher and Student,
  Willis D. Weatherford 276

Compromising on Coverage, *Ellsworth C. Carlson* 279

The Problem of Objectives, *Jackson H. Bailey* 284

Courses and Conferences, *John Meskill* 289

Conference Program 291

Part One: History

Chinese History for the Undergraduate

ARTHUR F. WRIGHT

Charles Seymour Professor of History, Yale University

> In truth, the interest in Far Eastern civilization has but just been awakened; the life of it, its strength, is yet to come. It is because the Far East holds up the mirror to our own civilization—a mirror that like all mirrors gives us back left for right—because by her very oddities, as they strike us at first, we learn truly to criticize, examine, and realize our own way of doing things, that she is so very interesting.
>
> *Percival Lowell, 1886*

A course in the history of China for the undergraduate finds its basic justification in these terms—the development of self-knowledge, understanding of one's own culture through the contemplation of a history that contrasts starkly with that of the West. Other arguments are often stated. Can one, it is asked, justify a "general" or "liberal" education that ignores the longest continuous record on earth of a people's effort to live together and build the good society? Or, and this seems to me more dubious, can we ignore the "background" of one-sixth of mankind, a sixth that appears to pose a threat to world peace? When the history of China is viewed mainly as "background" for understanding Mao and his regime, it will be distorted and undervalued.

Whether the arguments for them are specious or not, courses in the history of China have multiplied since World War II, and I would like to reflect on my own experiences in giving such courses, first at Stanford and now at Yale University. Many solutions are possible for each of the problems which I shall raise, and I make no special claims for my own. They are the product of a particular biography, of a cluster of interests centered on social and intellectual developments. Further, they have been hammered out in the effort to deal with Chinese history before 1800, with only sporadic attention to the history of China's response to the West. In each of the sections which follow, I raise what I think is a crucial problem and discuss what I have found to be helpful in working out a solution.

BEGIN AT THE BEGINNING?

My answer would be never! When I gave my first course, I began with the rise of the Himalayas; and, by the time I had laid the "groundwork" for a history of China, the students' eyes were glazed; and I had deservedly lost their interest for most of the course. I had been misled by what Marc Bloch called "the idol of origins." Several things now seem to me necessary preliminaries to a series of discourses on Chinese history itself. One is to tell the student why he is taking the course. He may think he has reasons, but they are likely to be dubious and ill thought out. I attempt to tell him what he is going to learn about China and about himself and try to arouse his intellectual curiosity about this immense sweep of human experience. Second, I think that we must all take time out at the beginning to deal with the clichés and stereotypes which are generally the students' only preparation for such a course. I have found that Harold Isaacs' *Scratches on Our Minds: American Images of China and India* is worth several hours of class discussion. The therapy is effective, for I hear no more in papers and discussions about "the inscrutable (or unchanging) East," "Asiatic hordes," "Oriental wisdom" (except from incurable Dharma-bums). The third step involves a statement of the instructor's approach, and this deserves a separate heading.

CLAIMS AND DISCLAIMERS OF OMNISCIENCE

I assume that it is every historian's business to make his own selection of the particulars and the patterns he has found in China's past.

This will be the product of his own study and reflection and of his own long-term interests. Some statement of what his selection will be and how he justifies it (without a discourse on the philosophy of history) seems to me an essential part of his introduction. And it should be here that he makes, once and for all, statements about the incompleteness of our knowledge, the inconclusiveness of scholarly writings to date, the necessary limitations to his own knowledge, and the like. If these are freely introduced in all lectures (and the temptation is great), the student becomes confused and loses confidence in his teacher. If, on the other hand, the instructor makes claims to have *the* approach or *the* theory, he will quickly become embroiled and undone by some average sophomore who has done the course readings. Occasionally, when major issues of interpretation arise, it is useful to summarize conflicting views and then to indicate which one the instructor finds most persuasive. For the superior student, these interpolations are enormously stimulating; for the average student, they are bemusing, often befuddling.

THE WILL-O'-THE-WISP OF COVERAGE

It was said of a certain Columbia course that a student looked out the window for a moment and missed the French Revolution. In a one-semester course in Chinese history to 1800, the instructor has approximately one-half minute per year of history. If he allows himself to expatiate on the rise and fall of all the political regimes in this expanse of time, and if he does not resist the temptation to mention the names of the actors in these dramas, the student will be overwhelmed by a plethora of meaningless detail, and, if he looks out the window, he will miss the rise and fall of some dynasty, he wouldn't know which, and probably he wouldn't care. Again, if the instructor indulges overmuch in his intellectual hobbies—technological developments, the history of the horse, or goings-on in the imperial harems—he will never reach his destination. The collection of many curious facts is not history, nor is it a lumbering chronology of dynastic events. If "coverage" in the vulgar sense is a delusion, then what is the historian to do?

NODAL POINTS, FORMATIVE EXPERIENCES

It is as characteristic of Chinese as of any other history, that not every year, every decade, or half-century is as decisive as any other. By decisive periods, I mean those in which events occurred or decisions were made that changed the course of a people's development. The decisive periods encompass the principal formative experiences that make a people what they are and not otherwise. To recognize this is the first step toward exorcising the will-o'-the-wisp of coverage. The second step is to try to identify such periods in Chinese history and then to concentrate attention upon them. Here, the great Chinese historians, especially the unofficial speculative writers of the old order and many of the moderns, Japanese specialists, and modern Western historians help us to identify these critical periods. Here is my choice:

A. The period of genesis: the emergence of distinctive features of a Chinese civilization in the Shang;

B. The later Chou viewed as a "classical age";

C. The unification of state and culture: the founding of the Chinese Empire by the Ch'in, consolidation and development by the Han;

D. The first experience of dismemberment and foreign invasions, cultural and political, c. 300–589;

E. Unification: a new centralized empire and its culture—Sui and T'ang, 589–750;

F. The breakdown of the second imperial order and the beginnings of the new society and culture—late T'ang, Five Dynasties, and Sung; proto-modern China;

G. The first experience of total conquest and of incorporation in a larger world-empire: the period of Mongol domination, the brutalization of politics, and the evolution of mass culture;

H. Reassertion of Chinese control over state, society, and culture: the Ming. The failure of creativity. With apologies to Toynbee, "the abortive effort to revive the ghost of the T'ang oekumene";

I. The second total conquest, continuation and atrophy of Ming institutions and culture under a Manchu-Chinese dyarchy.

Some of these periods are long, and further criteria of selection must be used. I tend, in many of these cases, to stress the transitions—of power, culture, and institutions—which bring one order to an end and usher in the new. Each historian, depending on his own interests, will emphasize the features of such transitions that he knows best and finds most interesting. And, as he does so, he will call attention, again and again, to the threads of continuity that knit this sequence of transitions into a single nexus of cumulative change. Finally, since Chinese civilization might, at any of these points, have taken another and different course, disciplined speculation on "what would have happened if . . ." helps to underline the character and significance of a particular outcome.

BLIND HISTORIC FORCES OR THE BREATH OF LIFE?

The easiest way to deal with Chinese history is to ignore those "ifs" and to assert that the Chinese were hustled along to their particular destiny by certain forces whose workings were blind, impersonal, and inexorable. On the most doctrinaire level, this subordinates events, cultural life, and personalities to such abstractions as "the contradictions inherent in the feudal mode of production." On a less theoretical level, one may talk of the dynastic cycle, the supposedly inexorable recurrence of set phases of the rise and fall of political regimes. This leads to the stereotyping of each period of dynastic decline, for example, so that the student imagines that precisely the same combination of forces: weakening of the imperial line, rise of taxes, engrossment of land, rise of eunuchs, and other events wrought the downfall of each and every dynasty. There are, indeed, recurrent patterns, but the differences amount to the cumulative changes that give China a history and not simply, as Granet believed, a static culture. And the best way to see the differences and to make vivid the cumulative changes is to turn away from abstractions (the vice of "reification" as the social scientist puts it) and give the breath of life to those periods and transitions that have proved decisive in the growth of Chinese civilization. This is the only way that a student can develop some "feel" for Chinese civilization, some empathy for the Chinese people, and, in some degree, what has been called the master quality of the historian—a sense of what cannot have happened. I venture a few brief suggestions which, I have found, help to give the breath of life to the decisive periods of Chinese history.

Recognizing that the setting of Chinese history—the stage and its backdrops—is utterly strange to our students, it is useful to make frequent reference to geography, the landscape, and to changes that time wrought in these. For example, it is significant that Chinese traditions were maintained in the south during the period of disunity—for the first time in a subtropical environment and in an area recently colonized. Again, one might mention the process of deforestation in the north that had driven the shipbuilders to the southeast coast by the fourteenth century, or note that Ennin, the ninth-century Japanese traveler, saw living glaciers in northwest China. These landscape and environmental references are most vivid when one can quote a contemporary description, in either poetry or prose.

To me, it seems essential to our purposes to let the Chinese speak for themselves and, wherever possible, to quote, in translation, their own discussions of a policy crisis, or their own arguments over political philosophy, their own evocations of life in a particular milieu, whether among scholars preparing for the examinations, in poetical or artistic coteries or elsewhere. Fortunately, we now have a rich collection of materials of this kind in *Sources of Chinese Tradition,* as well as in the fine translations of Arthur Waley and many others. A single poem may often do what a yard of prose will not—evoke a moment of crisis and recapture its conflicts of emotions and interests. Tu Fu's poems of social criticism do this, so does Wei Chuang's "Lament of the Lady of Ch'in" which captures forever the horrors of a rebel sack of a great capital.

The use of literary materials is one way of dealing with a problem of great difficulty—the elite and capital centeredness of Chinese historical materials. Students rightly ask what was happening among the eighty to ninety percent of the population who are only statistics in the official histories. Chinese poets, travelers, amateur ethnographers help us with the answer. So, for later periods, do stories, novels, and plays that evoke the life of the villages and lesser towns. A further resource, and one to be used to the limit, is found in the records of scattered foreign observers of the Chinese scene. Such observations as are found in the Sogdian letters recording the fourth-century sack of the northern capitals, in the writings of Arab travelers, in the diary of the traveler monk Ennin as translated by Reischauer, as in, also, the diaries of Matteo Ricci as presented by Father Gallagher, all help to correct not only the elite centeredness of most of our sources but also the ethnocentrism that pervades nearly all Chinese writings.

A biography often helps to capture in understandable human terms the problems and the atmosphere of an age, though the range of any life's involvements is always limited, and no one's is ever typical of the lives of all his contemporaries—even those of similar interests and temperaments. Mr. Waley's *The Life and Times of Po Chü-i* and *Yuan Mei: Eighteenth Century Chinese Poet* are excellent evocations of the ethos of an age and a milieu. In such works, the student is brought close to an individual's motivation, world-view, and standards of value, and stereotypes of "Chinese behavior" are effectively shattered.

COMPARATIVE REFERENCE: MEASUREMENT OR
THE FREE ASSOCIATION OF PLAUSIBLE IDEAS?

It is a sobering thought that nearly everything one may say in a
lecture in English on Chinese history has comparative implications.
But terms like "gentry," "middle class," and "religious faith" are
explicitly comparative for they imply that the phenomena named are
universal and that one is speaking of the Chinese subtype of the
named class. To take account of this as each term is introduced—
with disquisitions on Western history, the origins of the English
"gentry," and the like—will bring in abstract concepts and orders
of events which the student is ill prepared to understand. There is
no pat solution to the problem, but brief remarks that effectively
put the term "in quotes" are of some help. When terms are used
that have wide systematic implications, e.g., from Toynbee or
Spengler, then the problem is compounded. Did these great generalists err in grouping one or another Chinese phenomenon with
what they took to be analogues in other societies? And what of the
soundness of their systems generally? Consideration of such problems will lead to meanders away from the subject matter, and make
the student wonder whether he is taking a course in Chinese history
or metahistory. My solution is pragmatic and hardly defensible philosophically. I tend to use the formulations of generalists, not as theories
but as useful metaphors and to employ them with a rising inflection.
For example, leaving all questions of his total system aside, I have
found it helpful in discussing China's two assaults from without—
first by Buddhism and later by the West—to use Toynbee's "polari-
zation of reactions by societies assaulted from without," the Zealot
reaction, and the Herodion reaction. This can clarify the issues in
the Chinese context without overlong detours into the history of
King Herod and his conservative opponents, the Plains Indians,
or the Mahdi.

Comparative statements regarding specific characteristics of Chinese civilization are both possible and illuminating. For example, the Chinese monarchy is to be understood in its own particularity *and* by reference to kingship in other societies. Again, the structure and ethos of peasant villages—the cellular units of Chinese society —may be brought into relief by selective use of the generalizations found in such studies as Robert Redfield's *Peasant Society and Culture.* But all such references should be the result of distillation in the historian's own mind; they should be expressed in his own words and not in the technical terminologies of the social scientists he has read.

There are, of course, analytical systems that claim to provide labeled pigeonholes for all Chinese phenomena. But when we realize the primitive state of organized knowledge of Chinese history and when we see even the limited comparisons of yesterday modified or destroyed by today's new monograph, it would be folly to adopt some universal schema based on day before yesterday's knowledge. To do so would place the historian in an intellectual strait-jacket, lead him into arid terminological discussions, bore and confuse his listeners, and extinguish the breath of life that alone can make Chinese history real and memorable for his students.

THE PROBLEM OF ANCILLA

Textbooks are a necessary evil if the lecturer abjures coverage and concentrates on the critical periods and transitions suggested above. They reassure the student who wants "more facts" and the student who is uneasy without a connecting tissue of names and events ready at hand. Any textbook has the disadvantage of being a selection of historical particulars different from that of the lecturer (unless the lecturer wrote the text). This sets up a tension, not wholly negative in its effects, between what "the book says" and what is emphasized in class. A more serious disadvantage is that many textbooks are hack work often done to publishers' specifications and do not represent the best and most up-to-date synthesis that might be produced. Nevertheless, some sort of text is probably needed, and I find the Reischauer and Fairbank, *East Asia: The Great Tradition,* excellent and the best for my purposes.

Source readings seem far more important for reasons suggested above, and *Sources of Chinese Tradition* has proved to be a magnificent teaching aid. The introductions to each selection seem admirable in placing each discourse within its context of thought and history. The key ideas, habits of thought, and modes of argument characteristics of Chinese scholars and statesmen are brought home to the student in a way that comes near to being unforgettable.

For supplementary readings, our resources grow year by year. Paperback editions multiply, though one could wish that some of the revived titles had been left to moulder in their well-earned graves. Monographs and translations appear in growing number, and there are a few signs that the "China specialists" may fall in with a happy trend in American historical writing—a trend toward greater clarity, conciseness, and elegance in expression. When monographs are written with some thought to their possible use for course readings they will be better organized, less larded with academese, their footnotes will no longer dominate each page, and there will be fewer "Chinesey" translations from sources identified only by transliterated title. The new London volume, *Historians of China and Japan,* edited by W. G. Beasley and E. G. Pulleyblank, contains several chapters of the most useful and readable kind, and Burton Watson's *Ssu-ma Chi'en: The Grand Historian of China* is a model of lucidity. The masterwork of Joseph Needham, on the other hand, is almost useless for teaching purposes; for all its panorama of fascinating detail, it is highly technical and, much worse, is dominated by a particular ideology (including a teleology) that will mislead the student if he understands it at all. In general, I am inclined to reserve ideologically marked and polemical works for the graduate seminar.

Visual aids are now available in increasing variety. I have carried on only limited experiments thus far and can make only a few suggestions. One is that works of art chosen on aesthetic criteria should form only a small fraction of the total, for history uses art as document and can give only marginal attention to the evolution of style and taste. Thus a "bad" painting of a street scene may be more useful than a great painting of a mountain landscape, and prints and drawings in popular styles help to draw the student into the lives and tastes of the common people. Aside from paintings and sculpture, it is rewarding to use near-contemporary photographic slides of landscapes (particularly to drive home the variety of Chinese terrain), of techniques and ways of doing things, such as are found, for example, in the illustrations to Hommel's *China at Work*. I have not solved the problem of *when* to interrupt the lectures and have a session devoted to slides. Ideally, one should have a slide operator always courteously waiting and prepared to flash five minutes of carefully selected materials whenever they would support or illustrate the subject at hand.

Our tasks in developing a vivid and analytical history of China for the undergraduate are formidable. The uncharted periods of history are shrinking but slowly, ideological axe-grinding mars the pages of our journals and monographs, the vast bulk of new Chinese history writing is written in the unlovely and misleading jargon of Marxism-Leninism-Maoism. The land and the people of China are shut off from us. We wallow in ignorance and elevate hoary clichés to the dignity of interpretive hypotheses. We have none of the riches of translated materials that are at the disposal of historians of Europe, nor can we choose among ten or a dozen "respectable" textbooks. Yet, I for one would rather struggle year in year out to make some rough sense out of Chinese history than to give the most polished course in the world on the United States in the National Period.

Comment: The Japanese Perspective

ALBERT CRAIG

Associate Professor of History, Harvard University

After hearing Professor Wright, I feel that I would very much enjoy his course in Chinese history. I am in complete agreement with him with respect to his practical injunctions regarding origins, omniscience, and coverage and substantially agree with his view of history as a linked series of formative experiences. In this paper, I have been asked to consider the relationship between Chinese and Japanese history and, in particular, to comment on Professor Wright's approach to Chinese history as it would affect the presentation of Japanese history in an undergraduate survey course in Far Eastern civilization.

To see the relationship between China and Japan, we must first speak of the two major cultural transformations which Japan has undergone in the course of its history. In the first, which began in about the sixth century, Japan, a primitive society, came into contact with China and began from afar to participate in the Chinese zone of civilization. The following thirteen-hundred years can be thought of as the working out of Chinese and Sino-Buddhist assumptions and principles within Japan's native tradition and society. In this process, Japan developed a great art and literature and a fascinating history. At first, this impact was felt only at the capital and in centers of literate culture. But, by the thirteenth century, popular Buddhism— representing, in part, successive waves of thought from the continent —had penetrated to the lowest level of society, and, by the mid-eighteenth century, Japanese Confucian norms regulated family and society even in the most remote Japanese village. The second major impact on Japan was that of the modern West in the nineteenth century by which Japan entered into modern world culture. This change is obviously still continuing today.

In some ways, the processes involved in these two great changes were similar. Both involved what may be termed symbolic transformations: a process by which institutions, one's way of life, and even self were reinterpreted in terms of the concepts of a different culture. In each case, this adoption of new symbols sufficed to produce radical changes. In ancient Japan, the divine Emperor with his particular antecedents became, in part, the Son of Heaven with the universal cosmological and ethical functions of a Confucian monarch, a determiner of history. This theory of ruler and state continued with subtle modifications through all subsequent Japanese history to modern times. The Tale of Heiji for example, one of the early chronicles of the "feudal" wars and intrigues that prefigured Kamakura Japan, begins by attributing the disasters of the age to the ethical shortcomings of the Court. In modern times, the same process of symbolic transformation can be seen. For example, during the 1880s, Western ideas of human rights and representative government, by giving voice and a rationale to the inchoate strivings of well-to-do peasants and poor ex-samurai, led to the emergence of a recognizably modern political party movement. Such a movement could not have emerged from within Tokugawa society or traditional Japanese culture in a thousand years.

Yet, the differences between the first and second of Japan's great transformations are also striking. In modern times, the volume of Japan's contacts with the West has been far greater than its earlier contacts with China. More foreigners have been present within Japan, more students have gone abroad. Until the turn of the century, Japan was partially under foreign control through the unequal treaties, and industrialization has had its effect—the result of this has been not only the acceptance of much of the ideal culture of the West but also trends toward the duplication of the institutional order of the

West in most areas. In contrast to this, earlier contacts with China
were fewer and less coercive. The nomenclature and, in a few instances, the reality of Chinese institutions were borrowed during the
eighth and ninth centuries, but these soon passed away; what was
left was Chinese ideal culture applied to sanction a distinctly non-
Chinese society.

With this view of the relation between Japan and China, I would
like to turn to Professor Wright's use of "formative experiences."
Viewing these as the interaction of ideas and other planes of history
at crucial junctures in the development of traditional China, it seems
to me that this is just the approach best suited to provide a background for the subsequent study of Japan. That is to say, given an
appreciation of the relation between ideas and institutions in China,
one is then prepared to ask, how did the same ideas function in the
very different Japanese society. In particular, of the formative experiences discerned by Professor Wright, those that are most significant for the understanding of Japan are: the classical age of the Chou,
the assimilation of the foreign culture of Buddhism in the post-Han
period, the formation of the T'ang Empire, and the Sung synthesis.
It is worthwhile in preparing to treat these periods in China to keep
in mind what points are to be made in speaking of their cultural
significance in Japanese history.

Let me give two illustrations of the ways in which the common
ideal culture of the two countries was applied. I will take them from
the period with which I am the most familiar. The Neo-Confucian
philosophy of Chu Hsi formed the official orthodoxy of both the
Southern Sung Dynasty of China and of Tokugawa Japan. The
Southern Sung was a bureaucratic state *par excellence;* Tokugawa
Japan was a sort of centralized feudalism. That the same doctrine
could be used to sanction two such widely divergent forms of society
points up the sort of "fit" that often exists between ideas and the
society to which they apply. In Japan this "fit" was accomplished by
viewing Tokugawa feudalism as identical with the society of the
ancient sages of China's early classical age. By recreating such a

rule of virtue, Tokugawa society was good and, in fact, superior to that of China. In Chinese Confucianism, the Emperor received the mandate to rule from Heaven. In Japan, the Emperor was seen as the equivalent of Heaven and gave the mandate to the military hegemon. And it was in terms of this ideal polity that the military hegemony was overthrown in 1867, opening the way for Japan's modernization.

An even more interesting example is that of the scientific implications of Neo-Confucian metaphysics in Japan. Chu Hsi held that one must "investigate things," "investigate the principles of things," as one means of self-realization. In China, however, virtually all study was directed toward the civil service examinations. As a consequence, the scientific potential of this emphasis came to naught and Western science was largely rejected. In Japan, however, where position was largely hereditary and scholarship untrammeled by any but political restrictions, the same emphasis on the investigation of things was, I feel, one factor contributing to the eagerness with which the Japanese sought out a knowledge of the West. Both the vocabulary and the cosmology of the early students of Dutch science were those of Neo-Confucianism.

This type of possibility for comparisons between China and Japan leads to the second point that I would like to make in regard to Professor Wright's paper. I am probably somewhat more sanguine—perhaps rashly so—about the use of comparative history in undergraduate courses in Asian history. Where Professor Wright suggests implicit comparison, I feel that explicit comparisons are sometimes worth using. One such topic on which I lecture is Japanese feudalism. A useful book in connection with this topic is *Feudalism in History,* edited by Coulborn, especially the essays by Strayer, Reischauer, and Bodde. No one can read Japanese history without being struck by certain European parallels. Chinese culture stood in relation to the early tribal society of Japan as did Mediterranean culture to the tribes of northern Europe. In both Japan and, say, France, the decline of centralized authority led to the emergence of a manorial system, and a local military class. Each saw the development of a loyalty ethic (although the Japanese code omitted chivalry). Each saw the breakdown of the manorial system and the rise of the territorially united fief, the establishment of a hierarchical lord vassal relation within the aristocratic military class, the obligation of military service in return for a fief, the emergence of a system of single inheritance to protect the unity of the fief, and so on. At the lowest level of generality, these parallels break down. But, at a slightly higher level, the over-all similarity of structure and the fact that like institutions usually had similar functions suggest that comparisons will contribute a great deal to our understanding of either society. It also suggests a basic human response to a particular set of circumstances occurring in two widely separate areas.

This is not to say, in making such a comparison, that one can simply equate Japan with France at the appropriate periods under the common rubric of feudalism. The Japanese variant of East Asian culture was not the same as medieval Christian culture. However well these doctrines adapted to their respective societies, they cannot be lumped together as "feudal ideology." This can be illustrated by inquiring into the social consequences of cultural differences. Take, for example, the differing form of the feudal contract in Japan and Europe. In Europe, with the heritage of Greek and Roman thought, law was viewed as part of the natural order. As a consequence the "contract" (even if unwritten in the early illiterate phase of European feudalism) tended to have a legal character with specific reciprocal overtones: duties were spelled out, military service was often limited, and the vassal had legal rights against his lord. In Japan, on the contrary, following the Chinese conception, law was conceived of as man-made and inferior to ethical principles—which were a part of the natural order. Therefore, the feudal agreement— often a written pledge of loyalty—was not given legal character, but was rather the expression of an unlimited moral obligation of the vassal to the lord. Of course, in both Europe and Japan, formal differences in the statement of the feudal tie were often overridden by the *de facto* social situation. Parallels can be found in Japan to the

European baron who bragged that he had never betrayed an over-lord without a legal excuse. Yet at the most concrete level of history, many of the differences in the two societies can be explained as the practical consequences of their different conceptual guidelines. Ideas count. And in pre-modern societies, ideas embodying central values embedded in a cosmology counted even more.

I feel that the highly structured comparison, such as the one just touched on above, can be used effectively in lectures. Especially with the Reischauer and Fairbank text to carry the main burden of the narrative, such topical disquisitions can be used to present inter-pretations outside of a strictly chronological framework. Of course, to the bare frame that I have given here must be added the detail and examples that Professor Wright describes as giving the breath of life to history.

Still another type of explicit comparison is what might be called the point to point comparison. At Harvard, once each week, the students taking the course in Far Eastern Civilization are divided into smaller discussion sections. As preparation for these sessions, we use, almost exclusively, readings from primary sources or literature. Certain questions intended to guide the discussions are passed out at the beginning of the semester, and among them we try to include some that will lead the student to compare the traditional civiliza-tions of the Far East and West. When discussing Chou Confucian-ism, we ask: how does the Confucian sage-king compare with the Platonic philosopher-king or with the Jewish Messiah? We ask the students to compare the idea of the "gentleman" as it emerged in the writings of Confucius with that of the European Renaissance—say, of Castiglioni. They are asked to contrast the system of thought of the Chou legalists with the political thought of Hobbes. And on the Japanese side, similar sections are organized based for the most part on two splendid books: *The Sources of Japanese Tradition,* and Keene's *Anthology of Japanese Literature.* All such comparisons, of course, must be gauged to the level of knowledge that the students bring with them to the course. And, such comparative questions

Albert Craig

must be preceded by others that will first enable them to see, say, Confucianism in its own terms. Given these qualifications, I feel that such comparisons can be tremendously stimulating. The students discover that the problems with which the thinkers of Asia have attempted to grapple were not entirely dissimilar from those posed by the greatest thinkers in the West.

Indian History for the Undergraduate

ROBERT I. CRANE

Professor of History, Duke University

The subject of this paper raises, at the outset, fundamental questions regarding the role of historical pedagogy in higher education. It is difficult to establish what is "proper perspective" for the teaching of Indian history without facing basic issues concerning aims, approach, method, and value reference. The objectives of the cultural sciences, as Max Weber so effectively insisted, must be related to value references which are, in the last analysis, arrived at subjectively.[1] Criteria for deciding what is "proper perspective" involve judgments on the role of higher education, on appropriate methods of pedagogy, on the logic of heuristic devices, and on the relationship of one discipline or branch of knowledge to another.

In addition, judgments upon the character of history as an ideographic or a nomothetic science are fundamental to one's views on the teaching of history to undergraduates.[2] It is impossible within the scope of this paper to do justice to these issues. However, in assaying the role of Indian history in the undergraduate curriculum, consideration of these issues has served as a point of departure.

More precisely, the task required of this paper is to discern and explicate the pedagogical role of work on Indian history in two

[1] Max Weber discusses these matters in "Critical Studies in the Logic of the Cultural Sciences," in *The Methodology of the Social Sciences,* trans. and ed. by Edward A. Shils and Henry A. Finch (Glencoe, Ill., The Free Press, 1949), pp. 113–88.

[2] For some illuminating remarks see the review article by Bert F. Hoselitz, "On Comparative History," in *World Politics,* IX (1957), 267–79.

respects. First, there is the matter of what is relevant to presentation of the subject in its own right; second, what is relevant in terms of its larger function as part of a liberal education. The latter function of work on Indian history will be discussed first, before turning to internal problems of perspective in presentation of the subject matter.

Normally, the undergraduate comes to a course in Indian history or to an Asian civilizations course, which includes systematic presentations on the history of India, without any prior training in the subject. More than that, he will rarely have had any experience in the field of non-Western studies. If he has had previous work in what is often carelessly called "world history," close investigation will reveal that "world history" begins with the Greeks and comes down through medieval Christendom to the modern nation-state system of Western Europe.

This point is not made in order to be churlish. The problem is: (a) he has had little or no chance to step outside of his own cultural tradition to study one that is alien and (b) he had hardly been exposed to the use of comparisons—whether in terms of the use of ideal types or in a more direct fashion—in the learning process.[3] He knows almost nothing about the major characteristics of a civilization other than his own and is virtually unfamiliar with the use of comparisons or of other conceptual tools. Moreover, the parochialism and ethnocentrism which have been so conspicuous in his background make it difficult for him to pass over the divide between the known and the unknown.

An initial problem, therefore, stems from the lack of preparation of the student for learning about the unknown and the alien—the

---

[3] This is essentially correct, it is here argued, even if he has been exposed to a cursory introduction to non-Western civilizations. When such introductions are dubbed into a course whose orientation is Western, the extent to which the non-Western material is perceived in its own light almost always turns out to be minimal. All too frequently the presentation will use schema, such as nomenclature and periodization, derived from and valid for Western experience but misleading and unproductive when applied to non-Western experience. The student is permitted to assume that he has begun to grasp Indian history because it has been summarized in categories derived from European history. In fact, he may be worse off than if he had begun *de novo* and by himself to attempt to grasp Indian history.

paucity of his experiential and conceptual apparatus. This applies whether he is to be exposed to the art, belles-lettres, and intellectual history of the alien culture, or to a study of its social structure and organization, its family system, and its functional characteristics. It applies whether he seeks to comprehend the alien by imbibition of its "essence" or whether he aims at a sociological analysis of its system features. Though this point does not deserve to be belabored, it is mentioned because it requires thoughtful consideration of viable techniques which can help the student to make the leap from the familiar to the strange.[4]

Were this paper expected to suggest specific means to solve the problem—presumably such is not the case—I would propose two ways to facilitate the transition. The first depends upon immersing the student in the literature and plastic or graphic arts of the alien culture in the hope that a direct confrontation with the visible symbols of an alien civilization will pull him abruptly into the beginnings of a new context of appreciation. Such immersion can be forwarded by a skillful process of leading the student into the alien materials by a series of deft comparisons with *known* art forms, graphic media and literary works. The second method of making the transition relies upon plunging the student into an analysis of the characteristic forms of social organization of the alien culture, also by the comparative method, stressing the similarities and dissimilarities between social organization and structure in his own culture and in the alien culture.

The previous remarks serve to emphasize a major element in the presentation of Indian history to the undergraduate. That is the use of comparison in pedagogy. Comparison is urged not merely or primarily because it can be a bridge in the learning process from the known to the unknown; rather, it is urged on its own merits as an important intellectual tool. The act of viewing the history, the art forms, the world-view, the social organization, and the major philosophical systems of two or more societies in a comparative manner

---

[4] The fact that this seems usually to be poorly done does not logically require that it must always be poorly done.

can be a major adjunct to the achievement of comprehension. Whether the use of the comparative method be systematic and based upon the Weberian method of ideal types or whether it be pursued more closely and directly, comparison provides powerful means of judging, evaluating and grasping.[5]

The making of comparisons forces the scholar or the student to reflect upon the mass of material at hand so as to discern what is relevant to his inquiry. It requires of him a continuing and sophisticated process of ratiocination. To be able to compare, one has to be certain that one has selected comparable items, structures, or processes. Comparison is not an end in itself and should not be thought of as such—though there is a legitimate field of intellectual endeavor concerned with comparison—but rather is a means to an end. For this reason, in a statement regarding proper perspective in the teaching of Indian history, initial emphasis is placed upon its function in the context of comparison. Equally, emphasis can be placed upon the role of comparison in the study of Indian history.

The comparison and contrast of Hindu metaphysics and Christian metaphysics, for example, requires of the student the knowledge and the ability to grasp what is unique, characteristic and significant in both systems of thought. That is no mean accomplishment by itself. In addition, it requires that even what is most familiar be re-thought in the light of new analytical and evaluative propositions derived from the making of comparisons. As Bert Hoselitz has remarked in his essay,

it is indubitable that their use of the method of comparative history led to a deeper penetration of the subject than would have been possible without it, and new and significant questions were posed and possible solutions for them proposed which further our understanding of the functioning of social systems.[6]

---

[5] Max Weber formulated the role of ideal types in his essay, "The Meaning of 'Ethical Neutrality' in Sociology and Economics," in E. Shils and H. Finch, *The Methodology of the Social Sciences*, pp. 99–105. It must be stressed that Weber used the ideal type construct as an heuristic device, not as an end in itself and not as an "explanation."

[6] B. F. Hoselitz, "On Contemporary History," p. 270.

Unless it be argued that the function of higher education is the memorization of masses of information, room must be left for training in the use of analytical techniques and in the formation and testing of concepts. The mind is not a blotter, it is a potentially powerful mechanism capable of imaginative and provocative probing. But the capacity to probe, to ask meaningful questions, and to work toward sound and discriminating judgments has to be developed. This paper assumes that the study of an alien culture, as for example India, can be a means toward such training and that higher education demands it.

Now, whether the procedure followed in studying Indian history from a comparative point-of-view be direct or whether it be based upon the use of ideal type constructs, it must be systematic. Not only must we be sure we are comparing similar entities or systems, we must also make the comparisons in a rigorous manner. Comparison is a means of testing and cannot be carried forward in a haphazard fashion. One compares like entities in order to discover in what respects they are similar and in what respects they are dissimilar. One is then in a position to formulate fruitful questions which seek to account for the similarities and the dissimilarities. One achieves awareness of patterns of thought, organization or behavior and probes more deeply into the reasons for dissonances or for variations from the expected and for explanations of the unique.

In addition to its direct results in learning, the process bears fruit in several ways, each of which is important to a proper perspective for the study of Indian history in a liberal education. To begin with, such study dissipates the parochialism and ethnocentrism mentioned previously. This is a major task of higher education in all of its branches. Moreover, it provides the student with a better understanding of his own traditions. He has reflected upon them while studying them in comparison with the characteristic norms and behavior patterns of a totally different culture. In addition, by so doing the student has become a better informed and more knowledgeable citizen. This, too, is an aim of higher education.

It has been remarked that pedagogy is concerned with the relationship of one discipline or branch of knowledge to another. While this is a constant challenge to higher education, it is thrown into clear relief by the problems of teaching Indian history. The very fact that the student knows so little about an area such as India, when he begins his studies, forces the "area" course to be consciously concerned with matters of a disciplinary nature in attempting an adequate coverage of the material. In order to make the subject matter meaningful to the novice it has to be placed in the larger context of a grasp of social, intellectual, artistic, and economic factors. In order properly to explain a little, it becomes necessary to explain a great deal. Teaching Indian history to undergraduates requires due emphasis on art history, intellectual history, economic history, history of philosophical systems, social organization, political structures and values, and the dynamics of culture change. The historian has to transcend the usual boundaries of his discipline and include elements of such instruction in a history course.[7] This raises in an acute fashion the matter of the relations between the various branches of knowledge and the pedagogical issues involved in the presentation of non-historical materials by the historian. This paper is based upon the view that the student should be encouraged to acquire familiarity with the approaches of the several disciplines and that this will enhance his ability to handle the materials of Indian history.

The teaching of Indian history cannot be isolated from the rest of the curriculum for another reason. During the modern age, India has been closely associated with Western Europe and has been materially influenced by Western ideas, medicine, law, administration, economic practices, technology, and artistic forms. To understand modern India, one has to be aware of the complex of European institutions and patterns of behavior which were exported to India. This is true even if it be argued that these "exports" have been so

---

[7] Thus, for example, the excellent history of classical India by A. L. Basham, *The Wonder That Was India: A Survey of the Culture of the Indian Sub-Continent* (London, Sidgwick and Jackson, 1954), includes a considerable amount of invaluable material on a wide range of aspects of Indian culture and civilization, including information on styles of daily life.

internalized as to become part of modern India. To understand modern India, we must know what—and under what circumstances —was imported from the West. This means that the teaching of Indian history involves due recognition of the role of the West in modifying the traditional culture. By implication, the offering of Indian history is part of a larger curriculum which describes the sources of the novel instrumentalities which have so influenced the course of events in India.

The matter of relations between branches of knowledge vis-à-vis an appropriate perspective for the teaching of Indian history is important in another way. As an example, one may take a typical problem of conceptualization faced in the offering of Indian history. Reference is made to the use of the concept of a feudal age. Derived from the study of European institutions, the concept of feudalism is an effective device for examining an important period in Europe's past. Is such the case when the concept is applied to Indian history? The answer depends not only upon an exercise in the comparative method, but also on the careful use of insights and concepts from more than one discipline. Feudalism was a complex of legal, economic, social, and political arrangements. In order to determine the relevance of the concept for the study of Indian history, one must make use of insights from several disciplines.[8] Thus, the study of Indian history poses questions which require answers based upon the use of more than one discipline.

From what has been said, all too hastily, it will be seen that the teaching of Indian history raises a series of questions relevant to judgments about the appropriate means of pedagogy in higher education. It is argued that the use of comparison is important both in bringing the student to an understanding of India's past and in relating the study of India to other bodies of knowledge. Moreover, the study of Indian history requires exposure to the approaches and findings of several disciplines, drawn from the humanities as well

[8] The problem of feudalism in Indian history has been dealt with quite effectively by D. Thorner, "Feudalism in India," in, R. Coulborn (ed.), *Feudalism in History* (Princeton, Princeton University Press, 1956), pp. 133–50.

as the social sciences. These comments have sought to place the teaching of Indian history in the larger context of higher education. Equally important, however, is a proper perspective in teaching Indian history in terms of the presentation of the subject matter itself.

As was noted in the preliminary planning for these papers, there are certain basic questions which may be asked about any civilization. Though Indian history has its own discrete materials and presents certain unique problems of interpretation and periodization, it shares with the history of other civilizations an amenability to the posing of such basic questions. Rather than discuss the questions which might be asked, as such, it seems advisable to turn directly to a consideration of the problems and topics essential to an understanding of Indian history. Two categories will be discussed: (a) general problems of inquiry which underlie the subject and (b) the kinds of topics within Indian history which merit treatment.

It should be emphasized that in the discussion which follows there is no intention of proposing a comprehensive treatment of the subject matter. On the contrary, the true art of the historian rests upon the ability to be highly selective. The discussion which follows suggests a variety of topics which could be touched upon and a variety of themes around which the presentation of Indian history could be organized. It is assumed that each teacher will select those topics on which he has the most to say and those themes which seem to him most fruitful for organizing his presentation. Intellectual indigestion would be the result of any attempt to cover all or most of what will be referred to in the remaining pages of this essay.

An important issue for the study of Indian history is the *level* at which the study is to be pursued. The foundations for the recovery of India's past were laid by certain eminent classical scholars including Sir William Jones, James Prinsep, H. T. Colebrooke, and H. H. Wilson.[9] While the debt owed these men is great, the fact is that

---

[9] On these pioneers see the following titles: A. J. Arberry, *Asiatic Jones; the life and influences of Sir William Jones* (London, Longmans, Green, 1946); C. E. Buck-

their researches set the stage for a difficult problem. Their work was largely directed toward the discovery and translation of important Sanskritic texts. The reconstruction of India's past which stemmed from their efforts was derived from the study of Sanskritic and Brahmanical sources. This gave scholars a view of India based upon the high intellectual tradition and upon the formal codes for Indian life found in the classical writings.

The result has been both gratifying and misleading. As in most societies, the gap between the codes of the lawgivers and the life of the people was substantial. Research in Indian history provided a rich and fascinating account of how the system was supposed to work and of the leading ideas of the priestly and intellectual elite. The assumption was made that the world-view of the seers was the way-of-life of India. Knowledge of India's past was limited, primarily, to the materials found in such sources. Attention was fixed at the level of the high intellectual tradition, to the detriment of studies of a more catholic and broadly conceived nature. The actual life of the bulk of the people tended to be overlooked. Popular Hinduism lacked students while attention was fixed on the sophisticated metaphysical speculations of the elite. Understanding of India's past was tied too closely to *one* level of Indian experience.

In recent years, the corrections for the older, partial view have begun to appear. Work in anthropology and social history has progressed and has created an awareness of the existence of other levels of Indian historical experience. But one is still caught between the attractions of the self-contained splendor of the high intellectual tradition and the desire to probe more fully into the less heroic and more mundane experience of the carriers of the low intellectual traditions. In teaching Indian history, one has to decide which level or levels to focus on and why. One has, also, to make clear to the student the existence, the significance and the interrelations of the

land, *Dictionary of Indian Biography* (London, Swan Sonnenschein, 1906); H. T. Colebrooke, *Miscellaneous Essays* (3 vols, London, Trubner, 1873); Lord Teignmouth, *Sir William Jones: Works* (13 vols., London, J. Stockdale, 1807); J. Prinsep, *Essays on Indian Antiquities* (3 vols., London, J. Murray).

various levels. It is entirely legitimate to study the Brahmanical world-view of classical times; it is incorrect to give the impression that it was the only world-view which has developed in India, or that all Indians shared in it.

Another vexing general problem for the treatment of Indian history is the matter of periodization. It has been customary to use the standard periodization derived from European history in describing Indian historical epochs, but it is obvious that this is substantially misleading. References to the Indian "middle ages" cause the student to assume certain things about the era so designated because he knows what is meant by the "middle ages" in Europe. It is, however, quite doubtful that there was a constellation of events and circumstances at any time in India's past which corresponds to that set of conditions which we subsume when we speak of the "middle ages" in Europe.

There is, in fact, no agreement on the periodization of Indian history. Furthermore, a periodization which would suit the events of north India would not suit the events of South India. Each historian, presumably, must be his own guide in this matter. In my own presentation of Indian history (which happens to be in good part anchored to an analytical account of society and culture in north India), I tend to break the presentation up into the following flexible periods: the Vedic Age; the Classical Brahmanic Era—the Period of Development of High Hinduism; the Post-Gupta interregnum; the period of Muslim ascendancy; the period of European intervention; the period of the East India Company; and modern (post-mutiny) India. I find these rough divisions useful in organizing my presentation, but they are offered here simply as a suggestion of how Indian history might be divided.

Closely allied to the matter of the level at which interpretation is to be pitched is the problem of discerning and defining the Indian cultural tradition. This difficult task involves painstaking judgments on several subordinate issues. Following from the early emphasis on the high intellectual tradition, there has been a tendency to interpret

Indian history in a unitary, evolutionary manner. Generally this interpretation has been based upon the assumption summed up in the phrase "sanskritization." In this view, the bearers of the classical Brahmanical world-view spread over the subcontinent and diffused their cultural tradition and value system to all or most of the varied peoples who inhabited the region.[10] It is argued that the world-view of high Hinduism has, through the sanskritization process, filtered down to the various levels of Indian society so that their ways-of-life have been increasingly influenced—if not dominated—by the unifying force of a single, central cultural tradition.[11]

Unfortunately, we still know far too little about the complex and variegated relationships between the central tradition of high Hinduism and the existing local and regional traditions. Even now there is considerable disagreement among scholars on this issue and a variety of viewpoints are advanced. Some see sanskritization as the diffusion of the great tradition among the parochial little traditions, while others discover evidence of a neglected process in which elements of the little traditions are reified and incorporated into the great tradition in a "reverse" process of borrowing.[12]

It is difficult to decide whether there has been *one* Indian tradition or *many,* and equally difficult to decide how far the high intellectual tradition has permeated and transformed the low intellectual traditions of the masses in various localities or, indeed, to what extent the high intellectual tradition embodies elements of local traditions which have been absorbed, reinterpreted and integrated. This is by no means an academic issue. Analysis of critical divisive tendencies in the contemporary scene or of the effects of foreign rule depends upon one's treatment of the bewildering foliation charac-

[10] On the relations between the great and the little traditions, see V. Raghavan, "Variety and Integration in the Pattern of Indian Culture," *Far Eastern Quarterly,* XV (1956), 497–506.

[11] For a discussion of "sanskritization," see M. N. Srinivas, "A Note on Sanskritization and Westernization," *Far Eastern Quarterly,* XV (1956), 481–96.

[12] This has been explored by McKim Marriott in an article which has been published in, M. Marriott, ed., *Village India, Studies in the Little Community* (Chicago, University of Chicago Press, 1955).

teristic of India's past. In the presentation of Indian history, it is necessary to formulate questions on these issues and to analyze a maze of evidence and interpretations.

An example may be given of the extent to which these questions influence scholarly judgments upon a major topic in the presentation of Indian history. It is impossible to deal with India's past without discussing and evaluating the role of the caste system and the nature of caste.[13] In the light of the high intellectual tradition, as embodied in the Sanskritic texts,[14] one can define and describe caste as it was formulated in Brahmanical law. This gives an ideal and a static picture of caste as it was supposed to be when the law codes were formulated. Until recently it has been considered sufficient to study the ancient texts or secondary works based upon the ancient texts.

It is, however, increasingly apparent that the classical version of the caste system and of other aspects of Hindu social organization is far from adequate. Even if it be imagined that caste was once like the authoritative statements in the Hindu law books, it cannot be argued that such is the case in modern times. Thus, to understand how caste has changed and developed, as well as to comprehend its many local variations, one has to turn from the classical texts—valuable though they are—to a study of caste and social organization in action in various parts of the sub-continent. There are relevant and systematic observations which can be made about the institution of caste, even in view of regional variation, but not if the account be based solely upon the classical sources.

Fortunately, the materials for a careful study of the caste system in Indian life are becoming available, but the historian has to undertake a painstaking examination of a voluminous and growing body of literature in order to arrive at an effective and reliable syn-

[13] The same thing can be said for other aspects of Indian history. One cannot, for example, deal adequately with Indian history without examining the nature and effects of the major systems of landed relations and of property in land. But the same problems of interpretation exist.

[14] See, for example, Manu. *The Laws of Manu,* trans. with extracts from seven commentaries by G. Buhler (Sacred Books of the East, Vol. XXV, Oxford, Clarendon, 1886).

thesis of the data from several different levels of conceptualization. An adequate account of Indian society requires such analysis while the interpretation of many facets of Indian history depends upon it.[15] Caste and social organization are among the fundamental problems in the study of Indian history, about which basic questions of the kind which would be raised in the study of any civilization must be asked. In presenting Indian history, it is necessary to expose the student to the leading interpretations offered by modern scholarship.

In a like manner, a basic problem for the understanding of any civilization is the nature of the structure, organization and distribution of power and of the political order. In studying power and the political order, one is concerned with the justifications for the use of power and with the ways in which it is exercised and shared. Moreover, the study of the use of power cannot be confined to the level of the state but must be undertaken for various levels of society. Some of the thorniest issues for an understanding of Indian history concern the valid interpretation of the Indian political order and the use of power. This is true whether one is concerned with formal description or with the analysis of process; it is true whether one studies power and political phenomena in the village, in the region, in the vice-royalty, or in the kingdom.

Hindu ideas of the state, politics, kingship, and political organization are sufficiently different from our own to make any simple comparisons exceedingly difficult and fraught with danger. The tendency has been to interpret Indian political phenomena in terms derived from Western experience, or to write them off under a general rubric such as Oriental despotism. Either way, the student is

[15] Among the more valuable works on caste may be included the following: J. H. Hutton, *Caste in India* (Cambridge University Press, 1946); G. S. Ghurye, *Caste and Class in India* (Bombay, Popular Book Depot, 1957); F. G. Bailey, *Caste and the Economic Frontier* (Manchester University Press, 1957); F. G. Bailey, *Tribe, Caste and Nation* (Manchester University Press, 1960); A. C. Mayer, *Caste and Kinship in Central India* (Berkeley, Calif., University of California Press, 1960); McKim Marriott, *Village India, Studies in the Little Community;* Max Weber, *The Religion of India,* trans. and ed. by H. Gerth and D. Martindale (Glencoe, Ill., Free Press, 1958).

misled or misinformed. The dynamics of the indigenous social and
political process are passed over in favor of phrases which seem to
explain more than they do. Whatever position one adopts to explain
the Hindu concept of the state—or the Islamic political system imported into India—and the justifications given for the use and distribution of power, as well as the organization of the state system
and of the hierarchy and bureaucracy, it is necessary that the student
be exposed to problems of interpretation and to the difficulties of
using terms derived from the experience of other civilizations.[16]

   While the student should be exposed, I may add, to various interpretations of Indian political phenomena, this should not be done
merely for the sake of presenting different viewpoints. The amassing
of contrary opinions, as such, bears no charmed significance. The
purpose of studying a variety of expositions is to enhance one's
ability to make discriminating judgments by weighing and evaluating conflicting claims on the basis of the evidence they adduce. At
the same time, the student ought to acquire by these means a degree of intellectual sophistication concerning the usefulness of various approaches to the study of complex social phenomena.

   A course on Indian history can hardly rest content with exposition
of social structure and political institutions. An introduction must
also be given to the main currents in Indian thought, religious and
secular. Intellectual history stands alongside social and political
history and can, in fact, make an important contribution to the
understanding of political and social systems. Unfortunately, Indian
intellectual history is in the same situation as other branches of Indian history. There are the great tradition and the little traditions,

[16] The literature of Indian political thought and practice is extensive and includes
a variety of interpretations. Some of the more helpful titles and collections of read-
ings are: D. M. Brown, *The White Umbrella: Indian Political Thought* (Berkeley,
University of California Press, 1953); Wm. T. de Bary, ed., *Sources of Indian Tradi-
tion* (New York, Columbia University Press, 1958); H. G. Rawlinson, *India, a
Cultural History* (London, Cresset, 1952); A. L. Basham, *The Wonder That Was
India;* R. C. Majumdar, *Ancient India* (Benaras, Motilal Banarsidasa, 1952); U. N.
Goshal, *A History of Indian Political Ideas* (Bombay, Oxford University Press, 1959);
R. L. Park and I. Tinker, eds., *Leadership and Political Institutions in India* (Prince-
ton, Princeton University Press, 1959).

the orthodox and the heterodox, as well as discrete regional and local traditions, such garbed in its own distinctive language and literature. The problem is to be selective without doing violence to adequacy of treatment. In the selection of materials from the local traditions and from the central stream of Indian thought, the effort needs be to uncover pervasive and characteristic themes as well as the significant local variations which mark out important divergencies. Unifying elements which would constitute a common intellectual tradition must be given due consideration along with vigorous instances of particularisms.

Study of the history of Indian thought has two major results. To begin with, it exposes the student to a direct statement of the Indian world-view. This lends added comprehension of the social, economic and political institutions in which that world-view has been embodied. In addition, it helps to illuminate the milieu in which Indian institutions took shape. The reciprocal relationship between social milieu, institutions and the growth and modification of ideas can thus be studied. This places ideas in their context.[17]

A course in Indian history must also pay attention to the leading features of the economic organization and performance characteristic of India's past. Presentation of Indian economic history is hampered by the poorly developed state of this branch of Indian studies. Nonetheless, certain important attributes of traditional economic life in India can be described and the student can be brought to see the intricate relationship between Indian social organization and economic behavior. The forms of economic activity in an agrarian based and predominantly village society have to be outlined as well as the

[17] For material on the intellectual history of India, see: S. Radhakrishnan and C. A. Moore, eds., *A Source Book in Indian Philosophy* (Princeton, Princeton University Press, 1957); H. Zimmer, *Philosophies of India* (New York, Meridian, 1956); J. N. Farquhar, *Modern Religious Movements in India* (London, Macmillan, 1915); K. W. Morgan, ed., *The Religion of the Hindus* (New York, Ronald Press, 1953); Wm. T. De Bary, *Sources of Indian Tradition;* A. L. Basham, *The Wonder That Was India;* Max Weber, *The Methodology of the Social Sciences;* A. A. Macdonell, *India's Past* (Delhi, Banarsidasa, 1956); D. M. Brown, *The White Umbrella;* B. Majumdar, *History of Political Thought,* Vol. I (Calcutta, University of Calcutta Press, 1934).

traditional restraints upon innovation and capital accumulation. The role of the Indian state in regulating the use of the economic surplus should be depicted as well as the allied function of the great temple in guiding economic activity. The student needs also to be made aware of the function of secondary production within the village economy and of the significant differences between such secondary production and the specialized handicraft production which was destined for consumption in more cosmopolitan markets.

Given the facts of Indian social structure, examination of economic behavior involves a discussion of the function of caste as a means of organizing the production and exchange of goods and services. Social structural analysis is also required for a survey of the traditional Indian town economy, the role of gilds, the status of entrepreneurs in marketing and financing production and trade, and the relations between secondary producers and the consuming elites. At the same time, the student may be introduced to those provocative questions which seek to explore the reasons for the limited development of a money economy in India, or to assess the extent to which and the reasons why the Indian economy continued to reflect pre-capitalist forms in several of its sectors.[18]

The explication of Hindu thought and the tracing of economic behavior is, of course, not enough. The coming of Islam, and later of

[18] The literature on Indian economic performance is singularly inadequate. The following titles will, however, provide a basic introduction. S. Bhattacharya, *The East India Company and the Economy of Bengal* (London, Luzac, 1954); S. M. Edwardes and H. Garrett, *Mughal Rule in India* (London, Oxford University Press, 1930); S. Lane Poole, *Medieval India under Mohammedan Rule* (New York, Putnam, 1916); W. H. Moreland, *From Akbar to Aurangzeb* (London, Macmillan, 1923); R. C. Dutt, *Economic History of India in the Victorian Age* (London, Routledge and Kegan Paul, 1956); H. Furber, *John Company at Work* (Cambridge, Harvard University Press, 1948); T. G. Spear, *Twilight of the Mughuls* (Cambridge, Cambridge University Press, 1951); A. Tripathi, *Trade and Finance in the Bengal Presidency* (Bombay, Longmans, Green, 1936); R. C. Dutt, *Economic History of India under Early British Rule* (London, Routledge and Kegan Paul, 1956); H. R. Ghosal, *Economic Transition in the Bengal Presidency, 1793–1833* (Lucknow, Newel Kishore Press, 1950); Wm. Logan, *Malabar* (3 vols., Madras, Government Press, 1915); F. J. Shore, *Notes on Indian Affairs* (2 vols., London, J. W. Parker, 1837). Some of the volumes cited elsewhere in this paper include materials on Indian economic history past or present.

the Europeans, profoundly affected Indian history and modified the course of events. This does not mean that one has to become a specialist on Islam in order to deal with Indian history—though such specialization would not be ill placed—but it does imply sufficient knowledge of Islam so as to be able to understand the ways in which the Islamic impact modified Indian patterns of thought, art, organization and behavior. The effects of Islam were felt in India primarily at the level of government and administration, hence one must seek understanding of Muslim ruling institutions. But Islam also affected Indian religion, thought and art. One of the greatest achievements in the history of the sub-continent was the development of an Indo-Muslim architectural tradition which found its highest expression in the world-famous Taj Mahal.[19]

The establishment of Muslim rule in much of the sub-continent was followed by the coming of the Europeans, the beginnings of their territorial influence, the contest for domination of India, the emergence of the English as the leading power and the consolidation of their military and political supremacy. This is a fascinating story in its own right. But more than that, it requires judicious handling in order to explicate the dynamics of the process which led to the building of an empire by a trading company.

It had often been alleged that the empire was acquired quite by accident, but such a view is superficial and misleading. Good and obvious reasons impelled trading companies in the seventeenth and

[19] On the Islamic contribution to Indian history, consult: S. M. Edwardes and H. L. Garrett, *Mughal Rule in India;* Sir Jadunath Sarkar, *Mughal Administration* (Patna, University of Patna Press, 1925): Wm. T. De Bary, *Sources of Indian Tradition;* S. M. Ikram and P. Spear, *The Cultural Heritage of Pakistan* (New York, Oxford University Press, 1939): M. B. Ahmad, *The Administration of Justice in Medieval India* (Aligarh, Aligarh Research Institute, 1941); H. Goetz, *The Crisis of Indian Civilization* (Calcutta, University of Calcutta Press, 1939): W. Hasain, *Administration of Justice during the Muslim Rule in India* (Calcutta, University of Calcutta Press, 1934); S. N. Jaffar, *Education in Muslim India* (Peshawar, S. M. Sadiq Khan, 1936); W. H. Moreland, *The Agrarian Systems of Moslem India* (Cambridge, England, Heffer and Sons, 1929); R. Saran, *Provincial Government of the Mughals* (Allahabad, Kitabistan, 1941); Sri Ram Sharma, *Muslim Government and Administration* (Bombay, Hind Kitabs, 1951); K. M. Panikkar, *A Survey of Indian History* (New York, Hafner, 1956).

eighteenth centuries to move surely, even if hesitantly, toward territorial control. A disservice is done the student if he is not made aware of the cogent reasons for, as well as the difficulties of, creating an English dominion in India. One must understand the great trading companies and the context in which they operated in order to come to grips with their behavior, their rivalries, and their search for territorial control. This, of course, raises a thorny problem—how much English history must the student know in order to understand the milieu in which the East India Company functioned? While there is no easy answer to the question, it can be asserted that the student should grasp the basic facts concerning the aims, organization and procedures of the Company and the essence of its tangled relation with its rivals and with English political life. More than that can probably not be expected in a course on Indian history.[20]

A much more important matter, requiring thorough treatment, is the question of how foreign domination altered and transformed Indian life and institutions. As the Europeans imported their political and administrative system, their legal notions, their commercial and trading policies and their beliefs, values and norms into India there commenced a complex process of interaction between the ways-of-life of various segments of Indian society and the imported elements of English manners, customs and codes. The servants of the Company borrowed ideas and practices from the Mughals and from In-

[20] For the nature of the East India Company and the establishment of English power in India, see the following: C. H. Philips, *India* (London, Hutchinson's, 1949); C. H. Philips, *The East India Company, 1784–1834* (Manchester, University of Manchester Press, 1940); K. Ballhatchet, *Social Policy and Social Change in Western India* (New York, Oxford University Press, 1957); E. Stokes, *The English Utilitarians and India* (Oxford, Clarendon Press, 1959); Sir W. W. Hunter, *History of British India* (2 vols., New York, Longmans, Green, 1899–1900); F. J. Shore, *Notes on Indian Affairs;* B. S. Cohn, *The Development and Impact of British Administration in India* (New Delhi, Indian Institute of Public Administration, 1961); E. Thompson and G. T. Garratt, *Rise and Fulfilment of British Rule in India* (London, Macmillan, 1934); P. Spear, ed., *The Oxford History of India* (3d. rev. ed., Oxford, Clarendon Press, 1958); B. B. Misra, *The Central Administration of the East India Company, 1773–1834* (Manchester, University of Manchester Press, 1960); Lucy Sutherland, *The East India Company in Eighteenth Century Politics* (Oxford, Oxford University Press, 1952).

dian society but in doing so they transformed what they had haphazardly borrowed. At the same time, they engrafted thereon ideas and practices they had brought with them. The result was the piecemeal and unplanned creation of a new, but incomplete, amalgam. The study of modern India cannot avoid a searching inquiry into the dynamics of the process by means of which elements of two alien ways-of-life were juxtaposed in an acculturative encounter of great depth and complexity.

The analysis of the uncertain and unpremeditated engrafting of European patterns of thought and behavior onto Indian society is in its infancy, lacking even an adequate conceptual and theoretical approach. This enhances the difficulty of dealing with the process while, at the same time, it cries out for intensive scholarly effort. There is, moreover, an additional hazard to be faced. The writing of the history of British India is handicapped by the distortions of partisan bias. Many English authors have consciously or unconsciously sought to provide justification of and rationalizations for English rule in India, while Indian authors have been engaged in the refutation of the British point-of-view and in an understandable but unsound effort to glorify their own past while denigrating the British accomplishment.

The protagonists of each side have entered the lists unable or unwilling to understand the assumptions and the values of the other side. Though there are, of course, exceptions to this generalization, the exceptions are too few to materially affect the basic situation. As a result, the innocent bystander has to thread his way through a body of historical writing which is penetrated with apologetics and their counter irritants. The tone of a good part of the literature is such as to induce the reader to choose sides or to engage in a somewhat sterile attempt to cast up a "balance sheet," highlighting either the credits or the debits of foreign rule. Complacent justification or angry denunciation seldom make good history and the student, especially the novice, must be alerted to the situation as he begins his reading. It should, however, be made clear that the study of polemical writings is important as a means of testing the extent to which and the ways in which bias influences the creation of historical judgments.

Meanwhile, what is needed is a substantial scholarly effort to rewrite the history of British India in analytical terms designed to avoid partisan controversy and to understand the underlying processes of change which have been at work. Modern India has emerged from the interaction between foreign rule and indigenous traditions and the task of research and pedagogy is to comprehend what has emerged rather than to bestow praise or level accusation. In this effort one asks legitimate questions regarding the major characteristics of the interaction, the leading effects of foreign domination and the principal kinds of native response.

The impact of Europe on India was many-sided and affected Indians in a variety of ways and at several different levels. There is, therefore, no simple and straightforward account to be given. Rather, the historian must analyze the extent to which and the ways in which various elements of Indian society were affected. For an undergraduate course on India it is, of course, impossible to do this in depth and detail. But the presentation of the leading characteristics of the interaction, although necessarily selective, should rest upon a detailed study of various aspects of this complex and uneven process. This means that the historian has to be conversant with studies of modern India which have been produced by anthropologists, demographers, sociologists, social psychologists, economists, political scientists, philosophers, humanists, art historians, and specialists in Indian literature.[21]

[21] The literature on modern India is by no means satisfactory for the study of the issues posed here. Too much ink has been spilled in narrative political history and in reports of viceregal affairs and too little on the process of change, adjustment, and response. The following titles will, however, aid one in getting at a range of events and circumstances not dealt with in the traditional political histories. Wm. T. De Bary, *Sources of Indian Tradition;* Sir C. Y. Chintamani, *Indian Politics since the Mutiny* (London, Allen and Unwin, 1940); Sir Henry Cotton, *New India, or, India in Transition* (London, Trubner, 1904); M. L. Darling, *The Punjab Peasant in Prosperity and Debt* (New York, Oxford University Press, 1947); A. R. Desai, *The Social Background of Indian Nationalism* (Bombay, Popular Book Depot, 1954); Sir P. J. Griffitsh, *The*

The central theme of the study and of its presentation can well be the change and transformation which has resulted from foreign domination. Within that organizing framework—which asks how the emerging civilization of contemporary South Asia has been created by the process of interaction—the scholar may divide the account into a number of topics in one of several ways. He may choose to discuss the process of change as it has affected social organization, political systems, intellectual currents, economic behavior, religious thought and world-view. Or he may choose to discuss the subject in terms of changes in village society, changes in urban life, changes among the indigenous elites, and changes in the degree of cosmopolitanization which have come upon a formerly parochial and particularistic society.

Alternatively, he may select certain key themes of change, which cut across various levels, and organize the presentation around these themes. This could include a concentration upon the movement from a society based upon ascription toward a society based upon achievement, or the movement from political diversity to national unification and the consciousness of nationhood, or the movement from a social system in which the individual was immersed in his primary groupings such as family, clan, and caste toward a society

British Impact on India (London, Macdonald, 1952); B. T. McCully, *English Education and the Origins of Indian Nationalism* (New York, Columbia University Press, 1940); V. P. Menon, *The Transfer of Power in India* (Princeton, Princeton University Press, 1957); L. S. S. O'Malley, *Modern India and the West* (New York, Oxford University Press, 1941); Tarlok Singh, *Poverty and Social Change* (Bombay, Longmans, Green, 1945); M. Brecher, *Nehru: A Political Biography* (New York, Oxford University Press, 1959); W. N. Brown, *The United States and India and Pakistan* (Cambridge, Harvard University Press, 1953); N. C. Chaudhuri, *The Autobiography of an Unknown Indian* (New York, Macmillan, 1951); K. David, *The Population of India and Pakistan* (Princeton, Princeton University Press, 1951); S. C. Dube, *Indian Village* (Ithaca, Cornell University Press, 1955); McKim Marriott, *Village India, Studies in the Little Community;* R. L. Park and I. Tinker, eds., *Leadership and Political Institutions in India;* M. Weiner, *Party Politics in India* (Princeton, Princeton University Press, 1957); Sir Stanley Reed, *The India I Knew, 1897–1947* (London, Odhams, 1952); Taya Zinkin, *India Changes* (New York, Oxford University Press, 1958); M. Weiner, "The Politics Of South Asia," in G. Almond and James Coleman, eds., *The Politics of the Developing Areas* (Princeton, Princeton University Press, 1960).

in which the individual increasingly achieves autonomy and self-determination. Or, the central theme around which the presentation is organized could be the creation of modern Indian nationalism: the factors which made it possible, the circumstances which called it into being, the hurdles it had to attempt to overcome, the responses to foreign domination it had to symbolize and express, the methods it had to develop, the aims and objectives it set before the Indian people, the various stages through which it passed, the leaders who emerged within its ranks, the animosities it created, and the kinds of success it achieved.

Another organizing theme could be a concentration upon analysis and interpretation of the kinds of changes which have produced contemporary India through a study of modern Indian intellectual history. Though this is not easy to do because the range of materials available in western languages is limited, the modern intellectual history of India can reflect and exemplify many of the significant kinds of change which have taken place in various sectors of Indian life. This is especially true of autobiographical materials and of a number of interesting titles in recent Indian fiction. Even if the presentation be organized around another set of themes, the use of materials from modern Indian literatures can materially enhance one's grasp of the subject.

Whatever format is chosen for the presentation of the subject matter of modern Indian history, the central issues are clear. Foreign domination initiated a variety of important transformations in South Asia. Incomplete though these transformations may be, South Asia is quite different today from what it was two hundred years ago and equally different from what it would have been if there had not been a prolonged period of foreign rule. In order to understand modern South Asia, we must study the changes which have taken place. Even if we were to opt for a straightforward chronological account of the past two centuries, such an account would have to pay attention to major changes. The one thing which should not be done is to try to confine the account within the traditional scope of political history which seeks to describe only the apex of the political system. The meat and the heart of the British impact on India is lost if we look only to political history and constitutional development.

A special problem needs to be noted in connection with this matter of studying social change in modern India. We face a peculiar and not insignificant kind of limitation on our ability to study the subject. This limitation is inherent in the kinds of source materials which are generally available and have been most widely used to date. Most of what is in print on modern India is the product of the European minority who governed India or of the tiny handful of western-educated Indians. For India's past, we have relied upon the record left by the Brahman priesthood and for modern India we rely upon a record bequeathed us by an almost equally minute segment of the population. Of the views, behaviors, aims, and understandings of the masses under foreign rule we know very little. Only recently have village studies begun to explore at that level and to present their findings in readily available form. For earlier years, there is somewhat similar data deposited in census reports, administrative reports, settlement reports, district gazetteers, and the like, but those sources have hardly been used in producing histories and the original reports usually had a limited publication and distribution. The historian has to take special measures to get below the record as left by the elites so he may probe the *terra incognita* of the populace. Furthermore, he has to get below the record left by the rulers and the Western-educated so as to get at matters in which they were not interested. Official sources, however valuable they may be for certain topics, were normally not concerned with a range of issues on which enlightenment is required if modern Indian history is to be written in all of its richness.

The little which has been done so far to get at underlying phenomena, as in modern village studies, suffices to show how limited the older knowledge was. So many things which were blandly assumed to be true for India, or for Hinduism, or for caste, have turned out to be far less universal than had been assumed. The gap between the high intellectual tradition and the varied expressions of the low intellectual tradition is greater than had been imagined. The result is a need to revise and reconstruct many of our opinions about Indian society. We are learning that we know too much about the viceroys or about the college graduates who wanted posts in the Indian Civil Service and too little about the leatherworkers of Madhopur.

By saying this, I do not mean to suggest that the leatherworkers of Madhopur are more important to history than the graduates of Cambridge University or of Presidency College. I do mean to say that we cannot be complacent about a history which is the record of the activity of the latter and is almost entirely silent about the former. Actually, it is impossible to see the record of the Western-educated elite in anything like proper perspective unless it be placed in the proper context, and that context must include various levels of social structure and the relationships characteristic of the system.

Throughout this essay, emphasis has been placed upon the need to study social process and upon the proper concern of the historian with an understanding of process. That emphasis reflects the bias of the cultural historian in favor of the analysis of structure, and of interrelationships and movement in structure. Social process, as seen by the cultural historian, can be defined as change in the interrelations between the elements of a culture through time and from one state or condition to another.[22] If one is to grasp social process it is necessary that all of the relevant elements of society be included in the analysis. If part of the structure is left out—not to mention the interrelations characteristic of that part of the structure—the analyst will have at best an incomplete grasp of the phenomenon un-

[22] For an introductory discussion of social process see the chapter by R. L. Carneiro, "The Culture Process," in, G. E. Dole and R. L. Carneiro, *Essays in the Science of Culture, In Honor of Leslie A. White* (New York, Crowell, 1960), pp. 145–61. The same subject is dealt with by R. E. Turner in, *The Social Sciences in Historical Study; a report* (New York, Social Science Research Council, 1954).

der study. The understanding of India's past has suffered precisely from this kind of incompleteness.[23]

Perhaps it should be stressed that the study of modern India should not be confined to the processes of change alone. It is necessary to ask what the changes imply. What have the effects of change been and how does the emergent civilization alter conditions and potentialities for its carriers? As culture changes, how are men's views of what is possible, feasible or necessary changed? What new alternatives can be said to confront the actors upon the scene? How, in effect, do men respond to change?

Change may mean, as it has in recent India, new tools, new skills, new occupations. It may mean new freedoms—as is implicit in the new individualism—and the risks that go with new freedoms. It may include new values, goals, and justifications. Change usually involves new possibilities in social, economic or political behavior. Social change can be studied as a set of new potentialities and one can ask how men react or respond.

In modern India, foreign agency has been responsible for much of the impetus to change. Presumably, this complicates the indigenous response. Autochthonous change may be adjusted to rather readily. Change which springs from alien domination may be resisted vigorously, because it bears the stamp of foreign inspiration. Resistance to foreign domination may well take the form of opposition to the new ways associated with foreign rule. All of those segments of native society which suffer from change can agree, even if on nothing else, to blame the trauma upon the foreigner.

---

[23] The reference to incompleteness does not mean to suggest that an adequate historical account can or should aim at exhaustive detail. Not at all. Careful and rational selection of the relevant from the vast mass of detail is essential to sound historical writing or pedagogy. The point is that the "incompleteness" should not be the result of chance, of unavailability or of an unwillingness to examine the data for the relevant. The comparative method proposed early in this paper is, of course, based upon selection. But it is based upon a self-conscious selection of what is relevant to the task at hand and it presupposes the willingness of the historian to submit his selective criteria to critical testing.

Whether the response to change exhibits this negative reaction or not, the matter of the native reaction to change is of major importance to the study of modern India. The difficulty, of course, is that there has been no single, neat pattern of response to change or to foreign influences. There have been, as has been indicated, a variety of responses and the problem is to make sense out of the variety and to discern the *directions* in which the characteristic kinds of response seem to be leading. If change provides new alternatives, the response to change implies some choice among the alternatives. In order to understand the emergent civilization it is necessary to ask which alternatives are being chosen and with what potential outcomes. Indian society is being reshaped through the choices that are being made, and the student will need to know what the reshaping implies.

Let me hastily provide an instance, taken from recent Indian history, to illuminate this matter. British rule meant the introduction of Western education and the introduction of at least some of the institutions and practices of representative and parliamentary government. The education imparted under British rule contained justifications for the parliamentary system. These justifications were sufficiently persuasive to cause Western-educated Indians to demand representative institutions for themselves. Even if parliamentary procedures had not been initiated by the British, the educated demand for them would have grown apace.

Both Western education and representative institutions implied new alternatives and new potentialities for segments of the Indian population. For reasons which need not be specified here, certain upper castes among the Hindus turned with alacrity to the new learning and the new careers based upon Western education. For a variety of reasons, the Muslim community lagged far behind the Hindus in the acquisition of Western education. New potentialities were present but, in general, the Muslims stood aloof.

Because of English presuppositions and because of the nature of the skills required, it was the Western-educated class which had any hope of entering the embryonic legislatures. Furthermore, parliamentary institutions were based upon the idea of majority rule. When the development of the legislatures in a meaningful fashion took place, the backward Muslim community came alive to the possibilities of the new situation and realized their own disadvantages. The immediate result was the formation of a new political organization to defend Muslim interests and the demand for separate electorates to guarantee the election of Muslim candidates. From these modest beginnings—aided by other factors which need not be cited—dates the political organization of Muslim separatism which ultimately became a major phenomenon in the life of the subcontinent, leading to partition and the creation of Pakistan.

The story of the events which led to partition is an important aspect of the presentation of modern Indian history in its own right. But it is also important as part of the larger story of the Indian response to changes induced by foreign rule and it illuminates the thesis that one is less interested in change for its own sake than in the implications of change and the responses to change. In this connection it may be remarked that an adequate treatment of the evolution of nationalism in the sub-continent rests upon the view that it is a special case of the more general matter of Indian response to a process of change which was in good part induced by foreign rule.[24]

[24] This is particularly true because this vantage point helps the student grasp a vexing aspect of contemporary India. As is known, independent India is governed by the Western-educated elite who are imbued with modernizing values. There is, however, the paradox of ambivalence toward modernization and a counter-current of criticism of the basic postulates on which modernization rests. This raises the question regarding the source of ambivalence. By regarding nationalism, which enunciated the goals of modernization, as a response to foreign-induced change one is able to discern an important source of the ambivalence. Nationalism, while it favored modernization and a secular order, included strong overtones of negative reaction to foreign rule. The ambivalence in the nationalist posture is seen in its proper light and can be related to the post-independence disagreement over the goal of modernization. In part this is so because the nationalist movement had to seek effective popular support and this required the leaders to speak in terms familiar to the masses. The "Indianization" of the nationalist demand enhanced the ambivalence regarding modernization. Thus Gandhi, the most effective leader of the Congress, largely rejected modernizing goals and suggested a return to an age of pristine rural simplicity.

Emphasis on the indigenous response to changes wrought by foreign agency is, moreover, an important corrective to the typical reading of modern Indian history which lays its stress upon the achievements of British rule. Without in any way denying the British accomplishment, reflection on the characteristics of the Indian response help us to round the picture out and put it in proper perspective. Many of the innovations associated with British rule made perfect sense within the context of Western values, but their effects on the Indian scene were rather different than their proponents imagined. If we are to get at a realistic picture of their effects, we must include in our interpretation some reference to the ways in which they bore upon the Indian context and the Indian value system. Otherwise, we get an interpretation which is so ethnocentric in its assumptions as to render most doubtful a number of its conclusions.

Finally, in the presentation of Indian history, certain questions arise regarding the underlying processes at work in contemporary India. In theory at least, one's reading of the past should equip one for an informed understanding of the present and of the seemingly contradictory trends which can be noted as Indians make independent decisions regarding the directions in which they will move.

While historians tend to treat the contemporary scene gingerly, they seldom disclaim responsibility for understanding it. It is admittedly more difficult to analyze current trends, because so much of the relevant information is lacking, but there is no *a priori* reason to suppose that a sound grasp of the processes at work cannot be secured as a basis for informed questions and hypotheses. Moreover, it is precisely in the current scene that the historian can find something like a "laboratory" for testing hypotheses.

Of India today, one may ask what are the major problems faced, what are the more obvious alternatives available for exploitation, what directions of movement seem feasible or likely in terms of the changes which have already taken place, what reorientations of the value system have been carried sufficiently far so as to be able to support new departures, and what elements of society seem to sit at or near focal decision-points in the network of decision making? From these kinds of questions, one may fashion hypotheses regarding the probable course of events under specified conditions. Even though the hypotheses may turn out to be less than useful in discerning the course of events or in reckoning the probabilities, it can be asserted that the rigorous intellectual task of formulating hypotheses and devising their tests will prove to be its own sufficient reward. In the attempt to raise questions of this kind, the student will have been trained to use his mind critically and will have learned a great deal—not only about India—but also about the study of society.

Previous sections of this paper have dealt with aspects of Indian history to which attention should be paid and with the kinds of questions around which a presentation might be organized. Such treatment, though necessary, tends to dissolve the whole in favor of its parts. But the task of tearing a subject into logically separate topics for the purposes of analysis is only a prelude to the reassembly of the parts into a meaningful whole. A course in Indian history is concerned with over-all development and with the leading features of the civilization.

For pre-modern Indian, we seek comprehension of the whole by understanding the reciprocal function of its parts. We characterize Indian civilization as traditional, based upon a predominantly agrarian, peasant society and dominated by caste, kinship and other parochial solidarities. One sees the Indian tradition as pervaded by religion and supernaturalism, while the Indian social system reflects an emphasis on hierarchy, on duty to one's group, and upon the essentially static assumptions of status by ascription. Undergirding a pre-modern society was a fixed and limited technology geared to an economic system which was encumbered by the rule of custom, by unwritten sanctions against innovation and individualism, and by the requirements of an exchange system which was primarily social and hierarchical rather than economic.

Into this relatively static culture came the carriers of a restless, dynamic and at times brutal socioeconomic order. Impatient, individualistic, and pragmatic, they pushed and pulled the older order off its epicenter, in the course of pursuing their own aims and assumptions. Progress, as defined in the bustling circles of Western mercantilism, came to be the order of the day. Its heralds little knew and hardly cared whether it was congenial to Indian institutions or not. Solving the new problems they faced in an ad hoc manner, they managed to reorient certain aspects of Indian life and thrust India into the modern age.

Before long, India was involved in the beginnings of a revolutionary transformation, actively supported by the new, Western-educated class. When British hands faltered, their Indian counterparts pressed forward the demand for modernization, for self-rule and for universal suffrage. Since independence, the interrelated processes of change, which emerged early in this century, have been given additional impetus as public policy pushes for rapid economic growth, universal literacy, functioning and mass-based parliamentary institutions, equality of opportunity for all, and the emergence of a secular-rational order based upon the rule of law and upon modern science and technology. The new goals are in direct conflict with many of the fundamental assumptions of the traditional order and the question continues: can the demand for a modernized society replace the older gods?

The goal of the study of Indian history is to see the changes which have taken place in proper perspective, to place them in their context, to understand how the traditional order functioned and how its functions have been transformed. The study of Indian history seeks to comprehend and evaluate the effects of the transformation, the directions taken by the emerging new civilization and the probable outcomes of new trends.

If the student is not given this perspective of the whole, his study of the various topics suggested previously will tend toward pedantry. Learning about India's past for antiquarian reasons can hardly justify the inclusion of Indian history in the undergraduate curriculum. Rather the student needs to understand how and why Indian civilization has been transformed and to learn how civilizations change and develop.

Comment: The Chinese Perspective

JAMES T. C. LIU

Associate Professor of History, Stanford University

The illuminating paper by Professor Crane is a welcome addition to his helpful pamphlet of three years ago on the study and interpretation of Indian history for teachers.[1] Indeed, little criticism can or need be raised. Given the assignment to discuss it from the standpoint of a comparable and allied field, the field of teaching Chinese history to undergraduates, my comments tend to be in general support of this approach, perhaps with some elaboration.

A few parallel examples may be given to show how many points made in this paper are applicable or have been applied to the teaching of Chinese history in general education. First, the use of the comparative method has at least three distinct values: the *tool value* of taking the known Western culture across the bridge of comparison into the novel territory of an Oriental culture, in this case, Indian; the *rebound value* of a deeper understanding of the Western culture itself through reflection; and the *bonus value* of learning how to apply the same analytical method to yet another unfamiliar culture, for example, Chinese. In this light, a comparison of Hindu metaphysics and Christian metaphysics, such as the paper mentions, may be advisably extended to include a brief consideration of Chinese metaphysics. The additional time necessary would be amply justified to show how the impact of the Indian thought through Buddhism enriched the Chinese mind and yet on the other hand the teachings of Confucius hardly interested many Indians at all. To do

[1] Robert I. Crane, "The History of India: Its Study and Interpretation" (Service Center for Teaching of History, American Historical Association, 1958).

so might not be essential in a course on Indian civilization. However, it is almost imperative in a comparable course on China where the Indian elements, not found in the ancient classics, eventually became an integral part of the syncretic tradition, and whereas Christian metaphysics was unable to accomplish the same.

A second example is the criticism of the old view in teaching which concentrated almost exclusively on the level of high Hinduism, as if it were the entire Hindu culture. The same criticism has been vigorously raised by many in the Chinese field with regard to the classical, indeed idealized, version of Confucianism. Notable among such critics is Professor Arthur Wright who has edited four symposium volumes.[2] A number of articles in these volumes demonstrate how Confucian ideals mixed in varying degrees both with the originally non-Confucian values as well as with realistic considerations; or in the sociological terminology of Robert Redfield, how the great tradition changed through the intermingling of the little traditions.[3]

To follow up with a third example, Professor Crane raises the question whether the Indian tradition is one or many and whether it evolves in a unitary manner. A similar question exists in the case of the Chinese tradition. The answer shared by many of us is a pluralistic one—it has a unity, some polarities, and a diversity all at the same time. The unity, especially in view of the long time span, is truly remarkable. However, the unity refers to some common grounds with unifying persuasions, rather than an entity thoroughly unified. On the contrary, from the common grounds upward, this complex tradition branched out in diverse directions, sometimes beyond the shades of unity and even in opposition to it. Most intriguing

[2] Arthur F. Wright, ed., *Studies in Chinese Thought* (Chicago, University of Chicago Press, 1953); D. S. Nivision and A. F. Wright, eds., *Confucianism in Action* (Stanford, Calif., Stanford University Press, 1959); Arthur F. Wright, ed., *Confucian Persuasion* (Stanford, Calif., Stanford University Press, 1960); and a last volume of this series, forthcoming. Also of this series, is John K. Fairbank, ed., *Chinese Thought and Institutions* (Chicago, University of Chicago Press, 1957).

[3] Hui-chen Wang Liu, "An Analysis of Chinese Clan Rules," in D. S. Nivision and A. F. Wright, eds., *Confucianism in Action*, pp. 94–96; see also Robert Redfield, *Peasant Society and Culture* (Chicago, University of Chicago Press, 1956), pp. 68–96.

is what lay between the unity and the diversity. There often appeared basic problems which, in the absence of agreed solution, led to divergent polarities. Such polarities impelled continuing tensions and struggles.[4] From this pluralistic view, the students will learn a proper perspective, by no means a static picture of the seemingly unchangeable Orient, but the dynamics of a living and at times lively tradition.

Other parallel examples are plentiful. In teaching any non-Western civilization, it is desirable to outline to the students such problems as social organization, power structure, intellectual trends, economic behavior, and the like. Many of these problems still await further research. This is a handicap, but, in teaching, it can also be turned into some advantage. Another proper perspective is to train the undergraduates to raise questions and to impress upon them what would be involved in research.

Nor can we afford to neglect in a general education course the vast problem of modernization common to all the non-Western or pre-industrial societies, indeed a most vital problem which requires tremendous research but to which, unfortunately, many high-brow scholars prefer to close their eyes. Here again, the comparative method must be used and even expanded.[5] Sometimes, it is unavoidable to discuss not only what a different culture has but also what it does not have. For instance, the question why India or China, where trade flourished, did not develop capitalism as such. Rather than avoid the subject, we should take it up, understandably at the risk of overreaching ourselves. It is permissible to do so as long as the students realize that this is not a conclusive but partly speculative discussion. For the proper perspective is to encourage the young inquiring minds, to stimulate them, rather than to stifle them.

[4] Benjamin Schwartz, "Some Polarities in Confucian Thought," in D. S. Nivison and A. F. Wright, eds., *Confucianism in Action*, pp. 50–62; James T. C. Liu, "On the Dual Nature of the Confucian State," *Tōhōgaku* (Tokyo, June, 1961), No. 20, pp. 119–25.
[5] Professor Cyril E. Black of Princeton University has a forthcoming book on modernization by comparative study.

In concluding, may I attempt to characterize the teaching method as discussed so far. First, it is based upon what has been generally accepted in recent decades as the cultural approach to history and the social science approach to history.[6] The cardinal proposition is to study culture as a whole and its various aspects in relation with one another through the integrated application of relevant social sciences. Second, how can this proposition be implemented in a beginner's course with neither the excessive burden of covering almost everything important nor the accompanying danger of becoming too superficial? One answer is the *key topics method*. A key topic is usually chosen on two grounds: it is a key to the understanding of the culture or a vital aspect thereof; and, at the same time, it effectively demonstrates how the various social sciences come together in an analysis. Third, this principle of selecting key topics allows the teacher considerable flexibility in deciding the amount of time he sees fit to spend on a topic. For instance, to discuss Chinese peasant life, he may well limit it to a relatively narrow sample of a single village or he may take up the whole range of rural control, exerted not by the local government alone but also by other elements—political, economic, social, and ideological.[7] Fourth, while the proposed values of such a teaching method are usually granted, one objection has often been raised. Isn't this level of sophisticated analysis way over the head of ill-prepared undergraduates? Experience indicates, however, that the solution of this difficulty lies in escalation. The point is really so simple that it is frequently overlooked. A general education course need not at all maintain an even level from the beginning to the end.[8] On the contrary, it should start in properly at the beginner's level and then gradually move upward, proceeding from basic oversimplifications to mature qualifications,

[6] C. F. Ware, ed., *Cultural Approach to History* (New York, Columbia University Press, 1940); and Social Science Research Council, "The Social Sciences in Historical Study" (Bulletin No. 64, 1954).

[7] C. Yang, *A Chinese Village* (New York, Columbia University Press, 1945); and K. C. Hsiao, *Rural China, Imperial Control in the 19th Century* (Seattle, Wash., University of Washington Press, 1960).

[8] James T. C. Liu, "An Orientation Course on Asian Civilizations," *Journal of General Education*, X (October, 1957), 228–35.

from inevitable generalities to more involved particulars, and from relatively simple exposition to more intensive analysis. In summing up, this is a teaching method based upon the cultural and social science approach, by key topics, of flexible magnitudes, and at escalating levels. This is by no means *the* way of teaching a general course on non-Western civilization; it is a Rome to which there are many ways. And in time there will be a second and a third Rome when both research publications and teaching techniques grow. It will always be helpful to compare notes and share experiences.

Reflections on the Study of
Oriental Civilizations

CHARLES ISSAWI

Professor of Near and Middle East Economics, Columbia University

In the last analysis, one's views on the study and teaching of the history and civilization of the Orient, and one's understanding of the relationship between Oriental and Western cultures, depends on one's philosophy of history. Or, if one wants to avoid grandiloquent terms and use instead the jargon of the economist, it depends on the simple model in terms of which one interprets the historical process. And, whether he is aware of it or not, everyone who is engaged in studying a foreign culture and consciously or unconsciously relating it to his own, uses such a model, just as everyone has some kind of metaphysics. As M. Jourdain learned from his teacher, we must all speak either verse or prose—that is unless we speak gibberish. And, if we try to represent the prevailing models graphically, we find that they fall into two groups: the linear, or continuous, and the circular, or closed-in. For the sake of completeness, one should add a third group, the equivalent of gibberish; this can be represented by scattered dots and really amounts to saying that history is just "one damn thing after another," one event alongside or following the other, with no necessary connection between them; I might add that this is a very widespread view at the present time.

The linear model represents the unity and continuity of civilization. It states, essentially, that there have been not several different civilizations but one Civilization, with a capital "C," which manifested itself in different peoples at different times. This view is generally associated with the doctrine of progress: the line moves upward on the chart, though it is admitted that its slope is not uniform, that there may be cycles around the trend, and that some very sharp drops have occurred. Further refinements are possible, for example, the line may be twisted around one's finger to form a spiral, the symbol chosen by Vico.

So much for the forms of the process; as for its content, there are several versions. There is the view of the eighteenth-century Enlightenment. There is Hegel's majestic picture, in which the world spirit expresses itself in a dialectical process, finding its final resting place in the Prussian monarchy, and its very different offspring, the Marxist dialectic. And there is the liberal view of history as the story of Liberty: here the culminating point is political democracy, of the British or the American type, according to the predilection of the author.

Now, all these linear theories are open to grave objections. And most of these objections arise from the fact that they were all devised by Westerners and explicitly or implicitly assume that European or, at best, Western civilization is the culmination of history and the consummation of the work of the ages.

This view is arrogant and parochial, and as such offends our susceptibility in this mid-twentieth century, with our "One-World" ideas. It is obvious that Chinese, Indian, and other civilizations are not merely preparations for Western civilization. They stand in their own right and would make sense even if Western civilization had never come into being—or if it were to disappear tomorrow. So, indeed, stands all the past. As a conservative nineteenth-century Russian writer, Leontiev, put it, we can hardly believe that "The Apostles preached, the martyrs suffered, poets sang, painters painted and knights glittered in the lists simply in order that the French or German or Russian bourgeois in his horrible and ludicrous clothes might live an individual and collective life complacently on the ruins of all the greatness of the past." [1] Nor is the suggestion less

[1] Quoted by Nicolas Berdyaev, *The Origins of Russian Communism* (London, 1937), p. 103.

ludicrous if we substitute "working class man" for "bourgeois."

Another objection is that, almost inevitably, any linear theory tends to be optimistic: the line moves up. But, in this age of neo-barbarism, concentration camps, and thermonuclear bombs, we tend to be skeptical of all optimistic views and of theories of progress. We are more inclined to agree with Rivarol that "The most civilized empires will aways be as near to barbarism as is the most polished iron to rust." Or with Ranke that "All generations are immediate to God."

It is therefore not surprising that, in reaction to such linear theories, circular theories of civilization should have been evolved. The most uncompromising of these is the theory of Spengler, for whom each civilization forms a closed circle. And, for those who find Spengler too repulsive—or merely too rigid—there are more appealing models. Thus Toynbee's theory may be represented by clusters of circles, since some civilizations are related to others by affiliation. Another possible variation is that of interlocking circles stretching out in a chain—provided it is made perfectly clear that the chain is not "leading anywhere," is not registering "progress." This picture is drawn to take account of the influence which some civilizations have, at certain times, exerted on others. But, whatever the variations, one essential feature remains: each civilization is self-contained, each is "philosophically equivalent" to the others.

Circular theories seem to have been widely accepted, explicitly or implicitly. They fit well with the cultural relativism preached by anthropologists. And they appeal to those who are trying, for the best of motives, to transcend Western egocentricism.

But, in fact, they also raise grave objections. The first of these comes from the religious believer, or at least the believer in a revealed religion; for him, history is ultimately one because all men share in its crucial events. Thus, for the Christian, all men participated in the Fall and all were equally redeemed by Christ. The message of the Gospel is addressed to the whole of humanity, whom it will one day reach. And the Final Judgment awaits all equally. Similar beliefs are held by Islam and Judaism.

Secondly, and at the opposite pole, there are the objections of those who stress the predominant influence of technology on history. For them, too, history has a fundamental unity, based on similarity of technological development. When mankind gave up food gathering and hunting as its main occupations and took up agriculture and handicrafts, it closed the first chapter in history and began the second. As for the third chapter, it opened with the Industrial Revolution, which is rapidly spreading all over the globe. Compared with the difference between food gatherers and farmers or craftsmen, differences between various societies of farmers or craftsmen are insignificant, and the same holds for differences between industrialized and pre-industrial societies.

And in between these two groups, and participating in the nature of both, come the Marxists, with their belief that technological development is one of the most important causes of change in the economic infrastructure—which in turn determines the social, political, and cultural superstructure—and their conviction that the gospel of Marx is addressed to the whole of humanity, which will embrace it in the not too distant future.

None of these three views, the religious, the technological, and the Marxist, is fashionable in academic circles, but all three, nevertheless, carry considerable weight. They should at least make us pause and consider whether the reaction has not been pushed too far.

It is at this point that the social scientist may have a small contribution to make. Surveying the work of historians and humanists engaged in the study of Oriental cultures, he cannot but be struck by the emphasis they put on differences rather than similarities, on what is peculiar to each civilization rather than what it has in common with others. Of course, they are right. Of course, they should try "to penetrate in all its individuality and uniqueness the development of one society, or one civilization, the behaviour not of men and women in general, but of one particular group in a given period of time." [2] But in doing so, they are in danger of for-

---

[2] Alan Bullock in Hans Meyerhoff, ed., *The Philosophy of History in Our Time* (New York, Doubleday Anchor Books, 1959), p. 298.

getting an even more important truth, namely that "The simplicity of man is great, despite his diversity."[3] They are liable to forget that the members of other civilizations were, and are, men like themselves, with the same passions, facing the same or similar problems, using the same reasoning process. And, by passions, I do not mean so much the individual passions, such as love and hate, awe, fear, and so forth. These are too clearly depicted in the classics of the Orient—the *Ring of the Dove* by Ibn Hazm, the *Tale of Genji,* the Chinese and Persian poems, and others—for anyone to have any doubts. I mean rather the social passions: the resentment of oppression, the craving for justice, the feeling of solidarity within a social group, the tensions between groups and classes, and the consequent struggles for power. Similarly, the reasoning process I have in mind is best exemplified in science and technology and in constructing, analyzing, and reflecting on social institutions—that is, man's reason applied to natural or social phenomena. One can illustrate this point from the study of Islamic history and contemporary civilization.

Islamic studies were sired by classical philology out of theology. We should, therefore, be duly grateful to these two disciplines, which were the only available parents. But it seems fair to say that they have kept their offspring too long in leading strings, that they have shut it off from contact with other disciplines. As a result, Islamic studies suffer from two great weaknesses: first, they have neglected some very important aspects of Islamic history and culture; and, second, their approach to many fundamental problems is often inadequate.

As regards the first point, much work has been done by scholars on such subjects as literature, theology, law, and, to a lesser extent, philosophy. But other, at least as important, fields have hardly attracted any attention. Take, for example, economic history. As a distinguished scholar put it, "Of all varieties of history the economic is the most fundamental. Not the most important: foundations exist

[3] Karl Jaspers in Hans Meyerhoff, ed., *The Philosophy of History in Our Time,* p. 336.

to carry better things. . . . But economic activity with its tools, fields, trade, inventions and investment is the basement of man's house." [4] Moreover, Islamic economic history is varied, complex, interesting, and quite rich in sources. Yet, singularly, little has been done on this subject. And until more work is done, our knowledge of the Islamic world is bound to be very imperfect. Incidentally, this also seems to apply to the other Oriental cultures, with the conspicuous exception of Japan. The same is true of the history of technology. Here, too, the Islamic world has some important inventions, or improvements, to its credit, but the history of Islamic crafts has yet to be written. And one cannot but suspect that when it is written it will raise some very interesting questions. Thus, to take one example, it is generally believed that the presence of abundant slave labor impeded technological progress in Greece and Rome. Did the fact that Islam relied to only a small extent on slave labor, then, stimulate its technological development? This and many other questions have not yet been raised, much less answered. And also waiting for an answer are several questions in the natural sciences, another field in which much work remains to be done.

Now, these neglected fields have two things in common, apart from their intrinsic importance. First, they deal with activities which cut across cultural borders. Literature, law, and theology are usually specific to a particular group, but methods of trading, navigating, weaving, and observing the stars have much in common in spite of differences of time and place. Their study therefore may lead to a less particularistic view, to more emphasis on universal characteristics. And, second, the study of such fields can be carried out only by people who have mastered the corresponding discipline. Only one with a thorough knowledge of medicine can write medical history and only an engineer can most usefully study the irrigation works of a past age. As another distinguished economic historian put it: "This relation of theory to the study of history is not peculiar

---

[4] John Harold Clapham, *A Concise Economic History of Britain from the Earliest Times to 1750* (Cambridge, Cambridge University Press, 1949), Introduction.

to the field of economics. On the contrary, it is necessary to historical study to base itself all along the line upon what has been found with regard to the general character of those phenomena which are studied: to take a parallel as remote from economics as possible, the study of the history of war has always been found to stand in need of a knowledge of tactics and strategy . . . And this essential unity in the treatment of warfare has been found to exist in spite of the fact that war has from some points of view been revolutionized through the use of powder and steam.

"As to economics, this necessary unity in the problem, irrespective of time and space, is considerably greater than is the case with war. It is here, if anywhere, a question of *necessités permanentes;* for the basis of economic life and consequently of economic theory is practically universal and all-embracing; it is the necessity for making both ends meet." [5]

For this reason, it seems particularly important to touch on these subjects in any course on Oriental civilization. For this may well stimulate some student of engineering, chemistry, or economics to seek at some future date to apply his knowledge to exploring the history of that subject in some Oriental civilization.

So much for the neglect. The inadequacy of the approach is also due to the failure to apply some of the findings of the social sciences to the study of Islamic history. We know, for instance, that Islam contained huge cities—in the tenth century, Baghdad may have had a population of 1.5 million,[6] and Cairo was probably not very much smaller. We know that there were vast differences between the rich and poor; we know that the city dwellers belonged to very diverse ethnic and cultural groups; we also know that important economic and social changes were taking place. Does not this suggest that we ought to reexamine the history of medieval Islam in the light of the working of pressure groups, group conflicts, and

[5] Eli Heckscher, "A Plea for Theory in Economic History," *Economic Journal* (Economic History Series, No. 4, London), January, 1929.
[6] *Encyclopedia of Islam,* 2d ed., article Baghdad (Leiden).

class struggles? If we can trace such movements in Greece, Rome, and medieval Europe, is it not *a priori* likely that they had their counterparts in Islam? And, if so, is it not worth looking more closely at such movements as the Khariji, Ismaili, and Qarmati, to name only the more conspicuous ones?

As an example, consider the story of the poet Al-Mutanabbi, who is traditionally believed to have posed as a prophet, "revealing" verses modeled on the Koran to simple Beduins, in the hope of establishing his rule over them. As related, the whole episode is rather puerile and, whatever his defects, Al-Mutanabbi—by any reckoning one of the three or four greatest Arabic poets—was not puerile. But a French scholar has made the whole matter look much more sensible by showing that the poet was a Qarmati, that is, he belonged to "one of those social movements which develop, as always in the Orient, under the cover of a religious reform," [7] a revolutionary movement which tried to reduce "the reality of all the rites and even all the cults claimed to be of divine institution sheltered by the Islamic state, to a certain number of human laws—to social, rational, rules designed to give happiness to all on earth—by the fusion of all religions, regarded as simple, selfish castes." [8] And a similar explanation seems to be applicable to that other great Arabic poet, Al Ma'arri. "Those who have read the recently discovered *Majalis* of his teacher and friend Muayyad Salmani of Shiraz, who was no other than the Grand Dai of Ismaili propaganda, know that the bitter scepticism of the *Luzumiyat* and the *Ghufran* can no longer be considered as an individual singularity but testifies to the development, in favorable psychological ground, of the germs of methodic doubt and insurrectionary sarcasm contained in the initiatory teaching of the societies based on Ismaili doctrine." [9]

These very brief allusions to Al Mutanabbi and Al Ma'arri suggest another point. Among the most important sources for the

---

[7] R. Blachère, *Un Poète arabe du IVe siècle de l'Hégire* (Paris, 1935), p. 4.

[8] Louis Massignon cited in R. Blachère, *Un Poète arabe du IVe siècle de l'Hégire.*

[9] Louis Massignon, "Mutanabbi, devant le siècle ismaelien de l'Islam," in *Al Mutanabbi* (Mémoires de l'Institut français de Damas) (Beyrouth, 1936), p. 2.

history of the movements and ideas of Islam are the works of the poets. For in many ways, Arabic poets fulfilled in their society the function of editorialists and columnists, advocating or combatting ideas, supporting or attacking different groups. A politico-sociological approach to Arabic poetry may therefore often prove very rewarding. Or consider a much more prosaic subject—inflation. The last four hundred years have shown what havoc a prolonged rise in prices can wreak in the most diverse societies, what dislocations it can cause, what tensions provoke, and what new ideas generate. Now, we know that there were several inflationary periods in Islamic history and we have evidence that at least some of them caused considerable concern to those who lived through them.[10] Should we not, then, use our painfully acquired knowledge not only to study the course of price movements in Islamic history but also attempt to trace their political, social, and other consequences?

Or take yet another social science—demography. There is no doubt that the findings of contemporary demographers cast much light on one of the main driving forces of the history of all civilizations, population movements. Any historian or student of a culture who fails to make the fullest use of the methods and conclusions of demography does so at his peril. Thus, to take only one example, recently a very distinguished historian, basing his study on the Ottoman archives, published some figures on the population of the Ottoman Empire in the sixteenth century. In the main, his estimates seem very reasonable and are in line with other available information. However, they include subtotals for the Syrian provinces, broken down by religion, and I was able to show that the figure for the Christian population was much too low. For, given our knowledge of emigration, immigration, and conversion in Syria, these figures would imply, between the sixteenth and twentieth centuries, a rate of population growth which, as far as we know, has never

---

[10] See, for example, the interesting and remarkably penetrating study by the fifteenth-century Egyptian historian, Al Maqrizi, *Ighathat al umma bi kashf al ghumma* (Cairo, 1940).

occurred in pre-industrial societies. They also, incidentally, would imply that in the sixteenth century, Christians formed a much smaller fraction of the total population than they do at present, a conclusion which contradicts what we know from other sources.[11]

Another point where social scientists may have a small contribution to make is in stressing the more universal aspects of the doctrines of some of the great Oriental thinkers. Of course this approach can be very dangerous. As C. S. Lewis put it: "When we select for serious consideration those doctrines which 'transcend' the thought of his own age and 'are for all time,' we are assuming that the thought of *our* age is correct: for of course by thoughts that transcend the great man's age we really mean thoughts that agree with ours." [12] And in this same conference, three years ago, a particularly well qualified scholar stated that: "It will be found in general that the peculiar obstacle in the way of understanding Ibn Khaldun's thought is not its alien or singular character, but an assumed similarity, if not identity, between it and modern thought." [13]

But these objections, though weighty, are not conclusive. Our knowledge of natural laws, social phenomena, and human psychology *is* much greater than that of our predecessors, and in this subject at least it would be foolish to let ourselves be unduly inhibited by false modesty. Similarly, although it is essential to remember that, say, Ibn Khaldun was a medieval Muslim thinker and not a Professor in the Columbia Business School, and therefore to relate him to the thought of his time, preoccupation with what is peculiarly Muslim and medieval must not be carried so far as to obscure what is human and universal. After all, Plato was a disgruntled Athenian aristocrat, but that is not the most interesting or enduring aspect of his thought. And, in these matters, the bias of the social scientist may act as a useful corrective to that of the Orientalist.

[11] Those interested can find the original estimates, the criticism and a rebuttal in the first volume of the *Journal for Economic and Social History of the Orient* (1957–58).
[12] C. S. Lewis, *The World's Last Night,* p. 96.
[13] Muhsin Mahdi, "Ibn Khaldun," in Wm. T. de Bary, ed., *Approaches to the Oriental Classics* (New York, Columbia University Press, 1959), p. 70.

But it is above all in the study of the contemporary East that this corrective is most needed. The professional Islamicist, Sinologist, and so forth, often tends to be so fascinated by the peculiar character of "his" civilization—which he has apprehended after long and arduous study of its past—that he forgets the equally important common elements which it shares with the rest of humanity. And he also tends to ignore, or underemphasize, the great changes that are taking place in it—and indeed its very capacity for change. Thus a most distinguished Islamic scholar assured me that, in the Middle East today, "plus ça change, plus c'est la même chose." I replied that, compared to the deep and many-sided revolutionary changes sweeping through the Middle East today, North America and Europe seemed almost stagnant! Another eminent Orientalist declared that what was happening in China was nothing new: China had witnessed many previous revolutions in which the landlords had been liquidated and so on. I pointed out as mildly as I could that this was the first time in its history that China was producing 12 million tons of steel (the present figure is higher) and that that fact made some difference. Again, some scholars have interpreted the present regime in Egypt as a reincarnation of the Mamelukes, and have sought to study it accordingly. And yet, more light can probably be shed on this regime by studying such phenomena as nineteenth-century German nationalism, and contemporary Peronism, Chinese Communism, and Titoism than by studying the history of fifteenth- or eighteenth-century Egypt.

In a word, the Oriental societies are being subjected to two sets of forces. On the one hand are those historical ties binding them to their past and preserving their own peculiar culture. On the other are those world-wide trends drawing them into the mainstream of twentieth-century history. The Orientalist tends to overemphasize the first, the social scientist the second, and it would be futile to argue who is nearer the truth. What is essential is that both kinds of approach be used.

And this brings us back to the starting point of this paper and may suggest yet another working model to represent the relation between the major civilizations since the beginning of recorded history: a series of roughly parallel lines, one or the other of which sometimes pulls away from one of its neighbors, or draws a little closer to it and may even touch it. This represents the distinctiveness, independence, and philosophic equivalance of all the major civilizations. In the last few hundred years, however, one of the lines, the Western, changes its course quite sharply and moves away from the others, in what I believe to be an "upward" direction, though the value judgment implied in that last point is not essential to the model. What is essential, however, is the fact that the other lines, as though drawn by the first, are now moving, at a greater or slower speed, in the same direction. In other words, the scientific, technical, organizational, and other changes which started in Europe some three centuries ago, and made it so much more different from other civilizations, are sweeping over the rest of the world at an accelerated rate, and bringing huge cultural changes in their wake. And it does not seem too fanciful to suggest that, in some not so distant future, the lines may gradually converge and humanity may see an increasingly rich layer of common civilization superimposed on the age-old diversity of cultures which it has known since the beginning of history.

Comment: Traditional Methods and Modern Needs

HELLMUT WILHELM

Professor of History, University of Washington

The purpose of these papers is to focus on two things: on the one hand, on teaching about the Far East in the social sciences as distinct from the humanities; and on the other hand, the teaching of the Far East to undergraduate students who do not want to specialize in this area. All three of the major papers have devoted considerable time to the first of these emphases and have taken this opportunity to appraise the way in which their own science can be brought to bear on the undergraduate student.

As a result, it seems that the particular tradition of the teaching of Oriental topics and the special emphasis of this conference, that is the social science emphasis, are in some way contradictory. It has been suggested particularly in the paper of Professor Crane that our whole scientific tradition in what is called Orientalism grew basically out of the discipline of philology, one of the last embattled ramparts of the humanities that still exists. This tradition has been attacked, of course, over and over again but I think none of the major representatives of the Eastern field has entirely avoided the inferences of what Arthur Wright has called "the incubus of philological Orientalism."

This incubus is still with us and I must say that I am happy that it is. The great tradition of philology, growing out of classical philology but then spreading into Oriental philology, has at least provided Eastern studies with one foundation which is an anticipation of a rather modern approach, the so-called interdisciplinary approach. The great Orientalist in the past was not a specialist in economics or political science nor in history nor art. But he was made to take responsibility for all aspects of a civilization and to interlink and interrelate what is now dealt with under a great variety of different disciplines. This kind of universal approach to a region is something we should not, I think, look down on. It has anticipated some of the things that we are trying to do now including some of the relations that Professor Crane brought out in his paper. Among these are the interrelationship of the social and the economic aspects and particularly the interrelationship of these two with the religious aspect.

There are, of course, certain dangers to this basically humanistic approach—it leaves gaps which are not covered and have not been covered even by the greatest of Orientalists of the past. More particularly, the philological tradition deals with only one aspect of a civilization and as it is based on the readings of texts that, as Professor Crane pointed out, mainly or exclusively pertain to the so-called high tradition—the tradition of the literate and the tradition of what ought to be rather than what is. In this respect, we have to deviate from our background and try to take whatever tools our present age offers in an attempt to explain and to understand the civilization we are dealing with.

Another approach to Oriental civilization would be the disciplinary approach, the approach that Professor Issawi stresses in his paper. This, I think, is a remedy which we all stand in need of, which, however, the Oriental specialist is at times unprepared to utilize properly. Although we all have dabbled in the disciplines— reading discipline journals and grappling with discipline theories— none of us is as strong in any of the disciplines as a real discipline man. We might think we understand something about the workings of, let us say, the economy or the political structure but we still need guidance from the disciplines as such. And this is a point that I would like to take out of Professor Issawi's paper which appears to me extremely important: that the advances of the disciplines which have taken place in the theoretical field, particularly in this country, during the last ten years, may be of great help to everybody who is concerned with one of the Oriental civilizations. In other words, the Orientalist also has to keep abreast with the progress of the disciplines.

This gets us into one of the contemporary trends within the disciplines, which is to stress theory above facts and to sublimate facts into what the social scientists call a construct—an ideal image of the complex with which they are dealing. We Orientalists will not be able to avoid pondering these constructs that the disciplines offer and trying to see to what extent they fit a particular regional context. More perhaps even than the construct of a specific discipline, it may be of advantage to take into account theories derived from such constructs and apply them for the purposes of analyzing and understanding. This seems to be applicable particularly if we are talking to undergraduate students. To avoid having a student get befuddled by a great variety of different ways in which life manifests itself in any of the Oriental civilizations, it might be of help to look for the pattern first and then fill in the pattern with what Arthur Wright calls "the breath of life." Now, of course, the breath of life is the test. We ought to go after just that. But to look for the pattern first and then only point out the particulars and fill the pattern is a way of proceeding that I at least found very helpful in the courses on China's history and China's civilization that I have been giving during the last ten years.

A second short comment I want to direct toward the poor victim of our discussions—the undergraduate student. We have had references to the rather poor mental shape in which he enters college to grapple with the "mysteries of the East." I want to contradict this image of the undergraduate student somewhat. My experience with undergraduates, particularly on the more advanced level, is that while he is not always very well prepared, he is certainly very willing and able to deal with and to understand the problems of civilizations which are different from our own. If he is given some help, we have no reason to despair, and even if the sophomore occasionally comes with clichés and with questions of a kind we try to avoid, once he gets into the more advanced level, experience shows that he will be in a position not only to follow a course of the nature we are talking about but also to go on from there on his own. After all, what are we trying to do to the undergraduate student? We do not only want to make him listen. We want to make him read, think, and understand. The general level of the thinking and understanding of the more advanced undergraduate student in this country is, I think, quite gratifying. I usually rely on the undergraduate student to do his own thinking and to do his own understanding as soon as possible. I might give him my view, and what I understand to be an acceptable interpretation, but I also give him enough literature to read so that he will have conflicting views at his disposal not only to choose from but to stimulate his thinking and his understanding as well.

The Spiritual Form of the Oriental Civilizations

THOMAS BERRY, C. P.

Professor of History, St. John's University

When we think of the Oriental civilizations, we generally think of India as Hindu, Tibet as Buddhist, China as Confucian, Japan as Shintoist, Indonesia as Islamic. There is a central truth in this way of thinking. However, the reality of the situation is somewhat less simple. The major civilizations of Asia have been formed more by a complex of spiritual traditions rather than by a single tradition. A study of these complex spiritual formations is essential to any real understanding of Asian civilizations for it is through these traditions that Asian peoples have attained an awareness of their identity. Only through these traditions does any aspect of life have for them real significance. Asian peoples are most truly themselves when, in some spiritual context, they feel themselves, in the totality of their lives, caught up in a profound ontological communion with the entire order of cosmic and trans-cosmic forces. This, we see quite clearly in their life, art, and literature.

There is, of course, serious difficulty in presenting here any full account of that long series of spiritual developments that have given the Oriental civilizations their distinctive form. Yet these traditions must be considered. While no specialist or non-specialist could give adequate treatment of them in an ordinary college course, it should be possible to indicate the basic human experience which gave rise to these traditions, the main phases of their historical development, their interrelations, and the manner in which they have attained expression in the arts and in literature. In a college course on these civilizations, it is best to present each spiritual tradition in the civilizational context in which it appeared and to which it gave life, meaning and beauty. Here we venture only a listing of these traditions, a light treatment of each, and a series of conclusions that can be drawn from the manner in which they have functioned within the civilizational context of Asia. We include separate presentation of Yoga, Hinduism, Buddhism, Confucianism, Taoism, Shinto, Zen, and Islam.

YOGA

Among the earliest, most elementary, and most widely influential of spiritual disciplines in the Asian world is that of Yoga. Yoga arises from a profound experience of the human condition and from the desire to transcend this condition. The classical Yoga of Pantanjali is founded on a discipline that goes deep into the pre-historic past of India. Patanjali gave to the tradition a philosophical and theological context but this intellectualization of Yoga never attained the prestige of other thought traditions in India. The theory and technique of Yoga, however, became an integral part of India's spiritual heritage. Yoga was especially influential in the rise and development of Buddhism. Through Buddhism, it influenced the entire spiritual development of the East Asian and Southeast Asian worlds.

Because Yoga was deficient in its social, religious, ontological, and aesthetic development, it never provided a dominant form for any Asian society. For this reason there tends to be a certain neglect of this tradition in the general field of Asian studies. Yet no other tradition has presented the basic spiritual problems of Asia with such clarity and such directness. Also, none have gone further in the intensity of its psychological efforts to surmount this problem and to give man a means of overcoming those limiting conditions of his

life that constitute his deepest misery. The study of Yoga remains
our best introduction to a great part of Asia's spiritual formation.

HINDUISM

Hinduism as the basic spiritual form of Indian civilization is the
result of an amazing spiritual process that began in pre-Aryan India
and has continued after the Aryan invasion in a rich interchange of
Aryan and non-Aryan influences until our own times. It is a forest of
religious and spiritual growths so dense and confused in appearance
that it defies clear statement. However, we can say that the deepest
experience of Hinduism is the experience of Divine Being as the one
all-pervading reality that is both transcendent and immanent in the
phenomenal world. The clearest intellectual presentation of this
reality is found in the Upanishadic conceptions of Atman-Brahman.
Later, a new devotional experience in Hinduism brought into
prominence personal deities such as Vishnu and Shiva and their
incarnations, especially the Rama and Krishna incarnations of
Vishnu. A vast assembly of gods and forms of worship, of intellectual intuitions, and spiritual disciplines in the Hindu tradition
reveals a creative force of unique range and power.

Hinduism has given the basic form to Indian social life by its doctrines of caste and of karma, has provided a mythology adapted to
the spiritual needs of all the diverse groups within the society; it
has inspired an epic literature, has given expression to a profound
intellectual experience of reality in a vast spiritual and theological
literature, and has brought forth an exuberant art and architecture.
Yet, amid all these developments, it is difficult to find any unifying
principles. Everywhere in Hinduism itself and in the other traditions found within the Indian world we find a confused array of
forces striving in all possible directions. Indian civilization is rather
a process than an accomplished reality. We can best describe the
spontaneous forces of Indian civilization by analogy with the

luxuriance of a tropical jungle. The only unity within India is that balance of life forces that is proper to life in tropical regions. As this balance reveals a real order of life in the natural world, so this balance in Indian civilization reveals a real and dynamic order of life in the human world. Though the ultimate principles of this order are largely hidden from the scholar, whether native or foreign, they are entirely obvious to those whose lives are governed by these principles. It may even be that there is a more extensive though more complex and hidden order of life in India than in some of the other Asian civilizations. Every person and every deed has its own guiding norms in the context of a whole that functions as a completely integrated civilizational unit.

Because this balance of life forces was too complex a process for other peoples, Hinduism remained the proper form of Indian civilization without becoming a permanent civilizational form of other societies. Even so, Hinduism has been an extensive influence throughout southeast Asia and for some centuries gave to some of these peoples their introduction to those higher features of social life that we associate with the more advanced civilizations.

BUDDHISM

Buddhism, the most widespread spiritual tradition of Asia, arose from the intense experience of the agony and impermanence that is intrinsic to all existence in the phenomenal world. It provided a discipline of salvation that enabled a person to extinguish all attachment to this world and to attain bliss in the transcendent peace of nirvana. The development of Buddhism is hardly less complex than Hinduism. Its spontaneous and luxuriant growth is likewise a sign of its tremendous vitality and its correspondence with the needs of the societies in which it was received. It contained, from the beginning, extraordinary metaphysical insights that were later elaborated into some of the highest philosophical developments in Asia. Yet, Buddhism was also characterized from the beginning by its simple moral and humanist teaching that made of Buddhism a life discipline suited to all peoples of Asia from the most lowly to the most learned. Buddhism had a rare genius in its ability to transcend all political, racial, and social differences.

This new discipline first arose in northeast India and spread to central and northwest India. It extended northward and eastward outside of India to Tibet and Mongolia, to China, Korea, and Japan. In the south and southeast of Asia, it extended into Ceylon, Burma, and Thailand, to the region of Indo-China and to Indonesia. More than any other single tradition, Buddhism has given form and vitality to the arts and literature of all these regions. Indigenous social, religious, and intellectual forces later suppressed much of its influence in India, China, Korea, and Japan. It was rather to other more primitive societies such as Ceylon, Burma, Thailand, Laos, Cambodia, Tibet, and Mongolia that Buddhism brought a higher civilization, a new art and literature, new social structures and economic activities, and thus was able to establish itself as the dominant form in these societies.

CONFUCIANISM

Confucianism, the dominant form of Chinese civilization, is a tradition based on the perception of order in the divine, the cosmic, and the human realms of being. Yet, this original experience of order would never have been so thoroughly developed except for the opposite experience of disorder that took place during the period of the warring states in the middle of the first millennium before Christ. This prolonged and bitter experience gave to the Chinese a need and an appreciation of order in the individual, family, society, and the entire functioning of the cosmos, that has never left them. Eventually, this attachment to order proved the undoing of China for it later produced a static traditionalism unable to cope with the problems of social and cultural change.

Because of its humanist qualities, Confucianism has often been presented as a rationalist humanism rather than as a spiritual discipline on substantially the same level as that of Hinduism and Buddhism. Yet, a more thorough appreciation of its basic discipline reveals that it is a more spiritual and even a more mystical life formation than is generally recognized. It does have a reticence before the supernatural and a rare appreciation of the humanist aspect of life; yet, it also has a sublime sense of man's communion with the dynamic forces of the cosmic and heavenly orders. Its delight in the natural world as revealed by Chinese landscape painting is something more than the rationalistic or romantic naturalism found in the West in recent centuries.

As a civilizational form, Confucianism was most successful in the political and the social aspect of Chinese life. Its political achievements remain perhaps unmatched, for the Confucian political structure ruled more successfully over a greater number of people, for a greater period of time than any other political structure known to man.

This success of Confucianism in China made of it an ideal that was extensively imitated by other societies of East Asia. Its influence was particularly strong in Korea and Japan as well as in Annam to the south.

TAOISM

Taoism arises from an experience of the ontological and mystical qualities of the *tao*, the ultimate, all-pervading principle of reality. The real depth of this insight is revealed in the acute awareness manifested of the antinomic qualities of being and in the impossibility of reconciling those antinomies on the rational plane, though we can on the rational plane develop a way of dealing with these antinomies, a way which constitutes the essence of human wisdom. The expression given to this wisdom in the writings of Lao Tzu and Chuang Tzu provides us with one of the most soaring and most delightful forms of Asian spirituality. The depth of insight presented in these works can be matched only by the finest achievements of Buddhist metaphysics as found in the Madhyamika tradition founded by Nagarjuna.

While Taoism was unable to provide a dominant spiritual form for Chinese civilization, it did provide one of the most dynamic forces in that society and deeply influenced every phase of the intellectual, aesthetic, and literary life of the society. By intimate association with Buddhism, the Taoist tradition was largely responsible for creating the Ch'an tradition of China and the Zen tradition of Japan. By providing a pole of tension with Confucianism, it evoked from within that tradition a creative effort that it would not otherwise have produced. However, it was in the inspiration that it gave to the arts and to literature that Taoism made its highest contribution to Chinese civilization.

Taoism was of some slight influence in Japan but it never attained there any of the success achieved by Confucianism or Buddhism. Also, Taoism in its later superstitious and magical religious form became an influence in Annam. But in neither case was it of any great significance in the total formation of these societies.

SHINTO

Shinto arose from the Japanese experience of the all-pervading numinous reality that manifests itself throughout the entire natural world. This experience, though extensively expressed in the religious, literary, and aesthetic aspects of Japanese society, never attained that high intellectual development that we find in the other traditions we have mentioned thus far. Shinto had to wait until the eighteenth-century writings of Motoori Nobunaga before it attained that reflexive critical consideration that it needed. From that time, the development of Shinto into a higher intellectual tradition has been in process though it is still without the intellectual significance that has been attained by other Asian traditions. It is little wonder, then, that Westerners have found extreme difficulty in considering

Shinto as anything other than an undeveloped animistic folk religion of no great spiritual significance. Buddhism and Confucianism have been considered as the more powerful traditions in providing the spiritual form of Japanese civilization. This neglect of Shinto is a distortion that needs correction. Shinto is, indeed, a spiritual force that emerged out of a primitive society and has never been intellectualized so extensively as the other major traditions of Asia. Yet, its inner strength and influence, even its power of survival, rest precisely on the simple vision of reality. This vision has been so powerful that it has brought about profound modifications in every tradition that has been brought into Japan. Particularly as regards Buddhism, we find that Zen, the form of Buddhism that was most extensively affected by Shinto, has been the form of Buddhism that has survived longest as a creative influence in the thought, art, and life of Japan.

Shinto has not only provided the basic formation of the Japanese emotional, artistic, religious and intellectual life, it has also provided the fundamental sense of unity possessed by the Japanese people. It has given them a theory of political rule and even a sense of historical destiny. Thus the formation of Japan is primarily the work of Shinto. This basic tradition of the Japanese has never had any direct intellectual influence outside of Japan although its basic intellectual attitude has been communicated to the world through its art, its literature, and through its general life attitude.

ZEN

Zen arose from the subjective experience the mind has of itself and of its own limitations on the rational plane and of its higher possibilities when awakened on the trans-rational plane. Zen evolved as a meditation discipline seeking to eliminate the confusing processes of the rational faculty in favor of the higher intuitional experience the mind has of itself and of the unity of all reality in and through the mind. Zen arose within the context of Buddhism and can well be considered a Buddhist sect. Yet, Zen has proved such a distinctive thing in the history of Asian spiritual traditions that it seems best to accord it distinct treatment for the sake of clarity and convenience. Although Zen found its highest expression in the furthermost corner of the East Asian world, it has been deeply influenced by most of the spiritual traditions of Asia. It is influenced by Yoga and Buddhism, by Taoism and Confucianism, and finally by Shinto. Though the followers of Zen frequently like to consider themselves as bizarre, iconoclastic, and non-conformist, it is amazing to see the expression of Zen in the tea ceremony where it manifests a ritualism, a conformism and an order of etiquette that would do honor to the most dedicated Confucianist.

Zen did not become a dominant form of any society in Asia. Yet, it did supply much of the inspiration for Japanese intellectual and aesthetic life during the medieval and post-medieval periods. Zen seemed during its most influential period to have absorbed the Shinto mentality completely into itself. As an influence on non-Japanese society, it may be said that Zen has not been a serious influence in any other Asian society until recent times when Zen has suddenly become, in the twentieth century, one of the major intellectual influences of the entire world.

ISLAM

Islam arose from the awesome experience of Allah as the one supreme personal and transcendent deity in absolute control of the world through his providence who communicated to mankind through the prophetic revelation given to Mohammed and written down after his death in the Koran. Total submission is expected of the faithful to all the decrees of the Koran which contains a multitude of regulations concerning every phase of individual and social life. Thus Islam formed a new social and political order as soon as the faithful were gathered into a community. There was no state-church problem in the beginning for the demands of religion extended over the totality of life and all of life was consecrated in this new context.

But, while Islam provided the structure of an organized religious community, it had to absorb into itself the cultural achievements of the surrounding societies before it could enter into the world as one of the great civilizational forces. Thus, Islam at an early stage developed a capacity for entering into diverse cultural units and making of itself a vast multicultural unit held together by its religious faith. Yet, even while attaining high success in this endeavor, Islam began to feel almost unendurable tensions between its religious and its cultural allegiance. Until the twentieth century, it has been a constant temptation for Islam to turn against its cultural development in favor of religious orthodoxy and the legalistic demands of religiously controlled community.

Yet, while engaged in these inner struggles, Islam has spread extensively through the east Mediterranean region to Iran, Afghanistan, India, Malaya, and Indonesia, with important minorities in Ceylon, China, and even in the Philippines. In every case where Islam has been extensively received, it has asserted itself as a vigorous formative force in the society.

After this presentation of the origin, development, internal function, and external influence of these eight spiritual forces in the Asian world, I would add the following observations.

The entire civilizational complex of Asia should be kept in mind when studying any single civilizational unit for no part of Asian development has existed in isolation. This is a staggering assignment when we consider the difficulty of mastering some one phase of development in any one of these civilizations. Yet, there does exist an intimate relationship between the various civilizational units and between the spiritual forces at work in the lives, thoughts, and literature of the Asian peoples.

Each Asian civilization carries within itself an irreducible complex of spiritual developments that cannot be brought under any single designation. The full civilizational development of each society should be attributed to this complex spiritual foundation rather than to any single tradition even though a dominant spiritual tradition does seem to carry the main civilizational effort of the society. China has been formed by Taoist and Buddhist as well as by Confucian forces. Japan is the creation of Buddhist and Confucian as well as of Shinto tradition.

The Asian civilizations are formed not only by a horizontal complex of higher spiritual traditions. Each also includes a vertical complex of traditions that extend from the most primitive to the most advanced. Higher intellectual and spiritual developments have not suppressed the more primitive spiritual forces found in the various Asian societies. These primitive influences continue up to the present and most often remain in the lives of the people more powerful influences than these higher developments that we have here described.

Each of these civilizational forms has gone through many different phases of development so that to speak rightly of any Asian tradition we must be very clear about each phase of its historical development. There is both continuity and discontinuity in these traditions. It requires long and difficult study of each major tradition before a person can deal safely with the complex developments that have taken place. Indeed, the more influential traditions have developed diversities of expression that challenge all our efforts at understanding. Buddhism, for instance, by its division into the Hinayana and the Mahayana, and by its further division of both Hinayana and Mahayana into a wide diversity of schools of development, gives us a span of differences that require most careful attention if a person is to appreciate the elements of continuity and discontinuity in the tradition. The various phases of development in Confucianism and Shinto also force us to careful study in order to recognize the different phases of development through which these have gone.

No major Asian civilization is without extensive outside influences on its formation. This is true from the earliest period of these civilizations to the present. The entire history of Asian civilizations could be written in the light of these influences and the assimilation processes that have taken place as a result of this intrusion from without. In India, we have the intrusion of Aryan influences into the pre-Aryan Indian development. Later, there is the Islamic influence and more recently the Western influence. The higher development of Japan took place under outside influences, particularly the Confucian and Buddhist influences from the continent.

The intellectual and spiritual diversity within each civilization of Asia has constituted its most fruitful source of development. Without this diversity, every civilization in Asia would be terribly impoverished. Buddhism has been the greatest challenge to all the indigenous developments of Asia. Precisely, in virtue of this challenge, these other traditions have been forced to bring forth an inner richness of expression that otherwise they would not have brought forth. Buddhism in India, China, and Japan is as important for evoking responses from Hinduism, Confucianism, and Shinto as it is for making its own direct contribution to Indian, Chinese, and Japanese civilizations.

Diversity in the spiritual forces at work in each of these Asian societies has supplied for the diverse aspects of the civilizational life of these societies. No single tradition has been able to supply the total intellectual, aesthetic, moral, and religious needs of any Asian society. In so far as diversity has been eliminated, these societies tend to be weakened and to enter into a cultural decline. In its most vital period, China experienced a profound inner dynamism from Confucianism, Taoism, and Buddhism. Confucianism supplied a social discipline; Taoism, a metaphysical insight and aesthetic feeling; Buddhism, a religious devotionalism and new and more vast intellectual horizons. Later, when Confucianism became dominant to an excessive degree in the intellectual life of China, the cultural development of the society lost much of its earlier dynamism.

The general drift of Asian religious and spiritual influences has been from west to east. The Aryan influence entered India from the West. Buddhism moved from India eastward across Asia. Confucianism moved in all directions but its eastward movement into Korea and Japan constitutes its most significant movement outside of the territory taken over by China itself. Islam moved eastward across a good part of the Asian world. There has been no such cultural movement from Japan to China or from China to India.

Unity in the different Asian civilizations must be considered as a dynamic equilibrium of the many forces that are at work in these civilizations and that are constantly interacting on each other. At each stage of civilizational development, this unity has been something other than it was in the previous period, although it maintains a recognizable continuity with the past. We have no adequate way of understanding or describing the unity that is observable throughout this process of change. In seeking to identify certain distinctive and abiding characteristics of a civilizational process, we can only study these various phases of development and through observation of consistent tendencies in the midst of the change arrive at some idea of the main characteristics that distinguish each of the Asian civilizations from the others. On deeper reflection, we may find that our surest guide to understanding the Asian civilizations is that original experience of reality that occurred early in the life of each society and which gave to the people a unique intellectual formation so that all future influences were profoundly modified by this mode of conceiving reality. This earliest experience of reality and this earliest intellectual formation is never adequately presented in any of the classical or post-classical writings of the Asian traditions. At most, they are partial presentations to be valued and studied but they are not to be considered the total expression of this experience which is carried in the heart of the civilization as an ineffable mystery that we glimpse on occasion but never see in its full reality.

Ideas and the Power Structure

KARL A. WITTFOGEL

Director of the Chinese History Project, University of Washington

The search for regularities in the relation between the ideas and the power structure of Oriental civilizations is only part, but an important part, of man's search for regularities in human affairs generally. The very formulation of the problem implies that there are recognizable regularities in the structure of political power. It implies furthermore that there are regularities in the character of Oriental civilizations. Following widespread practice, I employ "civilization" to refer particularly to the totality of the cultural conditions—ideas and beliefs—of a given country, and I employ "society" to refer particularly to the totality of its institutional conditions.

It is certainly easier to determine the character of Oriental society than the character of Oriental civilization. This is so because the great systems of Oriental thought (especially the great religions) each have their definite singularity, whereas there is an ascertainable common denominator in the institutional order (and especially in the power structure) of the "Orient." This common denominator goes far to explain the growth potential of the various sets of ideas, but not always—and this is essential—the quality of their core features.

Since the days of Hippocrates and Aristotle, Western observers have been struck by the extraordinary strength of the state in "Asia." Machiavelli contrasted the monolithic power structure of Ottoman Turkey with the loose organization of feudal France. Montesquieu commented on the extraordinary strength of Oriental, as compared with Occidental, absolutism. And the classical economists found the governments of the Near East, India, and China engaged in a political economy which was lacking in the West. These governments, they observed, maintained large water works for the purposes of irrigation and flood control, which in certain hot and arid (or semi-arid) areas and also in humid regions suited to the growing of aquatic plants (mainly rice) were either necessary or desirable for the establishment and perpetuation of a productive and secure agrarian order.

The classical economists designated the thus conditioned institutional complex as an "Asiatic" or "Oriental" society. And following these insights—and Montesquieu's political distinctions—it became customary to view the peculiarly strong absolutisms of the East as representatives of a peculiar power structure, Oriental despotism.

The study of the Oriental power structure enables us to answer a number of crucial socio-historical questions. Contrary to the assumptions of the ecological determinists, the natural factor, though essential, plays a formative role only in combination with a number of equally essential cultural factors, some of which are decidedly non-material. Contrary to the assumptions of the economic determinists the "Oriental" power structure (the organizational and acquisitive state apparatus) can be transplanted to and perpetuated in areas that completely lack a hydraulic economy. The development of agrodespotic states in certain non-hydraulic regions of China and India, and the Orientally despotic character of Western Rome, Middle Byzantium, and Mongol and post-Mongol Russia are cases in point. And contrary to the assumptions of the general institutional determinists, the ideas that emerged in Oriental society do not all reflect the peculiarities of this society, nor are they necessarily limited to its borders. True, certain sets of ideas are functionally attached to the power structure, and some are indeed controlled by it. By and large, these differences are due to differences in the spheres of life to which the ideas pertain.

This point requires explanation. The human condition has three major spheres: man's relation to nature, man's relation to his fellow-men, and man's relation to his innermost moral and transcendent self. Each of these spheres has a quality of its own, and they overlap and interlink in a highly complex way. The sets of ideas that pertain to these separate spheres also have a quality of their own and they too overlap and interlink in a highly complex way.

Using the power structure (a special feature of the second sphere) as our point of departure, we can say that a given set of ideas (1) may be essentially indifferent to this structure, (2) may be related to it without being controlled by it, (3) may be controlled by it without being created and altered by its forces, and (4) may be created and altered by these forces.

With these possibilities in mind, we shall now try to determine in what form and to what extent they occur in Oriental society. In order to put the Oriental configurations into their proper socio-historical context, we shall point to corresponding (or contrasting) configurations among the multicentered societies of the West and Japan and to corresponding (or contrasting) configurations among the totalitarian societies of the Communist world.

The states of Communist totalitarianism and of Oriental society resemble one another in that both exert a monopoly of political power, and that, for this reason, the population in both cases is politically atomized. But even in hydraulic core areas, the organizational reach of the agrodespotic state in agriculture is limited: its managerial functions are restricted to certain productive and protective key operations (the peasants always individually till the land they possess or own), and private property and independent action may be widespread in handicraft and trade. Thus, despite its virtual monopoly in large construction, fast communication, centralized intelligence, and warfare, the agrodespotic state is only partially (semi-) managerial; and occasional totalitarian dreams notwithstanding, it is unable to exert total control over the country's economy, social life, and ideas.

In contrast, once collectivization is completed, the Communist state operates all major spheres of the economy, and increasingly it controls the people's social life (temporary limit: the family) and their ideas (temporary limit: certain popular religions). Thus, despite the just-indicated limitations, whose elimination is foreseen doctrinally and initiated as soon as practicable, the Communist regime is a total managerial state with totalitarian means for controlling the peoples' social life and ideas.

In the field of man's relations to nature, the Oriental civilizations have pioneered both practically and theoretically. The working out of a reliable calendar, the counting of people, and the measuring of land stimulated the rise of a rational astronomy, algebra, and geometry. Significantly, mathematics and astronomy did not originate in the free cities of classical Greece, but in the Orientally despotic states of Mesopotamia and Egypt; and both sciences have a long history in China and India. The early Greek mathematicians and natural philosophers owed their inspiration largely to the Oriental civilizations of the Near East. And even the two great "later" Greek mathematical schools, represented by Euclid, Hipparchus, Heron, and Ptolemy, flourished in Egypt.

Enormous advances in the natural sciences subsequently occurred in the late feudal, post-feudal, and industrial societies of the West, and these advances are as characteristic for the intellectual potential of these societies as are the limitations of scientific development for Oriental society. But faced with the recent technological accomplishments of the USSR, we do well to remember that man began to theorize about nature in an impressive way under despotic governments that had a decisive role in promoting these activities as well as their practical applications.

Turning to the ideas dealing with man's relation to his fellowmen, we find their dependence on the power structure varying in different societies. In classical Greece and republican Rome, communities of aristocratic or democratic citizens enjoyed great (and at times virtually complete) freedom to describe and evaluate social and political life (cf. Aristotle's three constitutions with their good and bad variants). The governments of the open Greek city states had little power to censure these ideas, except in such an extreme case as that of Socrates, whose political philosophy, however, was not in and of itself objectionable, as can be seen from the respect rendered to Plato who elaborated it. Even the more strictly hierarchical societies of medieval Europe had a deliberative and contractual quality. Understandably, their governments encouraged the restatement of key elements of Plato's and Aristotle's political philosophy.

The peculiarity of Oriental thinking about state and society is quickly apparent when we consider these Western developments. An institutional order in which political power was concentrated in an autocratic ruler and his officials had no use for discussions of controlled or contractually limited governments or for the politically active attitudes of free citizens toward such government. This does not mean that in Oriental societies there was no thinking on political, social, or economic institutions and actions. There was indeed. There was descriptive thinking with respect to conditions as they were, and there was regulative thinking with respect to conditions as they could or should be. The latter included idealistic as well as realistic and cynical (Machiavellian) ideas.

Of course, the descriptive and regulative ideas interlinked, since they dealt with the same institutional reality, and generally all types of regulative thought took the agrodespotic character of this reality for granted. Confucius, who strikingly represents the idealistic regulative position, is firmly convinced that "the people" are not qualified to participate in their country's government. They must, however, follow its policy even if "they cannot be made to understand it." The people are like the grass, the ruler is like the wind: "The grass must bend when the wind blows over it." To be sure, the good ruler must satisfy the people's legitimate needs—Confucius is greatly concerned with what may be called the rationality optimum of the absolutistic government—but the ruler's political problem is not an intra-societal one (his relation to legitimate, countervailing forces of society) but an intra-governmental one, involving the choice of proper councillors and aides and his own, and his aides', virtue and skill.

In such a genuinely absolutistic government, power tends to converge in a single center, the autocrat; and the presence of a councillor (or councillors) whose advice he solicits, far from threatening his supremacy, may well consolidate it. Optimally, according to Confucius, the top councillor should be a properly educated and morally mature gentleman-official; in Hindu India, he should be the ruler's personal priest, the *purohita;* in Islamic countries, the vizier should be a combination of secular wisdom and religious dedication.

Confucius' *Analects,* the Hindu *Law Books,* and the *Qur'an* outline the ideal behavior of the ideal ruler and his aides. But other thinking is differently oriented. The Legalists' writings, the *Arthashastra,* and certain Islamic manuals of policy are more concerned with the regime's power, revenue, and security than with the implementation of ideal norms.

The quantity and slant of descriptive thinking on administration and warfare depends on many societal and political factors. Their prevailing trend can often be inferred from the statements and behavior of the ruler's favored councillor or councillors. In China, where the education of the "superior man" included a detailed knowledge of past events, there developed a historical literature that contained the most comprehensive accounts of the administrative (bureaucratic) experiences of any pre-industrial civilization. In India, religious and religious-philosophical writings were, relatively speaking, much more numerous. In Mohammedan countries, we find a considerable concern for administrative and legal matters combined with a fair interest in history and a substantial interest in geography.

Did the political and historical ideas of these agrarian despotisms conform to the dictates of a totalitarian state doctrine, such as the Soviet theory of historical materialism? Governments that exert total political power can be expected to aim at total control of their subjects' political thoughts; and it may, indeed, be said that Confucianism and the political segments in Hindu and Mohammedan writings do have such a tendency. But, even where this tendency was present, it did not result in a policy that made the handling of political thought the monopoly of the state and its officials. The political and legal ideas of Islam were developed by persons who were neither necessarily officials of the caliph nor dependent on his directives. The political literature of Hindu India was written essentially by priests who, although respectful of the king's prerogatives, did not, as a rule, consider themselves the state's ideological functionaries. In China, Confucianism became the dominant political doctrine only in the second half of the first millennium A.D.; and even then other political ideas, especially those of Taoism, were tolerated.

Some students of Communist totalitarianism suggest that despotic regimes in general cannot, within their borders, permit the expression of unorthodox political ideas. The experience of Oriental society disproves this thesis. The agrodespotic state certainly did not favor the growth of social science as we know it, but neither did it monopolistically create and control all thought on society, economy, and history.

Manifestly then, in Oriental society, ideas concerning man's relation to his fellowmen did refer to this society; and they often dealt with its despotic regime. But, while in certain countries an official political doctrine was handled by representatives of the government, in general, state control over political and historical thought was haphazard and limited in contrast to the persistent and total control exerted by Communist totalitarianism.

In the sphere of man's relation to his innermost self, the contrast becomes extreme. There is, first of all, no necessary "uniformity of coexistence" between the institutional order (including the power structure) and man's religious thought. The great religions that emerged in various Oriental societies were neither created nor developed as a supreme state doctrine by the agrodespotic ruler and his ideological aides. This is true for Islam, whose grandiose monotheistic vision is not a reflection of the idea of conquest and rule with which it was intertwined. It is true for China's cosmic religion which

Confucius acknowledged by his profound respect for the time-honored public sacrifices. It is true for the religion of the Vedas as well as for Buddhism. And it is true for Christianity which originated within a Judaic enclave of Oriental society, flourished in Eastern Rome and Byzantium, and spread to non-Oriental Kievan Russia and Europe. The transfer of Christianity to these proto-feudal and feudal lands, like the transfer of Buddhism to proto-feudal and feudal Japan, demonstrates how indifferent these faiths were to the power structures that dominated the countries of their birth.

The Oriental state prevented the growth of an autonomous church (in Eastern Rome where a church emerged, the state placed it under its administrative jurisdiction); and it supervised and controlled the organizational and economic conditions of the representatives of the dominant creeds. But, except for some occasional and inconsequential attempts, it did not endeavor to alter the transcendent core of these creeds in order to serve its own political purposes. And it tried even less to manipulate the creeds of the secondary religions it tolerated.

To be sure, the agromanagerial state supported certain religions; and the reasons for this attitude and its effect on form and presentation, and, at times, also on certain elements of the creed, require realistic examination. Realistic examination is also required with regard to the philosophies of Oriental society.

The political segments of these philosophies were supervised just as were the political thoughts which were presented more pragmatically; not infrequently, however, they aroused less critical attention because they appeared in a wider metaphysical context. The metaphysical systems were generally linked to the religious tradition, and, like this tradition, they were not controlled by a power-oriented state doctrine—an agrodespotic dialectical materialism, as it were. The absence of such controls favored the spontaneous development of profound ideas (the *tao* in China and the *Brahman* in India). To close the circle, we may add that the absence of a state-imposed art doctrine (an "agrodespotic realism" comparable to the "socialist realism" of the Communists) favored the spontaneous development of large sections of Oriental art, particularly those dealing with man's private life and his relations to nature.

All this makes it clear beyond doubt that the state of Oriental society, despite its monopoly of political control, did not exert totalitarian control over all ideas. Extremely important segments of Oriental thought obviously enjoyed partial or full autonomy.

This does not mean that we should not study the functional and dependent segments of this thought—for a full understanding of Oriental society and civilization, this is vital—but it explains in a large measure why significant manifestations of Oriental thought (including art) appealed so strongly to many persons living outside the agromanagerial world.

We have already mentioned Japan, which, because of its acceptance of much of Chinese culture, became intensely associated with Oriental civilization, although it never developed an Oriental society. But recent developments go much further. The institutional peculiarities of Oriental society are not preventing members of our modern multicentered ("open") society from recognizing the value of many aspects of Oriental thought and from sharing fully in the great heritage of Oriental civilization.

THE INSTITUTIONAL APPROACH

Some of us have cautioned against a description of Oriental civilization that stresses institutional features and neglects significant historical detail. This warning is well taken and definitely helpful, if it does not imply a wholesale rejection of the social science approach.

The history of the Orient, like the history of the non-Oriental world, deals with institutional and cultural regularities as well as with singular events and personalities. These several phenomena are not sharply separated. Typical features interlock with others that defy stereotyping; and singular features contain typical elements whose identification helps us to understand the character and dimension of the singular elements. Shakespeare was part of a general literary development; but the way in which he introduced singular elements made his work unique. Muhammad, an urban Arab, was familiar with both Judaism and Christianity, but the combination of these and other typical features had a singular result. I submit that without Muhammad's unique personality there would probably not have been the religion known as Islam.

RELATIONS BETWEEN ORIENTAL CIVILIZATION AND ORIENTAL SOCIETY

Oriental (or hydraulic) society is characterized by the coexistence of several features:

Cultural: the knowledge of agriculture.

Environmental: aridity or semi-aridity and accessible sources of water supply, primarily rivers, which may be utilized to grow rewarding crops, especially cereals, in a water-deficient landscape. A humid area in which edible aquatic plants, especially rice, can be grown is a variant of this environmental pattern.

Organizational: large-scale cooperation.

Economic: large-scale (water) feeding activities and irrigation agriculture.

Protective: the productive hydraulic activities are usually supplemented by works of flood control that in certain countries, such as China, may be more comprehensive than the irrigation works proper.

Political: the organizational apparatus of the hydraulic order is either initiated or quickly taken over by the leaders of the commonwealth who direct its vital external and internal activities—military defense and maintenance of peace and order.

Social: stratification separating the men of the hydraulic government from the mass of the "people." The rise of a professional, full-time bureaucracy distinguishes *primitive* hydraulic society (headed mostly by part-time functionaries) from the state-centered forms of hydraulic societies (headed by full-time officials), who may have no important secondary classes based on mobile and immobile private property (*simple* hydraulic society), or which may have secondary classes based on mobile private property, such as craftsmen or merchants (*semi-complex* hydraulic society), or secondary classes based on both mobile and immobile private property (*complex* hydraulic society).[1]

The just-cited facts indicate that Oriental society cannot be explained in purely ecological or economic terms; and the spread of Oriental despotism to areas lacking a hydraulic agriculture underlines the limitations of such an explanation. Oriental despotism can operate beyond the hydraulic "foundation," but its power, which is complete in the political sphere, remains incomplete in man's economic and social activities. It is also incomplete in the realm of ideas. By and large, the Orientally despotic government exercises control over political thought, but it does not exercise a comparable control over esthetic, philosophical, and religious ideas. To be sure, these ideas have to be compatible with the despotic power structure, but they are neither created by it nor necessarily anchored in it. This fact deserves particular attention. At the same time, we do well to remember that, in virtually all dominant religions, the condition of the priesthood and many features in the presentation of the creed are functionally interlinked with the society in which they occur.

VALUES

In any discussion of Oriental civilization and Oriental society, the problem of values is an important one. The cultural relativists have avoided this problem, but, in many cases, their "value-free" position was shaken by the grim realities of the Hitler regime.

The three relations (realms), which I have emphasized here and elsewhere,[2] are basic to the human condition. Their careful examina-

---

[1] Karl A. Wittfogel, *Russia and China,* in preparation. For a discussion of this institutional order, see: Karl A. Wittfogel, *Oriental Despotism* (New Haven, Yale University Press, 1957), *passim.*

[2] Wittfogel, *Oriental Despotism,* p. 420.

tion provides a rational foundation for the recognition of both the positive and negative values in the life of man. A thoughtful critic has called this approach a "moral sociology." I accept this formulation.

An institutional order, in which man's relation to his fellowmen and to his innermost moral and transcendent self are dictated by an all-pervading totalitarian state, may produce all manner of technical improvements, but, in terms of the *conditio humana,* it is not a good society. The development toward such a society, far from being progressive, is decidedly retrogressive.

As stated above, Oriental society, although not totalitarian,[3] involves a system of total political power. Because crucial political freedoms are lacking, crucial intellectual freedoms are lacking also. In this respect, the multicentered societies of the West have values that are absent in the East. And this has been acknowledged in the East. The struggles of a Sun Yat-sen, a Gandhi, and a Nehru for a controlled (democratic) political order express their desire to correct this political deficiency. We show little esteem for these men if we hold their efforts pointless. On the other hand, independent philosophical systems and religious creeds, which the Orient has sheltered over time are being discriminated against not only by modern ideocratic totalitarianism (which eventually expects to eliminate them) but also by sizable groups in our own world (that find little or no value in them either). The technological revolutions in the West have greatly improved man's position by increasing his control over nature; but they have brought with them a nihilistic revolution which rejects crucial elements in man's relations to his moral and transcendent self, exposing him to the danger of becoming, in the core of his being, a hollow man.

Only by combining the great Western tradition in the political realm with the great Eastern and Western traditions in the spiritual realm can we attain the union between East and West which is made possible—and even imperative—by the present historical situation.

[3] See Wittfogel, *Oriental Despotism, passim.* Certain clarifying statements have been added to the third printing.

Comment: General Theories and General Education

AINSLIE T. EMBREE

Assistant Professor of History, Columbia University

The primary concern of that area of the college curriculum known, for lack of a more descriptive term, as "General Education" is to provide the student with courses which will aid in the integration of the values and experiences of human history into patterns that are meaningful and relevant in the context of the contemporary situation. Such courses should not be introductions or surveys—although they always tend to become such in the hands of those of us who teach them—but viable units within the curriculum that through their relationship with the whole academic enterprise give the student some understanding in a broad, and not necessarily superficial, way of the forces that have created our human society. This does not mean, one hastens to add, that general education courses should teach what "laws" govern society, or even that a philosophy of history should be expounded either explicitly or implicitly, but only that what Karl Wittfogel calls "recognizable regularities" in the development of societies should be examined and commented upon. As Thomas Berry points out, that while we have no adequate way of understanding or describing such regularities, it is possible to study them, especially in times of changes and during great movements, and thus to arrive at an idea of the main characteristics of the great Asian civilizations. In another paper in this symposium, Daniel Lerner suggests that it is possible to detect these trends and movements, if not by foresight, then at least by hindsight, and it is this kind of vision, not prophecy, that the teacher of general education courses seeks, in however a modest way, to acquire for himself and to use for the benefit of his students. Herbert Feis makes the same point in another way when he places stress in his paper on the necessity of self-knowledge as a part of education, since, in the process of studying the making of our world, one will surely come to a knowledge of oneself.

The persistent problem in all general education courses is to present material in a form that will actually fulfill any of these purposes. Whether one is teaching courses in Western civilization or Oriental civilization, two processes, it would seem, must be continually at work. One is comparison of events, ideas, and institutions existing in one geographical and chronological relationship with a similar series in other spatial and temporal relationships; the other is generalization, the attempt to make significant conceptual statements about events and institutions. The use of these methods, as every teacher knows or should know, is fraught with peril. This is true in courses dealing with Western civilization, where there is a long tradition of historical and sociological sophistication in scholarly writing, but the dangers are compounded in general education courses in Oriental civilizations, where there is no comparable body of analytic and interpretive scholarship. Yet, without some general conceptual statements, courses in Oriental civilizations tend to become collections of unrelated facts or, what is perhaps worse, generalizations about the mystic East or the unchanging Orient creep in to fill the vacuum.

It is against this background of concern and need that Wittfogel's approach to the great Asian civilizations—both in the paper given here and in his *Oriental Despotism*—is of special interest. He offers a conceptual scheme for comparing, not just Asian culture with the Western world, but of one Asian country with another, and of doing this on a level of knowledge that compels consideration even if it does not compel assent. The basic factor in his scheme, as I understand it, is the uncompromising claim that there is an ascertainable common denominator in the whole institutional order of the Orient, but more particularly in the power structure. On the basis of his analysis of specific historical phenomena, Wittfogel concludes that this common denominator is a method of organizing power. Oriental societies, in contrast to those of the West, have been characterized by a system of total power that colors all human relationships. This power, he insists, is not totalitarian in the modern Western sense, nor is it ever complete, but of its peculiar nature—a despotism that is based on the control and maintenance of an agricultural economy. This "agrodespotism" molds the three spheres of human activity—control of nature, social relationships, and religion, or what Wittfogel calls man's relation to his moral or transcendent self—in a variety of complex ways, but always in patterns that have recognizable configurations.

The question of the validity of Wittfogel's conceptual scheme is important, but not our present concern. It is sufficient to say that it stands in a great tradition and can bear the weight of criticism; and, even if it is not accepted in its general form, it can provide the teacher and the student with an organizing framework that is of value in general education. This is not to suggest that one should use *Oriental Despotism* as a textbook or even that one should "teach" its ideas, but rather that, as a daring intellectual construction, it can awaken interest even while its thesis is denied. Even as a whipping-boy, it is of value—just as Hegel and Spengler and Weber are made to serve their turn in courses in Western civilization. There is always the danger that great intellectual constructs such as Wittfogel's will prove so entrancing to students that they may be accepted with uncritical enthusiasm, but this is probably a danger worth taking, since exposure may also lead to reflective consideration.

One particular value of Wittfogel's scheme that may be mentioned is his discussion of the relation of scientific and technological achievements to the essential character of a civilization. In examining Indian civilization, for example, it is possible to point out the achievements of the ancient Indians in the invention of mathematical concepts, in surgical skills, and in metallurgical knowledge. There is, however, a certain unreality about such statements, for they do not fit into the general context of the culture as do the great scientific developments in European history. Wittfogel's suggestion that one wants to ask questions about the structures of power and social needs as the limiting factor in technological and scientific development is illuminating to the student. There is still a tendency for students to assume that Indians are in some curious way "otherworldly," and, hence, not concerned with technology.

Finally, Wittfogel's willingness to make comparisons, not just in descriptive terms but in relation to values, can be extremely stimulating in a classroom. His insistence on the necessity for a comparative study that is willing to make evaluations of orders of institutional power in terms of the possibilities they permit for the growth of human freedom and human creativity comes as a surprise to many students who have been taught that the making of value judgments is a sin against the academic spirit. At the end of our second semester in Oriental civilizations at Columbia College, we ask the students to read parts of *Oriental Despotism,* and there are always some who denounce what seems to be Wittfogel's Western chauvinism in suggesting that Western political values are in some sense "better" that those of the classical societies of Asia. One once said that since Wittfogel was so ready to pass moral judgments he must be a crypto-Christian. This tendency among some students to defend the East against the West is at least a refreshing change, and one that points up the possibilities of courses in Oriental civilizations acting as an agent of intellectual integration within the curriculum.

Comment: Generalizations and Chinese History

CHARLES O. HUCKER

Professor of History, Oakland University (Michigan)

All of us at this conference are concerned in one way or another with teaching about Asia (or some part of it) to undergraduates. I myself have been engaged in this business for a fair while, and, in my time, I have taught a wide variety of courses encompassing, at one extreme, a narrow advanced course on Ming dynasty history and, at the other extreme, a broad introductory "area survey" course on the Far East as a whole, including South as well as East Asia. Now, in a new environment, I am charged with developing an introductory course on China for upperclassmen in an area studies program that is required of all students in my university, as part of their general education. This new situation reflects a growing conviction in American educational circles that *all* educated people in our time should have some understanding of the non-Western world; and I expect that more and more of us are going to have to face up to the problem of presenting Asia to all students in some fashion.

Let me consider some of the ramifications of this problem, with specific reference to the role of China in a general education program. At the outset I must say I agree wholeheartedly with the view expressed in Professor Wright's paper that China is of value in general education not as background for current events and not for its own sake in an antiquarian sense but as a means for broadening the student's understanding of himself and his total environment. The educational impact derives from the contrast. Therefore, believing that one learns about himself only by seeing contrasts and comparisons in others, I disagree fundamentally with those who decry "comparativism." Paradoxically, however, it appears to me that in an educational progression from thesis (some grasp of the Western tradition) to antithesis (exposure to China) to synthesis (an enriched understanding of the student's own tradition in a broader context), the synthesis could easily be prejudiced by a "comparativistic" structuring of the antithesis. Like the Taoist sage, we can achieve our aim only if we do not strive for it. Therefore, China ought not be presented merely as a foil of the West. The aim should be, in my view, to present Chinese civilization as a rounded totality in itself and *as if* for its own sake.

As a historian, I am relieved that a course in Chinese history is the usual form suggested for achieving this end. But there is no reason why courses taught by sociologists, political scientists, economists, philosophers, or others could not have just as much educational impact as the history course. In any case, there are dangers. Too often, the student in the history course gets some impression of the progression of events but no grasp of the totality that is Chinese civilization; in other courses, a common pitfall is utilizing China only as subject matter for training in a particular methodology.

For these reasons, I have long suspected that the broad "area survey" approach to China has most to commend it for general education purposes. I have in mind a course that deals analytically with all aspects of the civilization from a variety of disciplinary points of view: the physical environment, historical patterns, thought patterns, aesthetic patterns, socioeconomic patterns, political patterns, and so on. Logically, perhaps, such a course could properly be taught only by a large team of cooperating specialists from the various disciplines. No one man could do it thoroughly. But is it utterly impossible for one good man to do it well enough, if he has a flexible mind? If he could, I suspect the educational impact on the student would be greater than that of a team presentation.

In any event, the historian in me shrinks from one inherent danger in this approach—the danger that the various aspects of Chinese civilization might be too neatly packaged in static generalizations, without concern for their changing qualities. Obviously, Chinese civilization is not a single integration of elements but a succession of different integrations. I would hope that an awareness of the danger might be sufficient to minimize it.

The other obvious danger is that the area course might become an unintegrated hodgepodge. I am afraid I have taught such hodgepodges and shall probably teach more of them. But I know better. No one could disagree with Confucius' contention that education should not be just a matter of learning and remembering much; there must be some thread that provides unity. Fortunately, the papers by Father Berry and Professor Wittfogel suggest excellent threads of this sort. Why not focus on intellectual values, for example, using them to inform the institutions and other cultural expressions of China while, conversely and concurrently, using the study of institutions and other cultural expressions to precipitate out, as it were, the basic ideological values in more and more meaningful refinements?

In other words, wouldn't the purposes of general education be served by beginning, for example, with Arthur Waley's *Yuan Mei* and proceeding from it to an interwoven analysis, one by one, of all the cultural elements that made the traditional Chinese literati what he was, just as well as by a course in Chinese history?

Part Two: Politics

The Modern Far East
and the Undergraduate

HERBERT FEIS

Career in government service and teaching

We have come together to exchange views about what should be taught in courses on Oriental civilizations as a component part of the undergraduate curriculum. My assignment, I gather, is to collect such thoughts as I may have about how such instruction can contribute to the conduct of American foreign relations and to mutual trust and enjoyment.

I have little but personal prejudice to guide me. Of one conclusion, I am almost sure: that an essential condition for a productive grasp of Oriental civilization and for its effective use in the formulation of our foreign policy is self-knowledge; I mean knowledge of the personal self. Unless the individual who devotes his college years to the study of Oriental civilization expends some of his private hours in self-examination, his efforts and knowledge are not likely to enable him to be a contributor to foreign policy who will be praised later by worthy men. Thus the aspiring student should be persuaded, by someone, somewhere, as he proceeds with his study, to seek to secure some rough impression of his reason for doing so, and his personal nature and problems.

I speak as a colleague, not a judge. Here are a few of the questions which the college tutors who strive to educate him might ask him to ask himself, while forbearing from asking him to confide that information to them. Does he find himself congenial with most

Americans and most American ways of life? Is it his impelling impulse to share his esteem for American ways with the peoples of the Orient? Or, to the contrary, is he seeking to escape from the life about him by immersing himself in studies of the Orient? Does he find that he can, without strain or anxiety, mingle intimately with Chinese, Japanese, Indians, Arabs, native Africans?

At some stage in his career either as an undergraduate student or more probably when he follows study with participation, he is apt to find that he must face up to these and related questions. So an early beginning on such self-examination is advisable. It may enable him to select the particular area or type of affiliation with Oriental peoples for which he will be well adjusted. Moreover, and this is the more important reason, it will make his study and his later effort more intellectually and emotionally self-supporting.

I am not suggesting that introspection take the place of diligence, ardor, and imagination. I am suggesting that along with the flow of these qualities, even the best student should have a measured look at himself in the mirror of self-knowledge at the start and end of the course.

There is another scarcely less hard and tortuous requirement that the student of Oriental civilizations should impose upon himself or have imposed upon him. It is that he try to learn quite a lot about American civilization—perhaps the most complex and varied in the world. This is not needed by those who study the Orient as a whim or out of intermittent curiosity, or as a collector of art objects or books. Nor by those who intend to remain merely observers of our relations with the Orient. And it may be upsetting for those who do not want to expose themselves to the hazards of judging their own country adversely in one or another conflict. For all such, it will be enough to bemuse themselves amiably by learning about the life of the Oriental peoples and, when issues arise, submit to the prevailing current of American opinion or to the wishes of those who may control their personal prospects.

But a comprehensive and vibrant knowledge of American civilization is vital for anyone who takes an active part in the course or conduct of American relations with the Orient, and is thus drawn into continuous and responsible contact with its officials and peoples. Lacking that, he will make mistakes of consequence.

Let me strive to convey my thought more clearly by enumerating some few features or facts about the flowing course of American civilization which, in my judgment, must be reckoned with by anyone, no matter how well instructed he may be in the affairs of the Orient, when he is concerned with our relations with that part of the world.

He should be cognizant of the varied ideals, faults, ambitions, and desires of the American people, their proneness to accept undisturbing, mediocre leadership, and their capacity to respond to noble and spirited leadership in times of crisis, their divisions and their unifying ties.

There is our tradition of national self-assurance and independence. Since the Revolution, we have been proudly sure that we need not submit to the intrusive action of, or unfair treatment by, other nations. This, for better or worse, still affects our stance in foreign policy, and continues to do so. It is a fine and proud heritage, but one that must be disciplined. For it may lead us to think that we are still immune from the need to be patient in the conduct of our foreign affairs. And it may cause us to construe any act of justified compromise or conciliation as "appeasement."

It tends also to cause us to be lax in the examination of our interests, and be satisfied with a mere restatement of certain abstract political attitudes or purposes. The Russians, of course, are much more fanatic practitioners of this type of obsessed diplomacy.

This tendency to talk in large terms, to favor verbalized conceptions and global plans, has thrived in part because the United States has not suffered from foreign invasion since 1812, nor destruction from the air, nor ruin of its cities, nor foreign occupation. Thus, though we are now all aware that planes and missiles and thermonuclear weapons have rent our immunity, we are apt to be unduly influenced by the sense that we as a country and as a people can not be vitally hurt or broken.

The political party in power may feel compelled not to expose itself to accusations by it opponents that it is being timid or heedless of the national interest or prestige. This, at times in the past, has caused the executive to disguise or aureolize his thoughts and intentions. For usually, the opposition finds it easier to gain supporters by being the more clamorous in its assertions about what is needed for American prosperity or due to American pride. Again, in order to avoid misunderstanding, I pause to remark that these streaks in American political life are a less grave threat to international peace than ways of dictatorship, where no corrective opposition is tolerated, and propaganda continually distorts truth.

It would be healthy if those, who as citizens or activists are concerned with our relations with the Orient, were aware of the fact that political and business groups and public personalities often appear before them not as their own selves, but transformed by image producers, commonly known as publicity agents, or in other circles as "public affairs officers." They protect their wards with fine phrases and pose them in favoring situations. Their assignment in government is to make all decisions and statements of their superiors defensible, wise, reasonable, and, at the worst, excusable. This presentation of official personalities and smoothed-out versions of our problems and incidents can be misleading. As we seek to probe beneath the outward guise and customs and avowals of the Oriental peoples, we should similarly probe beneath the exterior of our own actions and officials.

Even though the individual manages to retain his intellectual footing in the realm of instructed reality, he may well be puzzled at times to decide what is genuinely in our "national interest." History evidences that nations have often been mistaken about what is to their advantage, sometimes suffering greatly for what later turns out to have been a minor or even harmful end, sometimes failing to recognize situations or tendencies of genuine vital interest.

Historical inspection, alas, does reveal how often evil—real destructive evil—is abroad in the world, and this must be recognized and resisted; but it also shows how often foolish patriotic or ideological passion has left its friends and enemies in misery.

Your prospective student also might advisedly be made aware of the tendency of most Americans to identify the line of potential political and economic development for any and all countries for that which we enjoy and which has served us well. We have been thus over-optimistic about the chances of fostering a stable system of representative, or democratically controlled government, elsewhere. We have been over-zealous in our wish to nurture such political ways and institutions, which are probably the hardest in the world to sustain satisfactorily. Let law govern, let freedom ring, let all tyrants be deposed, let all men and women rule themselves through the ballot box. Certainly we ought to continue to praise and expound to all the world these precepts and means of justice and political liberty. But the well-taught student will recognize that our influence upon the peoples of the Orient can only be indirect, that each of them must stumble along their own hard road to some tolerable form of government.

The student may also be urged to assess critically, without beguiling phrases, when, where and how, our national security and international peace may be advanced by the undiscriminating extension of economic aid. I can not, on this occasion, go into the complexities of this matter, but will point briefly to a few of its neglected elements.

True, as George Eliot wrote, "It is seldom that the miserable can help regarding their misery as a wrong inflicted by those who are less miserable." True, people living in poverty and ignorance today are apt to respond to the appeals and bribes of Communists and/or their own national demagogues and fanatics. And it will be expedient, as long as our struggle against Soviet Communism is active, to provide some needed friends and allies with loans and grants even though their prospective use of them is dubious. But it has become plain that we can succeed permanently in helping only those who help themselves by being diligent, orderly, sufficiently honest, and thrifty.

It is hard to foresee when and where that gradual improvement of their condition will dispose an impoverished people to be less responsive to the seduction of hate and false premises which the Communists purvey. The traditional period from a state of resigned hard labor and poverty to one of aroused expectation, especially among what are called student groups, may express itself in a more, not less, challenging, if not hostile attitude toward the United States. It is not easy to keep the role, rate and kind of education which we must encourage in rhythm with the aptitudes and economic opportunities which a country provides. Yet failing that, the outcome may be chronic discontent and agitation rather than progress.

There are also the distressing and wasteful internal struggles between classes, regions, or religions—as at present in Vietnam and Laos. Or in displays of nationalist fervor, quarrels with neighbors, propaganda, and, above all else, competitive military expenditure.

My intention in calling attention to such elements of the problem is not to urge that we forego our program of foreign aid, but to warn the student of Oriental affairs that our experience should have taught us the need to strive hard to assure that our aid is used to good purpose, and to insist in return upon a steadfast friendliness, rather than diffuse it with good-natured largesse. Such called-for response will be condemned by all persons who want to see our aid falter or fail, and by those who dislike any restraint on their chances of economic or political gain. We will have to bear the charge of intervening in the affairs of others or restricting their freedom.

In the program named "Alliance for Progress" which we proposed to the other American republics, we may have adopted a promising technique—one enlarged and dignified by being converted into a joint effort and responsibility. The student of Oriental affairs will learn much by following its course, noting its successes and failures, and the reasons therefore, and whether the participants become cordial associates or turn into envious rivals. For ought we to be giving thought to a similar program for peoples of the Orient— possibly by extension and enlargement of the Colombo Plan?

Another phase of knowledge I think the student of Far Eastern affairs should have is of the personalities, ambitions and loyalties of the individuals elevated to high office in the United States. He should be encouraged to cultivate the habit of asking himself whether a selection was due to merit, or to the need to please some regional, racial or religious group, or to the accident of political favoritism or connection, and to spot the traits which nominees have shown in the past and for which they may be tempted, when in power, to compensate, for better or worse. It is hard to learn, despite the welter of publicity (and the false face which many popular publications present) and the essential facts about the fitness and wisdom (or shallowness) of men in public office, the qualities likely to determine their performance. It is harder still, unless one is at the very center—the high tension and temperature center—to know in association the views and natures of a group of officials that may influence one another. Hardest of all is it to know how these traits will affect the course of our foreign policy in particular situations. Yet, this is a very important area of interest for the student concerned with our relations to Far Eastern countries, a challenge to his ability to test prevailing impressions by assessments of his own. This task requires of the observer hardly less perceptive talent, judgment, and historic perspective than he looks for in the observed.

By my emphasis on the need for insight into personal selves and national ways and affairs, I do not mean merely conscious or textbook knowledge. I mean some qualifying sense that produces a cluster of perceptions; absorbed knowledge which should be the licensed guide for initiates; knowledge that becomes a kind of in-bred quality of the mind so that it may serve to regulate action without advance notice.

Even though a student may have only a distant and diminutive part in the determination of our relations with peoples of the Orient, he should have a sense of responsibility. For each and every point of contact between countries is expressive of the intricate interplay of act and response. Adequate although secreted knowledge of one's own self and of one's own country will instruct the native intelligence and the movement of the spirit, so that they will decide well when to be prudent and when to be bold, when to be silent and when to be outspoken, when to reprove and when to praise, when to give and when to refuse.

It is time, and more than time, to end my reflections on the accompanying knowledge which the aspiring student of Oriental affairs should be encouraged to acquire, and talk about some of the perplexities that will beset those who must determine and give the instruction. How can the students best be stimulated and taught in classrooms, seminars, sessions with tutors, so that each, accord-ing to his gifts and chance, may contribute to the effectiveness and justice of our foreign policy?

I will not venture to recommend a formal curriculum of study, or of contact, or of association, as having superior promise. I am inhibited by memory of the dialogue in one of Noel Coward's comedies in which suddenly the divorced wife shows an interest in the travels in the Orient of her former husband:

You were in China?
Yes.
How was China?
Very large.
And Japan?
Very small.
And the Taj Mahal, how *was* the Taj Mahal?

The first impulse is to seek to achieve comprehensiveness by arranging courses that span the whole area of pertinent knowledge. These have come to be known as courses in American civilization and the like. I still retain a hopeful belief in their potential effectiveness. But, like many others, I have been struck by the difficulty of making such courses coherent and thorough. You will have noted that Columbia University has decided to suspend the second year of its program in Contemporary Civilization, or more accurately, no longer to make it a requirement. As stated in the July, 1961, issue of *Columbia College Today,* the most explicit reason for the decision was "the difficulty of finding teachers who can encompass a range of materials as different in content and method and offering so many problems in conceptualization." If teachers able to convey this knowledge well can not be found, can the students be asked to strain for it? Paradoxically, I think so.

In a similar yielding to paradox, the same Committee that recommended suspension of the course in Contemporary Civilization proposed that among the alternatives to remain open is a course on Oriental Civilization, described as an "Introduction to the history and culture of Oriental societies."

My own notions seemed to me flightily high until I happened to read those passages in John Fairbank's book, *The United States and China,* in which he outlines what he thinks the student of Oriental affairs should know. I quote him:

Today, if we in America are to discharge the responsibilities which attend our power, we must know not only the conditions in which the Chinese [for he is writing about China, not the whole Far East] find themselves under Communism, but also their traditional patterns of response and aspiration, their mode of action when moved by hope or fear, their channels of expression for ambition, jealousy, pride, or love, their standards for the good life, of duty among friends and to the state, of loyalty to persons and to ideals. We can truly understand Chinese events and relate ourselves to them with wisdom only when we have become sophisticated as to Chinese motives.

Must we really accomplish these feats of understanding? I presume so even though we fail.

So how can we best try? I know no simple formula that could be the basis of a uniform regimen for all. For some, it may be best to spend long, long years in universities and libraries and in attending conferences. For others it may be lonely personal travel; for others it may be as a residue of personal experience in dealing with Oriental people as teacher, government official, businessman, or member of their families. For others, it may be reading over and over again the histories, novels, sermons and poems which are read or recited in the Orient. The task of the teacher, I presume, would be to try to guide each student in his effort to find, as best he can in his overworked days, whatever degree and combination of his activities and exercises contribute to his growth and correspond to his gifts.

I can not forbear from observing, in connection with Fairbank's wide-ranging description of our obligation, that I believe that Oriental peoples should be asked to make an equivalent attempt to learn about us. For every ounce of energy and of creative effort expended to improve our understanding of Oriental affairs, an equivalent exertion should be made by them. Let them be called on to devote an equal portion of their resources to courses in the understanding of the United States and the West, staffed by persons who believe that our merits and attractions exceed our faults and repulsions.

To the extent that available means and staff permit, there should be a disposition toward flexibility and variety. This is advisable for two reasons.

First, and acknowledged, is the difference between individuals: their temperament, aptitude, purpose, health, domestic condition, and economic prospects.

Second, is the great diversity of purpose that animates those who will assemble in the courses on Oriental civilization. "A" could

be really a perplexed dreamer who seeks to find in Eastern philosophies peace and wisdom. "B" may be a calculating and ambitious
young man who believes that by becoming a Far East specialist
he will enter upon a promising career in the Foreign Service. "C"
may be there because he wishes to teach the lore or the literature
of the Far East. "D" may have in mind the growing opportunities
in, let us say, the oil and aviation businesses in the Far East. "E"
may aspire to be a geographer, fascinated by the topography, the
strangeness of the great land areas and the seas and rivers, mountains, and jungles of the Far East. "F" may have his mind set on
getting into the C.I.A. "G" may have a strong desire to be of
service to poor and suffering peoples either as a religious or medical
missionary. There is no need, I am sure, to continue to run down
the alphabet of variation between those who may gaze at the ceiling
as you lecture.

Despite the variety and diversity of types and differences of
interests and purposes, there are some essential elements of knowledge with which all or almost all novitiates should acquaint themselves. My own thoughts of what these should be are commonplace.
So commonplace, in fact, that I feel impelled to preface them by an
even greater educational commonplace: that the skill and animation
with which any subject in the humanities is taught, the insight,
thoroughness, and stimulus with which it is developed to the listen-
ing student, is more important than the precise nature of the subject
itself. A great teacher of botany could make lectures on Chinese
trees or rice-growing in Thailand enduringly meaningful. For he
would color and inflate his subject until it was a great sphere reflecting many sides of the world. In contrast, a dull specialist can
make a course in, let us say, Japanese history or Confucian philosophy of no enduring value.

I favor, in general, the historical rather than the analytical presentation; for it is apt to be the more effective way of illuminating
the contemporary condition, tendencies, and prospects of a people.

Analysis so often turns into an exercise in sterile classification except as used to give greater meaning to the historical recital. Use it thus, not in lieu of history.

I have in mind an introductory historical course or group of courses which would acquaint all engaged students with the main vicissitudes of the Oriental countries: their affiliations and differences, their good times and bad, their triumphs and tragedies, their liberties and tyrannies, and the changes in their ways of livelihood as well as their social customs.

This would be the prelude to more specialized tuition—still with a historical bent. Between the various branches of study concerning geography, the economic conditions and problems of the area, its political and social arrangements and institutions and literature, the student should be allowed substantial choice, some chance to concentrate upon whatever aspect or element of Oriental life, and what part of the Orient has the greatest personal or professional meaning to *him* (it is time to include "her!").

My mention of geography has been cursory. I have in mind not the chance of memorizing the topographical details of any one small region or country, or the names of towns, harbors, rivers, and mountains, but a comprehensive comparative inquiry into the physical and human geography of the whole Orient. This will bring out the similarities and differences of its sections, and explain how they have affected the life and development of each country. It might well include brief forays aimed to make the student aware of how much more is to be learned about the influence of physical conditions on the ways, customs, plight, and motivations of the peoples of the Orient. I should think it well to have visiting specialists who could tell of the state of health, illness or well-being, vigor or weakness of the Oriental peoples, and of the causative conditions.

In one course which most students might be urged but not required to take, the essential features and events in the past associations—diplomatic, military, commercial and financial, and racial—between the United States and Oriental countries should be thoroughly reviewed. It should be selective rather than comprehensive, explanatory and interpretive as well as factual. This, I realize, is a fearsome assignment which can only be carried out in some beginning measure, enough, perhaps, to keep alive thereafter an inclination to study and analyze current experiences and situations.

To two areas of knowledge I should have to be persuaded to devote much official or classroom time. One is the history of art or literature of the Orient. For those who enjoy and care about art and literature will pursue their interest of their own free will and desire; and those who are indifferent or incapable of appreciation will find courses in them a dull drill. Similarly, in the set course, I would devote only as much time to the study of various Oriental religions and philosophies as may be needed to inform the student of the influences they have and are having upon present life and prospects. Beyond that, I would leave the subject to personal quest. For lecturing about these subjects may produce learned annotators but rarely results in true penetration. That can be nurtured only by self-initiated reading and reflection.

If these prescriptions were followed, the student, by now a junior, would have begun to accumulate some of the main elements of knowledge of his own country and of the Orient. It is then, at the latest, that decision should be faced as to whether he make the great effort needed to learn one of the Far Eastern languages, Chinese, Japanese, or one of the Indian or Malayan tongues. Any one who does so will improve greatly upon his chance of attaining a genuine acquaintance with the Oriental country and people, and should be much more able to play a valuable role in the formation or examination of American relations with them, as official, teacher or advisor. For mastery of the language enables the individual to communicate with at least one of the Oriental peoples, and to roam in their archives and literature, read their newspapers, periodicals, listen to their talk and enter into their lives.

But, alas, command of any of these difficult languages can be acquired only by prolonged application and determination. And in

the early stages of study much of this effort must be spent learning
tediously by rote, forms, signs, intonations. For at least two years,
I believe, study of any of these languages—oral and written—will
dominate the working life of the student, making greater demands
on him than any other course. As one young lady who learned to
read and speak Japanese fluently told of her own exertion: "for
over three years it governed my way of life, and was my only, constant and central purpose."

Thus, it would seem best, in an undergraduate course, to require
this language study only of those students who seriously intend
either to specialize subsequently in some branch of study about the
Orient or seek a career in some activity focused on or about the
area. Even for some of these an ability to converse in the language
will suffice; particularly for those whose interest is directed toward
Southeast Asia or India, about whose history and life most written
records are in English, French, or Dutch.

I will desist from the effort to collect my scattered thoughts about
how components and methods of a course on Oriental civilization
might best enable its devotees to contribute wholesomely to our national policy toward the nations of the Orient, and the conduct
of our relations with them. Even these meagre comments, I venture
diffidently, and with awareness that I have not adequately fulfilled
the assignment suggested by Dr. Embree that I talk about "knowledge of the modern Far East and foreign policy treated from the
point of view of ideas, concepts and factual information."

Tinting the outcome of all study of Oriental affairs will be the
way in which it is pursued. I should like to think that it might
be carried on and out in the spirit of the young men of the eighteenth century who went off on Grand Tours of the Continent
with tutors. During these years of discovery, they learned languages
by actual use; they enjoyed the chance to indulge in mild follies
or fancies out of sight and sound of families and faculty; they
were stimulated to compare what was familiar to them with what

was novel. The travelers through libraries and courses, through time over land and sea, will contribute most to our foreign policy who tincture their factual and analytical observations about peoples with a deep wish for peace and a sense of enjoyment.

Then, as sensible teachers, let us be satisfied if at the end of the course of study we can make a report similar to that which Adam Smith made to the elder Duke of Buccleigh as the two-year tour of the Continent, on which he had accompanied the son as tutor, drew near its end; in words that I remember somewhat as follows: "I am glad to be able to report, Sir, that your son shows improvement. However, in all truth I should add that there are few men at his time of life who do not improve."

Asia in the Study of World Politics

HAROLD D. LASSWELL

Edward J. Phelps Professor of Law and Political Science, Yale University

The study of world politics can be deepened as well as widened by incorporating more research material from the results of Asian scholarship and field investigation. Few doubt that in the years ahead the weight of Asia in the arena of world power will probably come closer to the potential suggested by the population figures. Already college courses focused upon global affairs are incorporating pertinent data and generalization, and encouraging the development of a larger corps of adequately equipped professionals who combine a competent command of the world scene with Asian specialties. We are adapting our institutions of college instruction to the urgencies of the time, and conferences of this character should expedite the process. The frame of reference required to give selective yet comprehensive consideration to world politics affords an opportunity to maintain and extend mutually beneficial communication among academic specialists whose training and accent is political and social or behavioral, and colleagues who are grounded in the history, geography, and society of Asia.

The scope and method of political inquiry reflect the vicissitudes of any academic discipline, especially one that is particularly sensitive to changing conceptions of the nation's place and prospects. A brief glance at the history of instruction in world politics may provide sufficient reminder of the sequence of development to identify the current posture of affairs. In the early years of the last century, college seniors were often exposed to the president of the college who made an attempt to interpret the civic significance of what had been learned. International law, practical ethics, and national government were the usual ingredients of the final brew. Evidently, they were regarded as potent enough to stimulate civic virtue though mild enough to prevent a binge of intoxicated agitation for utopian action now. In fact, of course, the impact was frequently tranquilizing, a result that depended in large part upon the personal qualities of the worthy gentleman who addressed the younger gentlemen present.

The brand of international law current in those days boldly affirmed universality. It was, as we now recognize, a parochial creation of the European state system, and reflected the perspectives current among European elites. Legal prescriptions were put forward in the name of Christian Europe, with marginal annotations to take care of such oddments as the Moslem states. At that time, the idea was not entertained that any trans-European power could make any significant contribution to or modification of the code. Their duty was to learn and perhaps eventually to earn admission to the elite. Scarcely anyone asked whether past epochs in Asia might cast the approach to international legal systems in a different light. Presently we shall pose some of these issues more explicitly.

With the exception of international law, world politics made little headway as a coherent discipline until the 1890s, when the United States stepped actively into the world arena by becoming the successor to the palsied power of Spain in the Caribbean and the Pacific. Courses called world politics began to appear; and while they dealt for the most part with diplomatic, imperial, and colonial history, they exhibited the taste and quest for analytic tools of thought that have become conspicuous features of the prevailing approach to the subject in departments of political science and international relations, and in some departments of history. The general tone has been non-normative, hence rather disparaging of legistic, ethical, or theological ways of examining the role of political power in human affairs. In practice, this has meant not hypocrisy but innocent contradiction or ambiguity. Between the two world wars, for example, the unmistakable bias of instruction was toward collective security arrangements. But the connection between analysis and policy recommendation was often left dangling in the classroom air. More recently, teaching has become more candidly attached to various interpretations of the power interests of the American nation state, or of the non-Communist bloc as a whole in its struggle with the Communist powers. Asian material has come into the picture with a rush. Scholars who are professionally focused upon Asia are collaborating in the preparation of general as well as special textbooks, often providing case studies of situations of direct concern to Asian powers.

The accent upon power in the study of world politics is to be understood as revolt against empty normative admonition. It is commonplace to say that the American cultural tradition specializes in ethical platitude, and that the chronic crisis of the age has built up a taste for understanding the alleged realities of power.

My view is that the study of world politics is likely to move toward a synthesis of the diverse emphases that are present evidence of the past of the subject. The current attempt to absorb Asian material, and to put it in an analytic and policy framework, may very well foster this intellectual synthesis.

I shall indicate briefly the components of a possible combination of elements. Let us think of five intellectual tasks that must be accomplished in the solution of any problem, including a problem in world politics. One task is the clarification of goal. What fundamental outcomes shall I seek to achieve (or block)? Another task relates to trend. Do the trends of the remote and recent past bring the world political arena nearer to the overriding goal or farther from its realization? A third task refers to conditions. What are the principal factors and constellations of factors that account for trends in any region or in the world arena as a whole? A fourth task is projection. Assuming that we do not influence the future, what is the probable course of future developments? Fifth, policy alternatives. What policies are likely to maximize the goals sought under various future contingencies?

The teacher faces these questions when he organizes a "course" in world politics and, among a myriad of alternatives, selects or rejects Asian materials as pertinent. The student faces these questions when he takes a course or decides not to take it, and when, once embarked upon a subject, he gives attention to Asian aspects, or plays up some other dimension of world politics.

What are the clarified objectives of the teacher of an undergraduate course in world politics? Each teacher who proceeds rationally is aware of his objectives, and has subjected them to the discipline of thought and discussion. Most teachers recognize a *minimum civic objective* for all students. Whatever the phraseology the aim can be approximately described as follows: To increase awareness on the part of the student of the processes of world politics and therefore to clarify the problems that confront him should he seek to participate actively rather than passively in world affairs.

Such an instructional aim is presumably acceptable to every teacher since it is phrased in terms of knowledge and affirms no preference for any other value than enlightenment. Many teachers go much further, however, and seek to arouse students to participate actively rather than passively in public affairs. This *positive civic objective* commits the teacher to recommending more than the pursuit of knowledge, since it is implied that the students should prepare to take action in policy matters even though available knowledge is insubstantial. Policy is a step into the future; and future events are only knowable after they have happened. It is necessary to deal with them as estimated contingencies on the basis of such historical and analytic knowledge as is at hand at any moment. To recommend a positive role as correspondent, editor, party official, diplomat, officer, or scholarly advisor is to assert that, given any state of ignorance, positive action is superior to the policy of passive action ("inaction"). Since American civilization favors the former solution, teachers who reject it usually find it expedient to adapt a strategy of deception and to proclaim the virtues of knowledge, while adopting a sneering tone of reference to civic enthusiasm of any kind, whether on the part of students, colleagues, or political leaders. Some teachers who sound this way are not aware of their value commitment or of deception. That they are proceeding without insight (hence non-rationally) does not of course mean that they do not have consequences of which they might become aware; and which, once perceived, might be endorsed or rejected. Is it helpful to Americans to have the Asian materials used to challenge an activistic orientation?

Among positive civic objectives, teachers differ in the weight they give to the pursuit of interests that they regard as *special* or *common*. The most candid special interest group affirms that the world should be dominated by a superior caste, and that the task of policy is to further the consolidation and perpetuation of a universal public order of caste. We are most acquainted with racist castes; but doctrines may be theological, for instance. In contemporary times at least, ideologies usually justify themselves in the name of the common good, whether they admit of power sharing or not. At the moment, all key elites of the globe justify their claims to authority and control by affirming the dignity of man (e.g., the Universal Declaration of Human Rights), and by asserting the principles of democracy. However, since ideologies are words *and* deeds, effective ideology is often far from proclaimed ideology, since no political opposition may be tolerated.

Most American teachers are willing to commit themselves to the traditional view that American national interests call for the perfecting of a lawful legal order that comprehends the globe, and is able to make itself effective against coercive violaters of public order. I agree to this; but I favor the opinion that teachers should communicate their postulates to students explicitly, and challenge the student to wrestle with the problem themselves. The Asian material regarding contemporary affairs is of obvious importance for any assessment of the factors that make for or against a truly universal public order that jibes with any conception of human dignity that we would accept as a satisfactory specification of the goal.

Undergraduate teaching in world politics often takes cognizance of the objective of *arousing interest in advanced study,* whether the object is formulated in terms of civic contribution or not. In this connection, the problem rises of how many special "courses" are to be offered at the pre-graduate level, and what they should be. I think teachers are entirely justified in opening the eyes of students to the intellectual and civic contributions that can be made by future specialists in world political studies, since any teacher who is worth his salt does speak with clarity and infectious earnestness about the place of his life work in the map of knowledge; also, our society needs to cultivate awareness among the young of the role of serious intellectual specialization. We can prevent abuses from arising in recruitment by the usual requirement of self-restraint, and by arranging for a faculty of sufficient diversity and personal strength to prevent one-sided emphasis upon a single field. World political relations can benefit from a larger supply of specialists in the years ahead, and if a college is seeking to call student attention to possible careers of intellectual and civic importance, it will be well advised to add to its staff in politics, especially in world politics, a professional in some Asian area who can help to motivate students to command the languages required.

Advanced study does not need to be justified wholly in terms of a career devoted to research, teaching, and consultation. I refer to these possibilities only to underline the view that professional alternatives should be made known to students in definite terms. We need to prepare better descriptions of professional careers open to students in every field. The legitimate role of these descriptions is not the "hard" or "soft sell" but clarity. Let me comment in passing that it is appropriate to make full use of student exchanges, summer semester field expeditions, intensive language courses, distinguished visitors in residence, simulated sessions of the United Nations, and the like, since these devices serve both motivational and subject-matter purposes.

Focusing attention upon the basic course in world politics, it may give point to the applicability of Asian materials if we examine some major topics. In this synopsis we consider the world political process according to participants, with distinctive perspectives, interacting in all arenas, possessing base values, employing strategies, affecting outcomes and post-outcome results. We move back and forth between the consideration of individual participants and of the aggregate.

PARTICIPANTS

It is traditional to regard national states as the principal participants in world politics and to give some attention to intergovernmental organizations like the United Nations. Because of the prominence of other transnational organizations, it is increasingly common to add to the list transnational political parties and "orders" (monopoly "parties"), pressure groups and gangs (the latter relying heavily upon coercion), and other associations that are often private (e.g., churches, businesses, educational and scientific bodies, mass media, humanitarian and health organizations, families). Finally, there is a disposition to give formal recognition to individual human beings as members of the world arena, with access to various tribunals. Many important groups are not necessarily organized to a degree that makes it convenient to treat them as formally responsible, despite the great influence they exert in shaping the political orientations. The reference here is to cultures and classes which enter the stage of world politics only to the extent that they condition organizations and individuals.

Any participant in world affairs seeks to maximize valued outcomes by affecting national and transnational policy. The task of the student is to become acquainted with methods whereby perspectives on policy can be discussed and explained. It is evident, for instance, that policy demands are affected by expectations regarding the present position and future prospects of each entity with which participants consider themselves identified. In contemporary affairs, the demand for independence from external tutelage has resulted in the emergence of many nation states whose culture is closer to a folk society than to a civilization. At the same time, older civilizations are reviving and making demands for unity, independence, and modernization. Asian studies are peculiarly important in disclosing constellations of factors that lead to such political demands, expectations, and identifications. As researches become more subtle, they are able to account for the receptivity of various societies to rival ideologies and systems of organization. If "Communism," "liberalism," or some other frame of reference is ostensibly incorporated into the upper, middle, or lower levels of a given society, what interpretations and operational patterns are affected by it? The remoteness of Asian societies from the world revolutionary centers of Europe makes it possible to follow the processes of diffusion and restriction in informative detail as well as to estimate the weight of factors that expedite or inhibit the spread.

ARENAS

An arena is a situation in which power is a significant value affecting and affected by the interactions that occur. Hence, we speak of the arena of world politics and of the arenas of each territorial component of the globe. Within each community are plural groups with arenas specialized to each phase of the decision process (intelligence, recommending, prescribing, invoking, applying, appraising, terminating). Not all arenas have established expectations about *who* is authorized to make decisions affecting *what* values by what *procedures,* and to use *severe sanctions* if it seems necessary to enforce decisions. That is to say, not all decisions are lawful; some are exercises of naked power.

It was remarked above that European nations worked out a system of international law that presupposes the existence of several nation states of approximately equal effective power, plus smaller states treated with formal equality. Although this system has never achieved sufficient enduring success to be regarded as a perfected public order—since the expectation of violence has been insufficiently modified to bring about the abolition of strong national armies—it has had some positive results in diminishing the inhumanities of war, and smoothing the way toward restoration of peacetime relations with minimum damage, especially to individual value positions. The recent tendency toward bipolarizing the world arena (USA versus USSR) has confronted the established order with structural problems that have not been overcome. At the same time, the extension of the practice of granting formal authority even to micro-powers has exacerbated the difficulties of unity by consensus. The rapid incorporation of powers whose predispositions are non-European (and in many cases pre-civilized; that is possessed of folk culture) has added to the confusion. Professor Bozeman, for instance, has suggested that the presuppositions of the limited world order worked out in Western Europe since the fifteenth century are not shared widely enough to maintain even the degree of order prevailing hitherto. The inference would appear to be that unity by imposition is essential (combined in the contemporary world with organized world conspiracy).

Asian scholarship has large reserves of case study material of great theoretical as well as contemporary importance. The history of China, for instance, would appear to afford an instructive case study of how a system of public order was stabilized at various periods on a set of presuppositions that differ from the European concert of powers. Does Asian experience provide other instances? Is the inference that the only alternative to attempted unity-by-concert is unity-by-imposition, supported by a highly centralized center capable of big-scale administration, vigorous policing, and intolerance of rival cultures? Given the parochial warp of European experience, it will presumably be enlightening to introduce such considerations into basic presentations of world politics.

BASE VALUES

By a base value is meant an asset that can be used to defend or extend the value position of a participant in world politics (population, resources, institutions). The Asian countries provide the most challenging evidence regarding numbers and power. Are there optimum population sizes for a pre-industrialized, an early industrializing, and a later industrializing society? Under what conditions, if any, can population be stabilized among people whose civilization and culture have rewarded them for biological multiplication? (The means already exist for cheap and effective contraception.)

Scientific enlightenment and skill would appear to be base values of the greatest importance for power as for many other value outcomes. Today we recognize that knowledge of nature may soon be sufficient to provide the flow of molecules needed to sustain life by technologies that permit the population to multiply indefinitely. How will the Asian elites employ such potentialities when they become aware of them? Will archaic agricultural methods be perpetuated as a means of providing work for the masses and consolidating the rule of a caste of politicians, police, administrators, scientists, and engineers who develop a special industrial culture? Is there evidence that Asian leaders are especially disposed to adopt "inhuman" political measures because of the supreme self-confidence characteristic of ancient civilizations and because of perspectives that transmit a view of the universe in which human beings do not make the significant decisions about life—decisions which come within the province of a plan of cosmic cycles that transcend human interference?

Another question about science, technology, and the role of Asia in politics relates to machine simulation of man. In European civilization, we already know how to automatize many production operations; we also know how to manufacture self-repairing man-like machines. It is freely predicted that these devices will be employed to supplement population limits in the West, if and when supplements are needed for power purposes. How will the elites of Asian countries view mechanical robots in terms of power?

In general, in regard to science, will it be possible for the power elites of Asia to obtain the political advantages that they seek from science and technology without dissipating their own control? Are there indications from historical situations of how the political man can keep other specialized types in tow?

STRATEGIES

A political strategy is the use of a base value to affect a power outcome. We have anticipated some questions of strategy in referring to population, science, and technology. A formally complete inventory would enumerate all the base values by which power outcomes can be affected, and examine the ways in which cultural predispositions affect strategic activities. A fourfold classification is often used for shorthand purposes in world politics: diplomatic, communication, military, and economic strategy. Do case studies justify the widespread view that Asian societies approach diplomatic negotiation with somewhat distinctive techniques at their disposal? What of military, economic and communication strategy?

When we look at the aggregate pattern presented by an arena in which many participants are employing individual strategies to pursue their ends, we perceive shifting patterns of coalition. In contemporary world politics Asian powers are non-polar powers and align themselves accordingly. Is it possible to demonstrate the conditions under which realignments occur? Assume further that bipolarization gives way to pluri-polarity, what orientation is to be expected?

OUTCOMES (AND EFFECTS)

An outcome is a culminating event such as victory or defeat in war or in decisions short of war. Examining the world as a whole we distinguish outcomes according to the changes that are made in the basic patterns of the arena, such as the number and strength of participants, or the system of public order. Constitutive changes— and less basic changes—can also be examined according to phases of the decision process. The impact of Asian powers upon the structures and functions of transnational intelligence, recommending, prescribing, invoking, applying, appraising, and terminating are in point here.

During a given period, post-outcome effects are open to appraisal from the point of view of any postulated system of goals that the appraiser regards as pertinent, such as movement toward or away from a universal public order of human dignity.

Whatever feature of the world political process is under consideration for curriculum building, all five intellectual tasks are relevant, namely, the clarification of goal, the description of trend, the analysis of conditioning factors, the projection of future development, and the invention, evaluation, and selection of alternative policies. The teacher may choose either minimum or positive civic objectives and accept responsibility for arousing interest in advanced study. Whatever the objectives articulated to the self or others, there is no doubt that civic and study objectives are necessarily affected to some extent. The suggestion here is that the incorporation of Asian materials shall proceed as explicitly and thoroughly as possible.

Comment: World Politics in the Study of the Middle East

J. C. HUREWITZ

Professor of Government, Columbia University

We are all placed in great debt to Professor Lasswell for his perceptive statement and for his many suggestions on how Asian studies might deepen and widen the discipline of international politics. Each of us engaged in the study of some corner of the vast continent of Asia must assuredly have known that our collective efforts had supplementary academic application. It is reassuring to have this confirmed by a master of that applied social science that devotes itself to the very essence of world society—the search for "laws" of state behavior in the international community, the resolution of problems of war and peace, and the role in this great drama of the individual, intrastate groups, and the state itself no less than transnational movements, intergovernmental bodies, and the world organization and its specialized agencies. Professor Lasswell has opened our eyes to ways by which Asian studies might enrich the discipline of world politics. I should like to turn his technique around to explore briefly ways by which world politics might enrich a branch of Asian studies—those relating to the Middle East.

So far, the Middle East has been neglected at the present conference. I shall seek somewhat to redress the balance. This raises the question of the region's precise location. A year ago Roderic Davison wrote a learned, indeed definitive, article explaining the variable geographic concept of "the Middle East."[1] I think I can dismiss that question in a single sentence: The Middle East is that zone of Asia and Africa that neither Asians nor Africans—nor for that matter the American Association of Asian Studies—wish to claim.

The Middle East differs markedly from the rest of Asia. It cannot boast, for example, of countries with populations comparable in size to those of India and China. The three largest in our region are the United Arab Republic[2] (a land that spills over from Asia into Africa) with some 30 million people; Turkey, with 25 million; and Iran, with 20 million. At the other end, appear Cyprus with only a half million inhabitants, and Kuwayt with about a third (well over 50 percent newcomers from nearby lands). Moreover, Israel is predominately Jewish and Cyprus predominately Christian, while Lebanon continues to rest its constitutional structure and political system on the fiction that a majority of its inhabitants are similarly Christian. Still, for purposes of analysis, bearing these exceptions in mind, we might think of the Middle East as a Muslim area. Also, it is often regarded as primarily Arab. Admittedly, the majority of the countries and residual British dependencies are Arab, but, of the region's estimated 110 million people, no more than half might be classed as Arab.

In other respects, however, much of what I have to say about the Middle East would have wider relevance throughout Asia. Here is where the discipline of world politics comes to our aid. The Middle East states are, as almost all those in the rest of non-Soviet Asia, newly sovereign. Even Turkey and Iran, which do not fall into this class, are new in their present guise. These two apart, all are inexperienced in the conduct of statehood, and most of them

[1] Roderic H. Davidson, "Where is the Middle East?" *Foreign Affairs,* XXXVIII (July, 1960), 665–75. The Middle East, for purposes of this paper, includes non-Soviet southwest Asia to the eastern frontier of Iran, plus Egypt, the Sudan, and Libya in adjacent northeast Africa.

[2] There comments were made on September 14, 1961, two weeks before the Syrian uprising that terminated the union of Egypt and Syria, which had been established in February, 1958.

are also uncommitted in a literal sense. They do not feel the tug of global issues. Nor have they in fact accepted formal obligations either in the degree or variety that the older states have, so that, at times, they behave in a manner that we are prone to label irresponsible. Actually, what they are striving for is status—or, shall we say, the symbols of status—in the international community. One such status symbol is nation-statehood, to which all Middle East lands aspire. Yet, what most achieve after independence is not nation- but nationalist-statehood, for the loyalties of the population at large have not been truly redirected. In the classical age of Islam, the state recognized not the individual but the group, which assumed responsibility for all its members. It might have been a religious group, a tribe (or one of its components), or a guild. In that period, Islamic society was in many ways far in advance of other countries.

These traditional patterns have been disappearing in the nineteenth and twentieth centuries. But the new ones have not yet taken shape. Little wonder then that confusion and frustration pervade the area. All its states wish to move ahead. They espouse economic development, seeking to modernize industry and agriculture. Obviously, this is a slow and uneven process. Iraq, for instance, has great development potential—ample reclaimable land, copious water supply, and steadily mounting oil revenues—and the army officers who overturned the monarchy advertised themselves as revolutionaries. Yet, oil revenues that once were put aside for public investment are now consumed not even for government administration but for keeping one man and his immediate aides in power, while laboriously assembled technicians have been dismissed.

As a whole, the Middle East may boast many economic accomplishments, but its individual countries are frustrated for another reason. Like emergent states everywhere in Asia, as students of world politics might expect, those in the Middle East desire military modernization. All want the latest military gadgets of the West—

rockets, jet planes, and electronic devices. We and the Russians, for our own respective purposes, have catered to—and occasionally even helped create—these whims. But the Middle East countries, instead of reinforcing their sovereignty, as they thought they were doing, by acquiring such weapons, have become more dependent on the outside world than before. Most of them cannot even manufacture parts for the imported equipment of the enlarged military establishments. Besides, every dollar invested in military modernization is a dollar withheld from economic expansion, which is already hindered by runaway population growth. In addition to nation statehood, economic development, and military modernization, a fourth status symbol is that of welfare statehood. There is no sovereign land in the Middle East, not even Yemen, that has not publicly obligated itself to promote the welfare of its people. These factors, clarified for us by the discipline of world politics, help account for the behavior of the newly independent states as they try to fashion viable societies and to find their places in the community of nations.

Professor Lasswell has referred to the parochial quality of international law as it developed in Europe, and the patronizing attitude of the European powers toward the non-European states. It would be worthwhile to investigate the rules by which the Asian lands were guided in their relations with one another before the initial imposition of European international legal principles. Such an inquiry would enable us to understand better the frictions that continue to divide the new states of Asia from the old ones of Europe.

Students of world politics have characterized the Cold War as a reflection of the bipolarization of international relations after World War II. Despite multiplying indications that the condition of bipolarity is weakening, the Cold War nevertheless lingers on, and, in the circumstances of unabating Soviet-West tension, there is still a tendency to pay close attention to what Professor Lasswell calls the base values—population, resources, institutions, and the like. Applying these rules to the states of Asia, we are likely to arrive at the conclusion that would suggest their continuing as pawns in international politics. Yet in more recent years, as the bipolar situation has begun to alter, we find that Asian peoples are playing a progressively more important role in world affairs. This is especially obvious in the UN General Assembly, where the young states of Asia and Africa carry greater weight—and certainly make more noise—than ever before. Moreover, it has been recognized that, in foreign aid to underdeveloped countries, the donors enjoy more influence before the terms for grants or loans are fixed, while the recipients begin to exercise stronger influence after the agreements are signed. This was well illustrated by Egypt's relations with the U.S.S.R. over Soviet aid for the Aswan Dam, which continued without interruption despite the recurrent quarrels between 'Abd al-Nasir and Khrushchev over the repression of communists along the banks of the Nile. These techniques of international politics enable us more clearly to evaluate the real status of the Asian countries in the contemporary world.

What is required for a deeper appreciation of Asia's role in world affairs is the study of the development of international politics in the continent at an earlier time. So far such studies have been written, by and large, with a European bias. To correct the distortion, it becomes essential to reconstruct the changing character of international politics in any region of Asia at least from the start of the European presence. I was interested to learn that students of India and the Far East feel that their materials for these earlier centuries are inadequate. Ours are woefully so. Even if we limit ourselves to the modern period, that is, from the fifteenth century to the present, there are wide gaps in our knowledge. Raw materials abound, it is true. Excellent archives may be found in Istanbul, whose collections are variously calculated to comprise between 50 and 200 million documents, covering more than a half millennium of history. But these materials are in a condition of such disarray that they cannot yet be handled rationally.

Suppose a scholar were trying to counteract a Western bias in

understanding a certain problem of the Middle East—how the Ottoman Empire handled a particular dispute, for example. He would
be able to procure only a glimpse of this from the disorganized
and unorganized materials in those archives now becoming increasingly available to scholars, Western and Middle Eastern. Once
we move out of the Turkish area, the situation becomes much
worse. In the Arab zone, which was largely subjected to Ottoman
control for four centuries, the records are far less plentiful and
useful. Nor is it accidental that in Cairo at the Institute for Higher
Studies of the Arab League courses on Arab history begin at the
dawn of the nineteenth century. Little effort is made to push them
back as far as 1517, when Egypt was taken over by the Ottomans.
Egyptians may teach courses on the earlier classical age of Arab
history, but the span between 1517 and 1798 is essentially unknown
and untaught.

The discipline of world politics is much concerned with the
impact of nationalism on interstate relations. If we apply the criteria
of this discipline to the study of nationalism in the Arab area, we
can understand why Arab nationalists do not seem to know whether
they are United Arab Republicans or general Arab nationalists,
whether they are Iraqis or Arab Unity nationalists. As they shift
back and forth between one and the other, this unknown history
of theirs plagues them. If we try to analyze why Arab nationalists
have framed the kinds of foreign policies they have, with well-
known effects on the international situation, we come to realize
that they are living, not in the present, but in the past and the
future. Of the past they have both positive and negative images.
The positive images hark back to the first century of Islam, when
Arabs spread out of the Arabian peninsula to engulf almost all
Southwest Asia, all North Africa, and the Iberian Peninsula. The
negative images are those of domination by aliens—first the Ottomans and later the Europeans. As the Arabs project themselves
into the future, they see similar images. Negatively, they are determined to kick over the traces of past subservience. This is why

all Arab nationalists, regardless of their governments' positions on the Suez crisis, could not help but take Egypt's side. In the nationalization of the Suez Canal Company, 'Abd al-Nasir's challenge to the Western powers was greeted with enthusiasm everywhere in the Arab world. Among the positive dreams for the future is that of the recreation of a single Arab state that would unite all Arabic-speaking peoples from Morocco to Masqat. In their view, the projected unified Arab state might in fact qualify as one of the great powers of the world. If they are living in the past and the future, it is understandable why they appear at times to be so irrational on contemporary affairs, why they often seem to be incapable of facing current realities.

With the postwar appearance of training centers specializing in the several regions of Asia, as of other parts of the world, there has come a growing demand for the application of the social sciences to Asian studies. A history of any region's international politics, usually under the rubric of diplomatic history, is a common feature of such programs. These courses have tended to break away from the traditional preoccupation with diplomatic correspondence as the source of information, to a use of all the tools of world politics. Indeed, those instructors of such courses who have engaged in research have had to draw upon the discipline of world politics to develop new techniques of inquiry and analysis to understand the unfolding problems in the relations between their several segments of Asia and the West. Still, it is clear that world politics as we have developed the discipline in the United States has concentrated overmuch on the special qualities of the great powers, the sources of their influence, and the effects of their behavior. But, in the Middle East none of the states as presently constituted can possibly become a candidate for great-powership. This would suggest the need for a further study of the techniques of small-power behavior in the world community, techniques experimentally devised by such scholars as Arnold Wolfers and Annette Baker Fox. Any such methods, to produce realistic results in Asia, would require the combination of a mastery of the discipline with a close knowledge of local history, institutions, and political systems, processes, and attitudes.

In closing, I should like to say a word or two about a survey that I am conducting on behalf of the American Association for Middle East Studies. In this survey, I am seeking to evaluate major trends and problems in undergraduate instruction on the Middle East in American colleges and universities. What the final results may show, it is still too early to know. But, in examining the responses to our questionnaires, I have been struck by many developments, some anticipated and others not. Institutions offering undergraduate courses on the Middle East have multiplied from fewer than a half dozen in 1950 to over 200 in 1961. Nor is there any evidence to suggest that the rate of growth has slowed down. Yet, while we have cause for cheer in such statistics, there are nevertheless many unattended or inadequately attended difficulties that beset the colleges and universities concerned across the country. Among the major problem producers are the generally low level of library resources on the Middle East in almost all schools offering courses on the area, the even more meager supply of textbooks and related teaching aids, and the prevalence of overtrained and undertrained instructors. In these circumstances, many institutions, instead of instructing their students, are simply turning the uninformed into the misinformed.[3] Germane to this audience, however, is the following question: Are these conditions peculiar to undergraduate instruction on the Middle East or do they reflect roughly the overall quality of such instruction on the remaining areas of Asia? I strongly suspect that it is the latter.

[3] J. C. Hurewitz, Undergraduate Instruction on the Middle East in American Colleges and Universities (New York, American Association for Middle East Studies, 1962).

Part Three: Economics

Economic Forces and
Social Change in Asia

WILLIAM W. LOCKWOOD

Professor of International Affairs, Princeton University

Asian studies by their nature call for a multidisciplinary (not to be confused with a no-disciplinary) approach. One major component is the economic, i.e., ideas and institutions concerned with the allocation of goods and services to supply a society's material wants.

This essay outlines three major themes around which to organize study of the material aspects of life among Asian peoples: (1) the economic-technological foundations of traditional societies, in relation to other social and ideological features; (2) early impulses toward change consequent on the intrusion of the West, bringing the technology and values of modern industrial society; and (3) the spread of the Industrial Revolution in the East today, in relation to other nation-building goals, and in the wider context of human freedom and well-being.

SOCIAL EQUILIBRIUM IN
TRADITIONAL ASIAN SOCIETIES

The student bred in the urban, industrial West can best begin the study of Asia with some empirical view of the difference between his own culture and the pre-industrial, agrarian civilizations of the East. This highlights the special character of modern industrial society which is his own heritage. Within the wholly different societies of

Asia, it affords insights into the interrelations of economic institutions with social structure, politics and ideology. And it sets the stage for analysis of the revolutionary changes.

Any stereotype of "Asian" or "Oriental" society is to be viewed with skepticism, of course. It can only gloss over wide disparities in the history and outlook of 1.5 billion people, organized in numerous distinctive cultures. Who speaks for the Punjab peasant, the Cantonese boatman, the Borneo headhunter, the Japanese industrialist, or "Miss Singapore" of 1963? There are many Asias, concludes O. H. K. Spate; far less than Europe has Asia with its great internal barriers ever developed a continental life of its own. Historically, it has included not only vast agrarian empires but also steppe societies, maritime trading kingdoms, and primitive forest peoples. Before 1850, the differences between China and India, or Japan and India, were hardly less than between India and Europe. Indeed, Arnold Toynbee dismisses the whole dichotomy between Asia and Europe as nothing but a myth invented by Herodotus, who claimed that the Persians made war on the Greeks to avenge Troy (which they never heard of).

Nevertheless, by contrast with modern industrial society, it is possible to generalize about the great traditional civilizations of Asia's alluvial valleys and coastal plains. Here, in East and South Asia, have dwelt most of her populations for a millennium or two.

This is a village society, first of all. Perhaps three quarters of its people live in small sedentary settlements dependent mainly on agriculture. Typically the village is 50–75 percent self-sufficient in its economic affairs. Beyond that it is oriented mainly to a market town within a day's walk. Its technology is handicraft—hoe culture, premachine manufacture, and transport by boat, by draft animal, or on the backs of men. Its productivity is correspondingly low, 5–25 percent of Western industrial levels. Life, therefore, imposes grinding poverty on the mass of people, with little hope of relief. Death rates balance uncertainly with birth rates at 35–45 per 1,000, rising or falling with the vicissitudes of famine and oppression. Livelihood on the farm is a perennial gamble with the weather, especially where irrigation is lacking. Margins are further narrowed by the drain of rent, interest, and tax incomes into the hands of privileged, town-dwelling elites.

Agricultural land comprised in this society the principal source of income, status, and security. But its control often depended more on birth or political privilege than on peasant industry. While urban business enterprise sometimes reached large proportions in favored regions, as in Gujerat or the lower Yangtze, by modern standards it remained stunted through lack of security and expanding opportunity. Its time horizons seldom encouraged more than short-term business ventures of quick turnover. Often, trade and banking were left to persons from special regions, castes, or other communal groups, who found strength in mutual arrangements of a self-protective and quasi-monopolistic character.

Cities like Peking might grow to tremendous size as administrative, military and religious capitals, with supporting trader-artisan populations. India is said to have been as urbanized in 1750 as England, France, and Italy. Edo (Tokyo) already boasted a million people, making it the largest city in the world. But such cities failed to develop into independent centers of commercial, political and ideological change that could overturn a society, as occurred in Europe after 1300. Tendencies in this direction were evident in late Tokugawa Japan, it is true. Yet even here it was discontented elements of the old feudal aristocracy, rather than a rising burgher class, that finally took the lead in abolishing the old order and pioneering the new. Functionally, moreover, as economic organisms, the cities of pre-modern Asia remained essentially different from the industrial metropolis of modern times. They lacked not only its internal specialization but also its complex two-way movement of goods, services, and factors of production between city and country.

Empirical accounts of such traditional societies are easily accessible today, since they still comprise so largely the framework of life in the Orient. There is no need to go in for archaeological diggings or extensive library research to discover their essentials. Anyone unable to visit them at first hand will find them abundantly written up and filmed, as modes of life still little changed throughout a million villages of Asia.

From descriptive study of this sort, one moves on naturally to analytical issues concerning the relations between economic institutions and other aspects of human existence. The survival of these civilizations over long periods of time suggests a stable adjustment between environment, technology and society. In their decentralized village economies, for example, social coordination and control are necessarily shared pluralistically by family, village, guild, caste, and other smaller groupings below the superstructure of the imperial state. Class structures present wide variations in detail—contrast, for instance, the nobility of Java and of feudal Japan, or the Hindu Brahmin and the Chinese scholar-official. Yet, all are societies of status in considerable measure. People are born to their place or bound by necessity, with a resulting lack of enterprise and mobility in economic life. Authority is ascriptive rather than achievement-oriented. Political power is for the high-born and the rich. It is subject to no constitutional restraints, though tradition combines with technology to limit and decentralize the functions of government. A wide gulf separates the mass of villagers and town-dwellers from the more mobile, literate, propertied minority that forms the political oligarchy.

The philosophical outlook pervading such tradition-bound societies tends to be consistent with these facts of life. It stresses the values of the small human group. It looks askance at venturesome defiance of the past. Its intellectual curiosities turn to philosophy and the arts, not empirical science. It idealizes harmony if not acquiescent fatalism—everyone in his place. Thus it contrasts with the spirit of striving and venture and perfectibility that sparked the modern revolutions of the West. To all this, the Eastern religions gave their tacit approval, even their divine sanction. "I am indifferent to all born things," says Krishna the godhead. "Acknowledgment of limits leads to happiness," reads the inscription on an old Peking gate.

In these traditional Asian societies, then, we have some of the world's great examples of stable social equilibria enduring through the centuries. Any movement away from the norm was apt to set in motion counter-movements that sooner or later re-established the orignal position or something close to it. Impulses to secular change were not necessarily lacking—invasion, invention, maritime enterprise abroad, and others. But they met with inhibiting influences that tended to return the system to the broad patterns of institutional equilibrium described above. One asks why this was so. How did these societies last so long? Why, for example, did no Industrial Revolution gather force indigenously to transform these agrarian orders in Asia, as in the West?

The classic case of traditional equilibrium is, of course, Imperial China, broadly from 850 to 1850. How explain the persistence of China's stable institutional base, and her essential cultural unity over vast distances and populations? Why did printing, gunpowder, and the compass change the face of Europe, but not the country where they originated? "A people the least revolutionary and the most rebellious," observes T. T. Meadows, watching the T'ai-p'ing Rebellion a century ago.

The British scholar-diplomat himself goes on to ascribe China's "unequalled duration" to three doctrines and an institution: (1) the ideal of government by moral suasion; (2) a belief that wise and able men should rule; (3) the moral right of rebellion; and (4) the competitive civil service examinations.[1] Meadows' famous dictum did not settle the question, of course, and since his time many another scholar has knit his brow over China's unexampled length of life. Was it enduring beliefs and moral values that made it survive,

[1] *The Chinese and Their Rebellions* (London, 1856, re-issued in Academic Reprints, Stanford, Calif.), pp. 401–2.

or a system of technology and social action peculiarly well adapted to material environment?

This issue of myth versus technique, of thought-system in relation to instrumental process, is an old one the world over. China offers only a particularly fascinating case for the student. Most historians, along with Meadows, have stressed controlling forces in the realm of ideology. They point to the Confucian code honored by the Chinese and handed on from generation to generation. Homer H. Dubs, for example, sees the key to China's national unity, not in economy, race, or territory, but in the Confucian moral ideal of one civilized world under Heaven—*t'ien hsia*—mediated by the Son of Heaven.[2]

Other historians, not all of them Marxist, explain China's stability mainly in terms of material modes of production and the forces they exert upon social institutions and beliefs. One such striking hypothesis is that of K. A. Wittfogel in his *Oriental Despotism*. Wittfogel postulates "Oriental society" (including China and a whole congeries of civilizations extending even to the Inca) as one in which the technology of water control yields major benefits from large-scale public works in agriculture and transport. Management of these hydraulic functions gives rise in turn to strong, "agrodespotic" government armed with "total" power. From this power base the bureaucracy can permanently dominate all other latent power structures founded not on political office but on property or religion or some other function.

The outcome, as Wittfogel sees it, is a single-centered society remarkably resistant to change. The managerial class in charge of the "hydraulic state" can "pulverize" all non-governmental forces and frustrate proto-impulses to revolution from industrial capitalism or any other quarter. The Confucian political ethic is viewed as a "benevolence myth" rationalizing an exploitive structure of power. Rather than an independent force that vitalizes Chinese culture and

---

[2] "The Concept of Unity in China," in Stanley Pargellis, ed., *The Quest for Political Unity in World History* (Washington, 1944), pp. 3–19.

makes it endure, it is essentially a control device that legitimates the two-class order and helps to stifle any latent impulse to change. Only the Industrial Revolution introduced from the West after 1800 could overwhelm this society. Even then, Wittfogel finds China's "monopoly bureaucracy" reborn today in its new Communist despotism.

Clearly, these views present us with a hen-and-egg situation. The reality is an institutional equilibrium in which social relations are determined both by myth and external circumstance interacting upon each other. But the nature of this integration poses absorbing questions of social analysis. And it leaves the thoughtful student still mystified as to the underlying causes of intellectual and material progress or stagnation.

THE WESTERN CHALLENGE: MODERNIZATION AND SURVIVAL

The second cluster of economic issues deserving attention in Eastern societies is their response to the West over the past century, particularly the forces impelling and retarding industrialization.

When the Western powers arrived in force on the coasts of Asia, after 1800, much of the region happened already to be in a stage of dynastic decay, with accompanying economic disorders. Yet, neither in Ch'ing China nor Mogul India, nor elsewhere in Asia—unless possibly in Japan—does it appear that endogenous crises left alone would have eventuated in anything more than a return, sooner or later, to the traditional equilibria of these societies.

At this point in history, however, powerful exogenous shocks began to be transmitted from the West with the arrival of its gunboats, traders, and missionaries. By 1910, virtually all of Asia was in political subjection, excepting Japan and Siam, and a China half-controlled by the powers. The first great organized reactions, of course, were rising campaigns of national liberation through which Asia began in time to strike back. But beyond and beneath them were other more pervasive responses that commenced to transform whole cultures in the direction of the goals and institutions of modern industrial society.

Foreign military aggression and foreign trade were the cutting edges of Western penetration. By the same token, they fostered leading sectors of change in traditional economies. Everywhere, modern arms proved irresistible, when backed by the efficient bureaucratic organizations of the West. Thus the subcontinent of India was subdued by a handful of British regiments exploiting its dynastic rivalries. Thereafter, it was ruled for a century by a civil bureaucracy that never numbered more than 5,000 Britishers. No leader of Asia's rising nationalism could fail to conclude that modern weapons backed by industrial know-how were the price of national survival. But they varied greatly in their perception of the change this self-strengthening would entail, and in their capacity to set it in motion.

Herein lies the contrast so often remarked between Japan's technical successes after 1868 and China's comparative failure. Of all Asian peoples, it was only the Japanese who moved swiftly to launch their country on the path of modernization, and to lay the foundations of modern industrialism and military power under the aegis of the nation state. Even where Japan's success was not duplicated, however, Western goods and ideas intruded progressively to subvert the old order. Foreign trade brought in new products from abroad, often superior to those of indigenous make. It opened export outlets for local industries, old and new. It attracted foreign and domestic capital into estate agriculture and factory industry. It created new urban centers of economic activity where the values and instruments of industrial capitalism began to re-shape the traditional economies of the East.

Except in Japan, this gestation took place largely under foreign political control. It tended, at first, to limit itself to treaty ports and colonial centers, where foreign business could pursue its aims and build supporting infra-structures free of the deterrents of the traditional hinterland. "A modern fringe . . . stitched along the hem of the ancient garment," said R. H. Tawney of China's treaty port system. Everywhere a dualism thus arose between modern and traditional. Its differentials and tensions were themselves the active force of change. But their persistence has handicapped integrated national development even to this day.

The agents of change and the channels through which they operated appear in kaleidoscopic array as one surveys this development over a hundred years and within a score of countries. At every hand are intriguing comparisons—China and Japan, just mentioned, but equally Japan and Siam, or Indonesia and the Philippines, or Bengal and Madras. The process of industrialization was generally halting. Usually, it was little more than a slow drift. So, too, with secularization, urbanization, and other aspects of what is loosely called the transition to modern industrial society. Lags and leads are easy to perceive—between city and country, between coast and interior, between large-and-small-scale industry, between impacts on different caste and class and communal groups. The penetration of various ideals and techniques was uneven, too. Those that are external to a culture enter more readily than those closer to its inner spirit. Slot machines are easier to learn to operate than joint-stock companies. Benny Goodman is more readily understood than Thomas Jefferson.

The sense of history gained from study of this whole process prepares one to approach the problems of contemporary Asia. On the one hand, with all the variations in rates and sequences from nation to nation, there appears to be a certain inevitability in the erosion of traditional economic life and the changes set in motion by exposure to influences from modern industrialism. On the other, the alterations necessary to a full-scale industrial revolution are found to be so radical and pervasive that it becomes easy to see why most non-Western countries are only on its threshold today. Five year plans and foreign aid programs may step up the pace of technical progress from year to year, but they need to be viewed in these longer perspectives of social transformation.

THE INDUSTRIAL REVOLUTION TODAY

Today there is a marked quickening in the determination of Eastern peoples to modernize, and the tempo of their efforts. Among twelve newly liberated nations of South Asia, with populations of 650 million, and no less in China and Korea to the north, rapid economic development is in the forefront of proclaimed objectives. The great issues of debate are no longer whether to modernize, but how to do so. Most leaders now look back on traditional institutions with the attitude of an American automotive engineer toward the old model T Ford. "My grandfather drove a model T, and he drove it pridefully and well," said he. "I mean no disrespect either to my grandfather or to the automobile when I say that today they both belong in the Smithsonian."

Economic development, in short, holds an insistent priority. Indeed, most other social ideals like democracy and national security must wait for their fulfillment on substantial economic progress. To assess Asia's prospects, or understand its problems, one requires some knowledge of the processes of economic growth. In particular, no amount of exposure to miscellaneous area study is any substitute for a grasp of the relevant disciplines among the social sciences.

Modern economic growth, or the Industrial Revolution, needs to be distinguished in the first place from economic changes of various kinds that have characterized human societies in the past. It means the application of modern science and technology, accompanied by growing use of inanimate energy, to achieve sustained, high increases in capacity to produce goods and services, with all the changes this entails in capital and skills, production functions, and industrial structure.

These are the processes now beginning to re-make the economies of Asia, as once they changed the West. National planners search for ways and means to raise savings from their traditional 5 percent or less to more than 10 percent of national income. Public and private investment is being turned to new products and processes, guided either by a redirection of market demands or by central, planned decision. Large-scale capitalistic enterprise is growing, with machine technology and organization borrowed from abroad. An industrial labor force is being trained in new technical and managerial skills. More slowly, capital and science and modern organization are entering the countryside, too, to generate progress in the agricultural sector. Radical innovations are taking place in international economic flows, including massive injections of foreign aid. And almost everywhere the early fruits of economic progress threaten to be swallowed up in population growth brought on by the fall of mortality in advance of fertility.

The details of these processes may be left to the specialist. But no serious student can avoid certain more general issues concerning the underlying determinants of growth or stagnation, and the consequences that follow. How do some nations succeed, and others fail, in changing vicious circles of poverty and low productivity into benign circles of cumulative, self-reinforcing growth? Again one returns to issues raised earlier in the context of pre-modern history.

The proximate conditions of economic development, in Asia or elsewhere, are readily identified. They include: (1) improvements in the quantity and quality of material resources, (2) additions to the stock of knowledge (skills) for utilizing them, and (3) the will and social capacity to organize these processes of growth. Underlying these direct determinants, further, are institutional propensities that favor or inhibit the kinds of behavior appropriate to such changes. Here lie the factors, material or human, that explain the difference between North and South America, Germany and Spain, Turkey and Afghanistan. Looking at the record, what can one say as to the characteristics of growth-oriented social systems?

One kind of insight is afforded by analyzing the nature of modern industrial society, with its marked capacity for economic growth. For example, Japan today displays a number of characteristics that clearly distinguish it from Tokugawa Japan a century ago as well as from present-day Laos. It is a society with goals that are more plural, with a stronger emphasis on material advance. It stresses instrumental efficiency more strongly, and distributes resources and rewards accordingly. It values people more largely in the light of universal norms of achievement in relation to specific goals. It is a more mobile and open society, affording greater freedom of choice. Recognizing these differences, however, we are still left with the question how a society moves from the earlier restrictive norms and authority structures to these more universalistic, achievement-oriented patterns. Especially, what are the economic aspects of the change?

Here, one issue much discussed today is whether rapid economic development by its nature must be an explosive process. In the crucial stage of transition—"take-off" is the fashionable word—is there a critical minimum speed necessary to break out of the traditional low-level equilibrium? This hypothesis can be supported by various arguments, technical and social. Thus observers anxiously wonder whether India's recent growth, about 2 percent per capita per year, is high enough to spring her out of her "low-level equilibrium trap," or whether some more massive effort is required.

Only Japan among non-Western nations offers a historical case worth examining on this point. Interestingly, her experience is not different from that of most of Europe and the United States on this point. Throughout her modern century, it is difficult to pick out any single decade or two as the period of economic take-off or breakthrough. On the contrary, one is impressed with the sustained continuity of her development after 1868, and the arbitrariness of any attempt to distinguish stages of growth, or even leading sectors. The great discontinuity was a *political* crisis, the Meiji Restoration, and the train of forces which it set in motion. So it has been more recently in China, too, though the economic consequences of the Communist take-over here can not yet be assessed.

A second issue in the strategy of economic growth revolves around the relative importance of new environmental stimuli to productive activity, as against broad cultural changes calculated to make people respond more vigorously to the opportunities before them. Is the development of Indonesia, for example, being inhibited by lack of appropriate personal traits, e.g., a reluctance to work hard in the tropics, or by dominant values in Indonesian society that place a low priority on economic enterprise and efficiency? Or, is it a matter of unfavorable environment, in the sense that markets and local leadership are lacking for peasant innovation, that new industrial ventures are unprofitable in a climate of political disorder and inflation, and that productive enterprise of any kind is discouraged by the lack of supporting facilities and inducements, just as it would be in any other country under similar conditions?

All aspects are no doubt important in principle, whether related to stimulus or response, to economics or morals. But it makes a difference in public policy where the emphasis is placed, as between the two approaches. One leads to a stress on changing the mind, on educating people to a new set of values. Since this is a long, slow process, it often breeds defeatism. Or, it prompts impatient nationalists to turn to dictatorial compulsion for lack of confidence in voluntary solutions. The other approach emphasizes the cumulative growth that may be generated even in seemingly stagnant economies if certain prerequisites can be provided like political security, currency stability, and attractive market opportunities. Vigorous advances recently in India and the Philippines, for example, argue for this latter point of view. Moreover, the variables in this realm are more strategic in the sense that they can be more directly attacked. But much debate goes on about the correct operational priorities in growth strategy in this respect.

A third issue in the foreground of policy discussions is the relationship between economic development and other social goals, especially political freedom. Here are choices decisively affecting the future of a nation. Yet development theory has little to teach that is both universal and practical in its application. Is the statesman entitled to look to the scholar for a lead on great strategic questions of this sort? If so, Prime Minister Nehru is right when he concludes that "the intellectuals have failed us."

Controversy centers around the political framework of economic development, and the responsibilities to be assigned to the public and private sectors. Economic growth in the West argues for the importance of dispersed private initiative within open and pluralistic societies. It has entailed vigorous leadership but not domination by the State. Prior to the Soviet revolution no successful case of development failed to be of this type; one may even include Japan here in considerable measure. Nor is the argument invalidated by the widening of State intervention in all such free economies with the new techniques and the new goals of the 20th century.

The opposing view dwells, of course, on the political and economic virtues of centralized control in the hands of an authoritarian if not totalitarian state. How else, it is asked, can an ambitious elite break down the rigidities of the pre-industrial order, unify its fragmented elements, and force the rapid introduction of the new technology? Freedom and private enterprise have "a bias for small change" that is obsolete today, it is said. Thus Communism makes a powerful appeal in Asia in terms of its capacity to drive lean, hungry nations into high-speed industrialization. Even non-Communists are generally skeptical that rapid economic progress is possible without more centralized, despotic regimes than have yet appeared in most of south Asia, Africa, or the Near East.

Totalitarianism is now receiving its first massive test in Asia. The Chinese record is still problematical. Meanwhile other nations mostly are experimenting with more flexible blends of state and private initiative organized under diverse political systems. As yet Communism has come to power only in the wake of prolonged disorder, international and internal. Elsewhere, powerful movements have not yet arisen to blot out political freedom in the interest of economic efficiency. Nor is it to be assumed that the two are necessarily in opposition. The vaunted capacity of totalitarianism to force economic growth may yet prove illusory in Asia; this issue is still open.

It might be added that even the Chinese did not choose Communism as the road to industrialization. Rather, it was imposed on them by a disciplined band of revolutionaries whose calculated objective was first of all to seize power for themselves. Having succeeded, amid the turmoil of World War II and its aftermath, they proceeded as rulers to impose a pattern of national development which, whatever its other merits or demerits, would destroy all latent opposition in both the city and the country and consolidate their grip. Elsewhere, too, as in China, Communism seeks power by exploiting all sources of latent disaffection and disorder with adroit opportunism. One powerful appeal is the promise of disciplined industrialization, of course. But this does not necessarily override all other values where viable alternatives are offered of a more temperate, pluralistic sort.

Experience teaches, in short, that successful economic growth can proceed under a variety of auspices. Most Asian nations are still groping for workable blends of public and private enterprise. One hopes that the decade of the 1960s will rid their leaders increasingly of ideological stereotypes of capitalism, socialism, and communism derived from the West. Instead, they need to turn to more pragmatic efforts to meet the structural requisites of growth within the framework of their national goals and capacities. One hopes, too, that in so doing they will not destroy their own cultural traditions, root and branch, by resort to extremist political ideologies. It should be possible to conserve things of value from their heritage, without blocking progress toward the goals of modernization that all peoples are now coming to demand. But the dilemmas posed in such choices are all too evident.

The Industrial Revolution continues to make its way slowly through Asia, despite setbacks and frustrations. Here live most of the world's peoples still waiting for science and technology to lift the age-old burden of poverty from their backs. Even as it advances, however, it leaves wide disparities between living standards of East and West. For the West, too, is pushing out the frontiers of technology, even more rapidly. The political issues latent in this gap between the have and the have-not are not likely to be relieved by any development in prospect, even if the flow of aid to the East is increased. In this economic realm, as in the political, the world still faces the problem of continuing to exist half-slave and half-free.

Comment: The Humanistic Uses of Asian Economic History

STEPHEN N. HAY

Assistant Professor of History, University of Chicago

The American student of Asian civilizations is commonly motivated by both humanistic and practical concerns. On the one hand, he (or she) is attracted to the ancient, exotic, and supposedly mysterious achievements in religion, philosophy, literature, and art enshrined in the Islamic, Hindu, Buddhist, and Confucian traditions. On the other hand, the American undergraduate often feels a responsibility to learn about the contemporary conditions of Asian peoples either because he realizes their strategic importance to the political and economic interests of the United States, or because reports of their almost unimagineable poverty have aroused in him a desire to help in some way to relieve their distress, and his own uneasiness about it.

The newly-inaugurated Peace Corps has already done wonders for such practically-motivated students as well as for the underdeveloped areas of the American conscience. Lecturing recently to a group of Peace Corps volunteers training to work in East Pakistan, I found their interest greatest when we considered the historical reasons for the low standard of living now prevalent in that part of Asia. In the future, as other American organizations, both private and governmental, increase their already substantial efforts to raise these living standards, the need for undergraduate study of the past history and present state of Asian economic life will continue to increase.

William Lockwood proposes a clear, three-part agenda for such study. As a historian, I cannot disagree with his chronological arrangement of major periods, or "clusters" of problems, in the economic history of Asia. I do feel, however, that these problems can be viewed from a somewhat different standpoint than that taken in his paper. Paradoxical as it may seem to the social scientist, I intend to argue that the study of Asian economic history may be conducted in such a way as to serve essentially humanistic purposes.

For example, in dealing with his first period, Lockwood reduces an enormous variety and complexity to a simple negative: nonindustrial. Unless I misunderstand him, he would paint a doleful picture of economic "stagnation" all over Asia as a kind of gloomy backdrop for the entry in the last act of the real hero of the piece, "the Industrial Revolution." Is there not a danger that such a foreshortening of some five millennia of economic history will perpetuate the nineteenth-century stereotype of a tradition-bound "unchanging East," and will merely imprison the student in his (to a certain extent also tradition-bound) belief that his own civilization is the highest yet achieved by man, all others being merely its unsuccessful forerunners?

As alternatives, I would suggest two possible themes for study. One would be the economic life of peasant societies, considered in the light of the higher culture or "great tradition" to which they subscribe. McKim Marriott's symposium *Village India* [1] offers much material concerning a country whose population is still today 80 percent rural. The considerable differences among the "traditional societies" and the types of "social equilibria" found in Southwest, South, Southeast, and East Asia deserve scrutiny, as do the changes through time within each society.

This is the more static, but still far from unchanging, side of pre-industrial Asian economic life. The more dynamic side emerges when we look at periods of great expansion in trade and commerce,

---

[1] McKim Marriott, ed., *Village India: Studies in the Little Community* (Chicago, University of Chicago Press, 1955).

for instance in Gupta dynasty India, Sung dynasty China,[2] or
Tokugawa Japan. J. A. B. van Buitenen's translations of *Tales of
Ancient India*[3] reverberate with the adventures of prosperous merchants, some of them winning great wealth with their trading
voyages to Southeast Asia. The teacher might attempt to recreate
the economic life of these dynamic periods and then ask: Why was
such vigorous growth not sustained? If it had been sustained, would
it have achieved the kind of economic modernization which later
took place in Western Europe? To what extent were external
forces—the expansion of Islam or the Mongol conquests—to blame
for checking such growth, and to what extent were internal factors
(unfavorable geography and climate, or the neglect of science and
technology) responsible?

Lockwood rightly emphasizes the fascinating possibilities for
studying the interplay in Asian societies between cultural and economic forces, but he illustrates this interplay by quoting two expressions of a passive attitude toward life. These demonstrate, he
says, that "the philosophical outlook pervading . . . tradition-bound
societies" was partly responsible for their failure to enter the Industrial Revolution before the Western intrusion forced them to
do so. This game of quotations is one at which any number can
play. Many exhortations to strenuous activity are also found in the
Asian classics. Does not the Buddha say, "Work out your end with
diligence?"[4] Does not Krishna remind Arjuna that "he who controls the senses by the mind, O Arjuna, and without attachment
engages the organs of action in the path of work, he is superior?"[5]
Does not *The Great Learning,* the portal through which every

[2] See for example Robert Hartwell, "A Revolution in the Chinese Iron and Coal
Industries during the Northern Sung, 960–1126 A.D.," *Journal of Asian Studies,* XXI
(February, 1962), 152–62.

[3] J. A. B. van Buitenen, trans., *Tales of Ancient India* (Chicago, University of
Chicago Press, 1959).

[4] Maurice Percheron, *Buddha and Buddhism,* trans. by Edmund Stapleton (New
York, Harper and Brothers, 1957), p. 37.

[5] S. Radhakrishnan and C. A. Moore, eds., *A Source Book in Indian Philosophy*
(Princeton, Princeton University Press, 1957), p. 113.

student entered upon the study of the Confucian classics, tell us that:

On T'ang's bathtub, the following words were engraved:—"If you can one day renovate yourself, do so from day to day. Yea, let there be daily renovation." . . . The superior man in everything uses his utmost endeavours.[6]

The crucial distinction to be made here, I would suggest, is not between a passive Asia and an active West but between the different goals toward which "the spirit of striving and venture and perfectibility" has been directed in each hemisphere. It was Max Weber, the great analyst of the rise of capitalism in Western Europe and of its failure to arise independently elsewhere, who pointed out that it is possible to use rational methods in many different areas of human activity, including "mystical contemplation . . . commerce, technology, scientific work, warfare, law and administration." Furthermore, each one of these realms "can be 'rationalized' from the most diverse ultimate viewpoints and directions, and what is 'rational' to one may appear 'irrational' to another. Rationalization in the different areas of human life has therefore occurred in all cultural circles in the most diverse ways."[7]

Students might therefore be asked to compare and contrast the *kinds* of perfection to be striven for according to Vedantic Hinduism, Islam, Buddhism, and Confucianism and then to attempt the much more intricate task of extrapolating from each of these systems of thought its possible consequences in the economic lives of its adherents. Weber's pioneering work in this field still deserves our attention, despite his tendency to over-generalize about Asia or "the East." Fortunately, the relevant portions of his *Gesammelte Aufsätze zur Religionssoziologie* are now available in English trans-

[6] James Legge, trans., *The Chinese Classics . . . Vol. I, Containing Confucian Analects, The Great Learning, and The Doctrine of the Mean* (Oxford, Clarendon Press, 1893), p. 361.

[7] Max Weber, *Gesammelte Aufsätze zur Religionssoziologie* (Tübingen, J. C. B. Mohr [P. Siebeck], 1920–21), I, 11–12. (My translation.)

lations as *The Religion of China* and *The Religion of India.*[8]
This complicated problem of the interactions and interdepend-
ences between cultural patterns and economic patterns takes on a
new dimension with the intrusion of the modern West. Here
again, as Lockwood points out, there are fascinating possibilities
for comparative studies, and he himself has contributed to an understanding of the reasons why Japan's leaders were so quick to take
the path to industrialization, and China's so slow.[9] Another fruitful
line of inquiry might begin with the question: Why did India and
Southeast Asia succumb so easily to Western power, and how did
their subsequent economic development differ from that of the
more autonomous areas, Japan and China? In the various initial
responses to Western power and civilization of the dominant elites
in different parts of Asia, the student encounters one of the grand
themes of modern history.

But the ambivalent character of economic change in the Southern
Asian countries which passed under colonial rule presents a special
problem, for there is little doubt that their domination by such
rapidly industrializing nations as Britain, France and the Netherlands had baneful as well as beneficial effects, and for sundry reasons
produced an even greater concentration upon agricultural production, relative to the total economy, than was previously the case.
This imbalance remains today a major obstacle to their economic
growth. For this reason and the quite practical purpose of understanding how Asians look at the nature of the continuing Western
intrusion into their own lives, the American student is thus brought
up against the thorny question of "imperialism." The question:
"Has the Western intrusion as a whole done more economic good
than harm?" is still much-debated by scholars in societies recently

[8] Max Weber, *The Religion of China: Confucianism and Daoism,* ed. and trans. by
Hans H. Gerth (Glencoe, Ill., Free Press, 1951); Max Weber, *The Religion of India:
The Sociology of Hinduism and Buddhism,* ed. and trans. by Hans H. Gerth and Don
Martindale (Glencoe, Ill., Free Press, 1958).
[9] William Wirt Lockwood, "Japan's Response to the West; the Contrast with
China," *World Politics,* IX (October, 1956), 37–54.

freed from colonial rule, and the student would profit from exposure to such influential theoretical writings as Marx's articles on India, Hobson's *Imperialism, a Study,* Lenin's *Imperialism, the Highest Stage of Capitalism,* and Schumpeter's *Imperialism and Social Classes,* as well as to such concrete studies as J. S. Furnivall's *Colonial Policy and Practice.*[10]

The intrusion of the modern West into the economic life of Asia raises many other questions whose significance transcends the Asian scene. What exactly was "the Industrial Revolution," and what role has it played in modern history? Was the industrial system of production really the principal source of the power the Western nations displayed in Asia between 1757 and 1941, or was it but a manifestation of other power-conferring components of what we may for lack of a better term call "modern civilization"? A chronological study of Western contacts with Asia would help the student to see more clearly the complex character of "modernization" as it has developed in the West and spread from there throughout all other civilizations. For example, the English East India Company was a joint-stock company created not to engage in industrial production, but to foster trade. The surprising ease with which it conquered India between 1757 and 1818 was probably due less to the weapons of its British and sepoy soldiers than to the qualities of individual initiative and group discipline displayed by its personnel within the framework of efficient military, economic and administrative organizations. These same ethical and social qualities later contributed to the industrialization of England in the nineteenth century, but they were also applied in such diverse realms

---

[10] See Karl Marx, *Articles on India* (Bombay, Peoples Publishing House, 1943; 2d ed., 1951); K. Marx and F. Engels, *The First Indian War of Independence, 1857–1859* (Moscow, Foreign Languages Publishing House, [1959]); J. A. Hobson, *Imperialism, A Study* (New York, J. Pott, 1902); Vladimir Il'ich Lenin, *Imperialism, the Highest Stage of Capitalism: A Popular Outline* (New York, International Publishers, [1939]); Joseph Schumpeter, *Imperialism. Social Classes,* trans. by Heinz Norden (New York, Meridian Books, 1955); John Sydenham Furnivall, *Colonial Policy and Practice: A Comparative Study of Burma and Netherlands India* (Cambridge, Cambridge University Press, 1948).

as law and government, banking and commerce, science and technology—all of which greatly facilitated the industrial mode of production, but all of which originated prior to it.

By beginning the story of the Western intrusion into Asia with the pre-industrial British conquest of India (or with the still earlier Portuguese and Dutch conquests in Ceylon and the Malay Archipelago), the student will be able to correlate the further spread of Western influence in Asia with the increasing power of the industrializing and modernizing West. As he notices the successive stages of its development at which the West has presented itself to different parts of Asia, he will form a differentiated picture of a sequence of intrusions by a series of different "Wests" into various parts of Asia. The next step in this study of comparative industrialism through time will be to add a spatial dimension by comparing, as Lockwood suggests, the "leads and lags" in the economic modernization of various countries and provinces. Why did some parts of Asia, and some sectors within each society, advance rapidly while others lagged, and to what extent were these differences due to the nature of the traditions or the types of social equilibrium obtaining in each civilization or society? Why have some minority groups—the Parsis, Jains and Marwaris in India, the Chettiars and Chinese in Southeast Asia, and others—taken such a long lead over the other groups in these areas? [11] These are some of the challenging questions which may be used to provoke stimulating classroom discussion.

Coming to Lockwood's third major theme, the economic transformations taking place in Asia today, the student will at last feel himself on familiar ground. Here he can see something practical going on, something in which he can perhaps take part. It is precisely at this point, however, that the student (and his teacher) should face a question which is essentially a humanistic rather than

[11] D. R. Gadgil has in progress a study which will throw light on this question; see his *Origins of the Modern Indian Business Class: An Interim Report* (New York, Institute of Pacific Relations, 1959), which forms the first draft chapter in a projected book carrying the story down to the present.

a practical one: Toward what goals, what *ends,* are men led to put in motion the interlocking processes which are necessary to achieve economic modernization? There seem to me at least three answers to such a question. The most obvious goal is certainly wealth, and the desire of private individuals and firms to increase their wealth has been the major spur to the economic modernization of the West and, in the main, of Japan. A second possible aim is to strengthen the state, and the concern for state power would seem to have been the principal drive behind the industrialization of the Soviet Union since 1928 and of the People's Republic of China since 1949. But what purpose does economic modernization serve in countries where high standards of living and adequate defense establishments have already been achieved? A possible third purpose beyond wealth and power is the promotion of human welfare, especially the welfare of those Asian, African, and Latin American societies which are still a long, long way from large-scale economic modernization, and whose bulky populations present formidable obstacles to their achieving it.

The promotion of human welfare in Asia, once accepted as a goal for action, presents an awesome array of practical problems. In some ways our much greater wealth imposes on us a severe handicap, for our actions may easily be misconstrued by those accustomed to regard the rich as their oppressors. The problems of *translation*—not merely between people speaking one language to those speaking another, but from people living on one economic level to those living on another—have been too little studied. Here, the economic component in Asian civilization courses, properly taught, can introduce the American student to a dimension which he must experience with his own senses to appreciate: what it means to live on 1,500 meatless calories per day; to walk or to ride a bullock cart whenever he needs to travel; to do without radio, without TV, without newspapers or books to feed his mind; and to live by his muscles instead of by his wits. Films and slides may help him to sense the great gap between his life and an Asian peasant's, and village studies will be more relevant here than reports on industrial growth.

Ultimately, then, the student's deepening understanding of the economic life of one or more Asian societies, and of the interactions among the economic, social, political, and intellectual traditions of each society, may serve both practical and humanistic ends. For such understanding can not only equip him to deal effectively with the problems of the developing nations, it can also help him to stretch his mind beyond the confines of his own familiar environment, to discover other ways of living in and looking at the world in ages past and present.

Some Basic Geographical Factors in the Study of Asian Civilizations

THEODORE HERMAN

Associate Professor of Geography, Colgate University

In order to point up some of the tools as well as the substance of this topic, I will open with a broad contrast. Let me generalize by stating that while the oldest of the great cultures began inland, those that have had the widest areal spread and most sustained vitality developed near the open sea.

Our own culture is the distant heir of this slow spread across the Asian land-mass out of interior river pockets and wind-swept grasslands. The pace quickened in the western projection constricted between the seas of Europe. Moving along and around the rocky coasts, up the open river valleys, and along the margins of the barrier forests, men increased their culture contacts and met the opportunities of several environmental factors in the narrowed reaches of central and western Europe. Exchange, enterprise, and innovation under Rome, followed by 1,000 years of interior evolution that since the Renaissance has burst over the world in a series of dynamic revolutions mark what today we call "Western culture."

By contrast, the major civilizations of Asia have developed inland where contact has been more uncertain and more selective. As one moves east across Asia, the land-mass spreads out into a series of oases, pocket valleys, and lowlands, often isolated from each other by distance, mountains, and desert. The pattern of land and routeways is the exact opposite of that in Europe. Basic change in the land-locked Asian cultures has been much slower despite the technical and intellectual flowering in certain parts at least ten to fifteen centuries before the European Renaissance.

A very marked difference was the lack of accelerating innovation in the practical arts over much of Asia. One is always fascinated by the question of why there was no sustained, expanding, multi-sided renaissance in the great south and east Asian cultures. That there was part of such a blossoming as Islam spread around the Mediterranean seems to sustain the thesis that opens this paper.

THE GEOGRAPHER'S VIEWPOINT

I have introduced this topic by focusing attention on a function of location in cultural development. Space and spatial difference on the surface of the earth are the geographer's concern. He is interested in both the facts of and the reasons for spatial difference. The reasons lie in the physical, the cultural, and these two inter-acting. Further, geography cannot be understood without reference to the past—geological, archaeological, historical—for these illuminate the processes of spatial change and of the use of area. The end of such study is an understanding of the significance of place or location in the affairs of men, shown especially by the relations generated between places.

It goes without saying that no culture can be understood apart from how its members use their portion of the earth's surface. Some features are obstacles, others are opportunities, and we do not have a single, one-way explanation to assure us that these are constant even in a given culture. Much less are we satisfied by generalizations that the physical environment *determines* man's use of an area or his institutions. There is some relationship, to be sure, for otherwise a group could not operate, but the connection is complex, two-way, and never entirely static.

In the following pages, four basic geographical factors have been selected to illuminate some points about Asian civilizations. While there are differences from country to country, several of the problems discussed apply widely. Also, they should be seen in historic context, since all these civilizations have been in their present areas for many centuries.

SOME CONSEQUENCES OF LOCATION

It is a common impression that most of the civilizations of Asia existed for many centuries in isolation from other cultures. No statement could be more mistaken, since at least around the borders and usually through the court contact with other peoples was constant. But the point is that contact was not highly effective and continuous with those cultures that had important contributions to make to progress.

Perhaps, one will ask what values, institutions, and techniques could have been learned, say, from the Mediterranean area during Rome's flowering. No one can state with certainty nor what changes would have occurred after arrival, but Roman law, the Roman senate, and patrician application to agricultural improvement are three possibilities.

The second point about the contact is that it was selective in kind as befits at least a three-year journey over the vast spaces of Inner Asia, and that the ideas and trade were largely restricted to the elite. For the most part, we do not know the story of early technological impact in traditional Asia. When and where, for example, did the stream-revolving Persian water-wheel enter China, and what changes did it make in land use and economic organization? The same question applies to other imported techniques, to useful plants, and the like. To what extent did material advances in one part of a country confer advantage there, and how did the ruling power in the core area respond?

These questions are important because they help us to understand the implications of culture contact for affecting spatial relationships, both between countries and within any one country. In every part of Asia today, this is apparent in the lopsided political, economic, and social evidences of Western impact, generally extending in from embayed coasts.

Lacking effective outside challenge, the great cultures maintained their ethnocentrism to such an extent that joining the modern world has been a most painful experience for many of their people. But the doors have also often been closed against the immediate neighbors, a problem attacked by the Colombo Plan of 1950 and examined again in 1955 by the Bandung Conference. This intra-Asian exclusivism is a fact of cultural geography that will be present for some time to come.

PATTERNS OF LANDFORMS

A physical map of Asia shows that most of the countries are divided internally by mountain ranges into separate lowlands and pocket valleys. Only the Indian sub-continent has a continuous open lowland of as much as 1,000 miles, and this spreads out from the center in opposite directions into vastly different climatic regions. Except for the Yangtze, there are no great river traffic arteries that integrate trade and other cultural manifestations as do the Rhine, Danube, St. Lawrence, and the Mississippi. Hence, the tendency toward political sectionalism induced by different cultural impacts and farming systems has been strongly reinforced by topography. This is as true for nineteenth-century Japan and Korea as in twentieth-century China and India, and in the new states of Pakistan and Indonesia.

These regionalisms were not *caused* by geography nor will they necessarily be forever maintained by geography, but the nature and location of landforms, drainage systems, climates, soils, and vegetation have offered opportunities and imposed obstacles at certain stages of development. Regional self-sufficiency supported the cultural hearths in the middle Indus and Yellow River valleys, from whence these cultures could spread into quite different physical environments. Yet, from region to region, trade did not develop to such an extent that the masses of people formed an internal market large enough to generate surplus investment capital. There was not the need for better roads and carriers to reduce the cost of distance and rough topography from region to region. Whether the emphasis on agriculture as the chief form of production was the result of cultural preference and long isolation or of a too-easy reward from favorable natural conditions, it certainly did not lead to a vast indigenous industrial growth that could begin to draw the sectional interests of the respective countries into effective national states.

Against such divisiveness, the traditional rulers used various ideologies and ceremonies, supported by bureaucratic elites and, as necessary, armed force. In the mid-twentieth century, the ideologies and ceremonies of nationalism, the civil service, the army, plus widened secular education, government investment, and improved transportation are all used for the same purpose. But such devices are costly burdens on heavily-populated agrarian states.

The upland areas have played another political role. In China and India, to name only two examples, the mountain borders and internal ranges have given refuge to dissident groups, both dominant and minority. In an effort to resolve the age-old animosities, both countries during the past six years have set up special regions in several of their barrier areas, while trying to draw them into the modern state. Although not all of these minority groups may have once occupied the fertile lowlands, it is true that none of them do so today. Asian history is full of the record of such displacement, and it is still going on.

PATTERNS OF POPULATION CONCENTRATION

The location of population concentrations is another important geographical feature. When we realize that most Asian concentrations are on limited fertile plains and lowlands, especially where water can be controlled, the contrast with the patterns in the United States or Western Europe, for example, is illuminating. It underlines the differences between an agricultural and an industrial-commercial society and reminds us of the strong hold of tradition in Asian farm techniques and settlement.

Except for India and Pakistan, the main population concentrations in most of Asia are on or close to the coastal lowlands. This permits the raising of high-yield crops in areas of sufficient summer rainfall and may provide economic opportunity with the establishment of multifunction cities on the coasts. It may also lead to the rapid spread of new crops such as maize and rubber that have been brought to Asia during the last 200 years. Such new crops change land use and market relations and, as in Java, support great population increases. They may lead to population shifts similar to the Chinese spread into the northeast provinces for the commercial production and export of soy beans in the first half of the twentieth century. Internal political changes occur with population shifts, shown in the rise of the coastal deltas for commercial rice growing and the building of Rangoon, Bangkok, Saigon, and Hanoi in place of older capitals inland. Economic investment in the politically unbalanced countries tends to cling to the new power centers, retarding, in turn, the balanced development of the interior. Examples of such concentrations under modern impact exist in almost every part of Asia.

The cultural effects are equally obvious. Social innovation of every kind changes the old ways, raising at the same time a leader class that takes the responsibility for reform. Living in the coastal centers and hence sensitive to outside pressures that would destroy their own interests, they are an important part of the new nationalist elite. They are evidence of a qualitative change in the population through outside contact that eventually affects the whole mass.

Another mark of population quality is the mass capacity for change. In an agrarian society, this is expressed by efforts to obtain higher output per unit of land and, hopefully, per worker on the land. But it also appears in man's initiative for conserving and renewing the land's output potential.

It is at this point that one raises a question about man's attitude toward the land, a basic matter in understanding spatial differences. Students of Asian civilization make much of the peasant's identity with natural processes: birth, death, and the eternal round of life despite the uncertainties of weather, calamities, and the like. From this, we are told, has evolved a strong sense of acceptance of whatever comes and has created a static society in which the individual shows little interest in improvement. This would partly explain the personal attachment to field and to place, the slowness of technical advance, and the lack of widespread efforts at resource conservation.

But I wonder how completely valid this over-all stereotype of a static society really is. How uniform is the outlook of all the farmers even in one village? Is it not possible that some are more resourceful and industrious than others? If there were not some individuals willing to try new seeds or new methods, because of their foresight, or just being better off, or some accident, how could *any* changes have come into Asian agriculture? What were the conditions under which new crops were accepted? Were such changes made in time of distress, or on the contrary, under relative prosperity when taxes, rents, and nature were favorable enough so that men could experiment? Or, is it that change occurs most readily where people have contact with outsiders who have different ideas and techniques to offer?

When one recalls that agricultural change has taken place in many parts of Asia, an understanding of the reasons for change becomes very important as a guide to inducing change today. Although not all countries have equal pressure of men on the land, change is nevertheless needed, and no matter what doctrine or incentives are introduced, men in the mass must be made to believe that they can improve their lot on earth. Only in changing the physical environment is there hope. Thus we say that man's values shape the land, as in the great modern water control projects of China, India, Ceylon, and Thailand, or the efforts to reduce shifting hillside agriculture in the Philippines and in northern Borneo.

Large-scale conservation efforts provide another example of the same, but these are large scale manifestations of a new attitude to the land. Forest conservation in Burma and Japan, and shelter belt planting in north China are two kinds of effort against the pressure of population and the limited resources of national treasuries. They are evidences of a new civic attitude toward the land derived, in part at least, from contact with others.

PATTERNS OF INDUSTRIALIZATION

There are two patterns of modern industrial location in Asia. The older, chiefly devoted to textiles and other light manufactures, clusters close to the coasts from its beginnings under foreign stimulus and for overseas trade; Bombay, Calcutta, Shanghai, and Tientsin are examples. The newer is for iron and steel and metal products, heavy industry that, except for Japanese investment in Mukden-Anshan and originally in Wuhan, grew on indigenous capital.

Of the dozen large iron and steel centers in Asia, only those in Japan, and now Shanghai, are directly on the coast, the former because of an early start in trade and handicrafts that had capital, skills, and easy transportation along the south Honshu shore. Elsewhere in China and in India, large complexes have been and are being built inland on local resources and with government capital. While the Chinese plan to make iron and steel complexes as the center of the seven or eight industrial regions of the country, the Indians are concentrating their construction on the eastern side of the plateau where coal and good iron ore lie close together.

The building of new industrial plants in formerly remote areas will not decrease population pressure in the older settled areas, but it will bring factory life and technical skills to many new places. It will challenge the local people to cope with rapid change and will cause many conflicts, especially on the frontiers of cultural impact. Industrial change cannot be resisted, although it may be true that not all those involved enjoy its fruits equally.

It is axiomatic that railway building goes along with industrial spread, so that, where previously agricultural commodities could not be shipped far by muscle power, the general internal flow should be quickened. If for no other reason than this indirect benefit from industrialization, one would expect that slowly the old regional separatisms within the Asian countries would decline in favor of new economic cores such as exist in the industrialized countries of the West. Likewise, urbanization should help to reduce sectionalism, although possibly it will bring a new cleavage in national life between town and rural dwellers.

ASIA'S ROLE IN WORLD AFFAIRS: GEOGRAPHIC NOTES

We in the United States tend to see Asia's role in world affairs largely in terms of Mackinder's land power versus sea power heartland pattern. In the world power struggle the Inner Crescent around the heartland power is regarded as passive, easy to control by one of the two superpowers. This notion contains a large element of cartohypnosis.

First, the former control of the sea lanes of Asia by Western powers has largely vanished not because of the development of aircraft but because the adjoining land areas are no longer under Western control. What has happened to Port Arthur, Trincomalee, and Suez can happen to Singapore, Taiwan, and Japan.

Second, within the ring of Asian countries there is not much functional unity or even common interests. Animosities based on historic grievances or recent experience or lack of knowledge divide one Asian people from another.

Third, as power bases for expansion within Asia, these countries vary greatly in resources and industrialization.

Fourth, one of the greatest changes that has come to Asia in modern time is the idea that individual welfare is an important concern of the state no matter what kind of social system the country has. It is not acted upon everywhere, but it is a vital part of Asian nationalism that is spreading against the traditions of the past. Such an idea is truly explosive and stands as a real check on any Asian government that would sacrifice economic and social welfare for forceful expansion.

All this does not mean that the independence of each country of Asia is forever assured. It does not mean that these countries can dispense with economic, social, and military help from other countries. It does not mean that some of these countries do not have influence on other countries in the world.

Sheer location on shipping and flying routes or as military bases is important, but the method today is to operate by treaties rather than by conquest. Production of export specialties needed elsewhere and serving as markets, both present and future, give them influence. Finally, they will have influence as they learn how and how not to apply foreign ideologies and institutions to their overcrowded, low surplus, extractive agrarian societies (except Japan) in the face of popular demands for both opportunity and security. The physical, historical, and cultural conditions of each country of Asia make each one unique, but they are important examples to the rest of the world. The essence of that example is change, and particularly to change their uses of space.

Comment: Geography and General Education

JOHN E. BRUSH

Associate Professor of Geography, Rutgers University

One might begin by discussing Professor Herman's treatment of China's geography, but I will direct my attention to basic themes and concepts suitable to the geographic study of any Asian civilization.

Modern geography has discarded environmental determinism, yet, sometimes I find that it is implicit in some approaches to Asian studies. Geographers will agree with Karl Wittfogel when he says in his paper that "man's relation to nature" is one important sphere of the study of civilization. But let it never be said that a particular economic activity or system of civilization has been *caused* by environmental conditions. We geographers no longer believe the facile theory that Norwegians are a maritime people because of their fiorded coast. We know that fishing and foreign trade are important aspects of their economy and we can not dispute the existence of fiords. Yet other people living on other fiorded coasts do not earn their livelihood from the sea, and many maritime people have no fiords. While crass environmental determinism is as indefensible as certain forms of economic determinism in cause and effect explanations of human affairs, the role of environment remains an important topic for study. I think we should always view the environmental complex as containing possibilities for human choice. The range of choices depends in part on man's own skills and goals. In other words, the potentialities of environment change as civilization changes.

This leads me to my second point about geography in Asian studies. An important part of the process of gaining historical perspective is learning about the dynamic relationship between man and the land. One of the best ways to accomplish this aim is to deal with population, settlement patterns, systems of agriculture, and the spread of cultivated plants or domestic animals in past periods. Extracts from travelers' accounts are helpful. I am pleased to see that Arthur Wright recommends in his paper that "One should make frequent references to the geography, the physical landscape and to changes in these."

A third geographic objective in the study of Asian civilization should be map-consciousness. What images come to mind when I mention the name of the important Indian state of Uttar Pradesh? Does one visualize its location and outline on the map of northern India? Is it flat or mountainous, wet or dry, densely or sparsely populated? These and other questions can be answered by a student who has developed the ability to think in terms of geography.

Geographers hope that students of Asia will gain a sense of place and area along with other concepts. I hope that those of us who teach Asian studies will not forget to place man's feet on the earth. I think this, and perhaps more, is what Herbert Feis must have in mind when he makes his plea for a "comprehensive comparative inquiry into the physical and economic geography of the whole Orient" in his paper.

Geographers today conceive of their task as the study of areal differentiation of the earth. It is the nature of geography to view natural and human phenomena in terms of spatial distribution and to organize findings in terms of regions. There is a certain parallel in this respect to history. Historians treat their subject in terms of chronology and organize their material in periods. In geography, it is the spatial relationships and covariance of phenomena in areas which constitute problems for study. In history, it is the sequence of events or the time relationship which receives attention.

Just as William Lockwood would like to see students of Asia gain a "sense of history" as a basis for the study of economic change and modernization, I would like to see them gain a sense of geography. This aim can be achieved through the concepts I have mentioned in the introductory course on Asia. Whether or not the concepts are put forth by a professional geographer at this stage of the curriculum is of secondary importance.

Professor Herman's treatment of Chinese geography exemplifies these new viewpoints as he endeavors to show how geographic relationships have developed and evolved in the Orient. One can not predict future geographic patterns on the basis of past experience, when the values, institutions, and technology of Chinese civilization are undergoing rapid change. One should hesitate to project parallel developments in other parts of eastern and southern Asia where neither the physical base nor the political-economic system are duplicated.

Part Four: Anthropology and Sociology

Asia via Japan:
An Anthropologist's Attempts

DOUGLAS G. HARING

Professor Emeritus of Anthropology, Syracuse University

The major dilemma of contemporary education—breadth versus depth—comes sharply into focus when teachers confront the endless diversity of Asian civilizations and our own complacent provincialism. What can be done about Asian studies? Curriculum planning faces the traditional urgencies of established departments, each convinced that education will fail dismally if it lacks the saving grace of the one and only vital specialty. How could anything be sacrificed to accommodate a new "field"? Things hardly could be otherwise, for department heads and deans have sought out teachers thoroughly grounded in—hence, evangelical about—the subject that each is paid to teach.

Conceivably, Asian studies could absorb an entire four-year curriculum plus years of graduate study without covering the salient details of the human variety that is called Asia. Even if anyone aimed to convert all of education into a monopoly for Asia specialists, this would not happen—even in Asia. Thus the dilemma of superficiality versus depth is inescapable. The best of teachers must decide what to treat in detail and what to leap over in generalities that—he hopes—might be verifiable. The issue is not whether to include or to omit Asia in American education; it is whether educators can think in terms of this culturally multiple world. Willy nilly, we are embarked upon the adventure of a vastly more complex curriculum that accepts cultural pluralism as a reality inherent in many departments of knowledge. The need for regional specialists will continue, but it is probable that they may not be herded together in Asian studies programs. More and more, they will be sought after as colleagues in many departments. Certainly in the humanities and social sciences, every topical specialty can enhance perspective by cultivation of Asian, Latin-American, and African aspects of their fields.

Our cultural and geographical nomenclature, however, is badly outmoded; it perpetuates the vagueness of old-time maps that attached romantic names to large blank spaces. Even the neologism "non-Western" denotes numerous complex and diverse entities scattered randomly over the globe. Only the North and South Poles are accurately "non-Western." This meaningless pseudo-geographical symbol vaguely denotes many different peoples and regions that have little in common beside the fact that they have not fallen under communist rule.

The term "Asia" has only antiquity in its favor. Even as a geographical term it is unrealistic; the European peninsula has as much in common with India as India has with China, while contemporary Japan is more "modern" than many "non-Western" countries. The Moslem peoples, sometimes included under Africa and sometimes under Asia, belong historically and culturally with the Mediterranean region. Clarity might gain if the word "Asia" could vanish suddenly and completely. The various cultural areas that diversify the human scene in Europe, Asia, and Africa could be denoted by specific names and children could be spared the vagueness that most of us absorbed with our first geography books. If one's theme be the oneness of mankind, such terms as "East," "West," "Asian," and "European" are best forgotten. If the cultural diversity of mankind be considered, these words mislead by lumping together peoples that would prefer to stand separately. Meanwhile, we talk about Asia—as I shall do in this paper.

My approach to Asia by way of anthropology may invite a personal explanation. I did not happen upon Asia as a professional anthropologist in search of fresh kinship systems and odd quirks of tribally-fostered patterns of personality. On the contrary, seven years of living in Japan—for which I had the dubious preparation of undergraduate engineering and graduate theology—drove me ultimately to anthropology in search of insight. Rudely plucked from Japan and thrust back into New York City, I turned to Columbia University; it is pleasant to acknowledge that experience in this setting. After groping in education, psychology, sociology, and statistics, I discovered anthropology. First under Leslie Spier (who was visiting here in the summer of 1926), then under Franz Boas and Ruth Benedict, I found what I had sought: a scientific technique for study and appreciation of alien civilizations. Experience had enforced a strong conviction that protracted residence is prerequisite to any real understanding of another culture; the training in anthropology—especially ethnology—provided techniques of analysis and perspective in the process of comparing the cultures of many different tribes and nations.

Shortly, I faced a nagging question, even now answered only in part. Why had this kind of research not been applied more diligently to Asian peoples? Asia had received attention from historians, linguists, philosophers, students of international politics, poets, artists, and—chiefly in German and British colonies—a few anthropologists. In the nineteen-twenties, however, American anthropologists still were preoccupied with the fascinating cosmos of pre-Columbian America, aboriginal Australia, Oceania, and sub-Saharan Africa. In subsequent decades, American anthropologists have gingerly approached the major Asian civilizations. An anthropologist no longer needs to build status by parading detailed knowledge of some isolated peripheral tribe. Asian ethnology has become respectable.

Let no one anticipate a magical solution of problems of Asian culture by some esoteric skill of anthropologists. Asia is too vast and diversified for any one discipline to encompass. Since the Euro-

American quest for self-knowledge has generated our whole panoply of intellectual disciplines, it follows that insight into Asia's peoples and traditions challenges the combined resources of Occidental scholarship, plus those of disciplines as yet unborn.

Anthropology, however, has gained much from concentration on peripheral, non-literate peoples. Granted that the borderline between ethnology and history is vague and that ethnographic studies become history by the time they are published, an ethnographer is an observer and recorder of the present rather than the past. If there are gaps in his report, they may not be excused by the absence of documentary records; he must accept responsibility for his own omissions and misinterpretations. The people whom he studies live before his eyes and he shares increasingly in their ways of living the longer he remains among them. When he moves from the study of non-literate tribes to a civilization that includes a literary tradition, he is in the position of observing that which the native literati have missed because to them their own culture is commonplace. As an outsider he sees the commonplace as the conspicuous. After he returns home to write a monograph, he becomes unhappily aware of what he has missed. If fortune grants him another visit, he is sensitized to the items that had escaped him formerly. A second visit also permits observation of the extent and rate of change— plus the advantage of the welcome that greets one who no longer is a stranger, but an old friend returning to renew acquaintance.

Ethnographic studies reveal the ever-present contradictions in human living. An ethnographer aims at accurate reporting, not at consistency in the record. The enduring paradox of universal human similarities in the face of local diversity stands out in comparisons of different cultures. All human beings are alike, but equally vivid are numerous incommensurable cultural differences. Personal bias tends to stress one or the other aspect. One observer is fascinated by the common humanity of all peoples, while another is impressed by the irreconcilable differences. Both aspects of human societies are real; neglect of either is as culpable in teaching as in field ob-

servation. Stress upon the exotic and unusual is no less a bias than
is the tendentious glossing over of differences in favor of the "oneness of mankind."

Thirty-five years of trying to introduce American students, through
anthropology, to Asian cultures prompts further personal comment.
I began by teaching a one-term undergraduate course on Japan. I
continue to approach Asia by way of Japan for a simple reason:
apart from my native America, the only country in which I feel at
home is Japan. This does not imply mastery of Japanese culture,
any more than the accident of birth in the United States implies
mastery of our own complex civilization. Students needed to be
exposed to a civilization different from their own, and I had to
start with Japan. India, China, Melanesia, or Korea might have
worked equally well in other hands. Still young enough to be
rash, I went ahead with meager library resources and no depend-
able textbook.

One cannot teach about Japan apart from the rest of Asia. Within
a very few years, I was prefacing my term on Japan with a term
on China. I blush at this confession, for I do not know China at
first hand and do not know the Chinese language. Japan, however, required a Chinese background and the students were almost
totally blank with respect to Asia. Before long, I learned that Japanese culture could not be explained without India, Oceania, Central
Asia, and Siberia. If one picks up the net of human affairs, he
ultimately deals with its remoter ramifications in space and time.

My philosophy of teaching has raised eyebrows among some professional educators. One can not browbeat or inveigle students into
working; example, however, is contagious. More than once I have
ventured to teach in an unfamiliar area; I have prefaced the course
with a confession: "This field is not one that I have mastered. I
want to learn about it and I invite you to join me. Don't ask me
for answers; hunt them up and bring them to class!" As soon as
students learn that such confession is sincere and not a pedagogic
trick, the response is enthusiastic. Moreover, if a student develops

real interest in a topic, that is the time for him to study that topic
—no matter where it "belongs" in a professorial scheme of things.
If the student "is not ready for that," he may surprise one by
zealously getting ready. When lecture topics are rigidly scheduled
in advance, there is slight room for riding a tide of interest at flood.
Obviously also, complete disorder in a course guarantees confusion
and boredom. I compromise by distributing an outline of my topical
intentions, and by requiring a textbook or two. A textbook, however, is something to shun in class; it should be seen and not heard
—or more aptly put, read and not reiterated. By hypothesis, students are literate. I blandly accept that premise, assign textbooks
for examination purposes, and conduct classes on the assumption
that required reading is actually in progress. In addition to textbooks,[1] the student is expected to read materials of his own selection. A bibliography of about 3,000 items, based on the holdings
of our University library, is available to students in any of our
courses on Japan. Students submit reports of such reading and are
examined on items they claim to have read—a laborious task for
the professor, who scrutinizes the reports and includes in the final
examination a specific question for each individual student. Grades
take into account the maturity of choice exhibited in each reading
report.

Rarely do I encounter a student who fails to find something in
Japanese culture that he wants to investigate in detail. Here is the
function of the term paper. The student chooses a topic and con-
fers with the professor; approval generally hinges upon accessibility
of source materials. The only restrictions are: (1) the student must
demonstrate the relevance of his topic to the course; (2) the topic
must give promise of leading to broader insight into Japanese

---

[1] In recent years, I have required George B. Sansom's *Japan, a Short Cultural History* (Rev. ed., New York, Appleton-Century, 1943) and Donald Keene's *Living Japan*
(Garden City, N.Y., Doubleday, 1959). R. P. Dore's *City Life in Japan* (Berkeley,
University of California Press, 1958) may come closer to the desired kind of textbook. My fellow anthropologists may comment that none of these authors is an anthropologist: Sansom is a historian, Keene specializes in Japanese literature, and
Dore calls himself a sociologist.

culture; and (3) the student should enjoy the necessary reading. The latter requirement puzzles some students. I recall one girl who, late in the course, burst out naïvely, "Why professor! You really meant that about enjoying it!" The range of topics is astonishing: biographies of Buddhist saints, formal garden art, the casting of bronze bells, contemporary scientific agriculture, the obsolescent apprentice system, demography, current Japanese novels in translation, Japanese communism, land tenure, the balance of international trade, mythology, cuisine, marriage customs, fox cults, sculpture, acupuncture, *et cetera;* I recall a really good paper on symbolism of styles of hair dressing. The upshot is that, to understand any exotic culture, one must follow its ramifications and sooner or later become aware of the pervasive ethos of that culture. Granted that term papers are major burdens of the academic life, even an inferior paper may enforce upon the teacher some lively reading in order to grade it fairly. One learns to be grateful to the student who, having waded beyond his intellectual depth, forces the professor also to dive on short notice into a new topic. With the years, I have learned also to be humbly thankful that students forget much of what one has tried to teach. There remains the rich reward of teaching: the numerous individuals who discover for themselves a world to explore and go far beyond those of us who imagined that we were doing the teaching. The Asian sage who said that the teacher lifts one corner of a subject, but his disciples must lift the other three corners, was profoundly right. Students who are worth educating do lift the other three corners. In the long run, they lift more than any mentor could have foreseen.

Since, at Syracuse, regional courses in ethnology are open to students who lack previous contact with anthropology, two opening lectures necessarily sketch the ethnographer's approach [2]: what kinds of facts are sought, how are they obtained, how are they verified or discarded, and how interpreted? Then—since I strongly

[2] This ethnographer's approach is summarized in his anthology, *Personal Character and Cultural Milieu* (3d rev. ed., Syracuse, Syracuse University Press, 1956), pp. 4–31.

disapprove of a hop-skip-and-jump survey of all Asia—I blithely contravene my own canon by devoting four or five lectures to general features of Asia. A quick geographical survey permits hasty introduction to the major Asian cultural areas: Chinese, Indian, Malay-Oceanic, Central and Northeastern Asia. So brief a discussion of entire regional modes of living is sadly deficient, but it introduces many students to the concept of cultural areas. As the study of Japan proceeds, students usually recognize features derived from other parts of Asia. Topics treated in terms of spatial distribution include: the implicit socio-cultural premises of Indian life that led to Buddhism; the spread of Hinayana and Mahayana; fertility magic; divine kingship and its magical foundations; status language in Oceania; shamanism; Greco-Indian elements in Buddhist art; Chinese Taoist and Confucian ideologies, including propriety and ritual government; Chinese familism and the ancestor cult; China's ancient multistate system and the Ts'in unification (this topic evokes analogies with contemporary China); the self-fulfilling Chinese doctrine of historical cycles; the ethnocentric "Central Kingdom" and its dealings with barbarians; and, especially pertinent to Japan, the "glory that was T'ang." A lecture on Oceanic cultures turns up at this juncture; frankly speculative, it notes Oceanic-Japanese parallels that fascinate me personally. During all this high-altitude flight over much of Asia, students supposedly are digging into the textbook assignments on Japan.

Specifically Japanese topics follow outlines that might occur to any ethnologist. Having treated Asia thus cavalierly, I insist that Japan may not be handled so generally and superficially. The fundamental pedagogical premise is that every student should know at least one non-Euro-American civilization as well as time permits. After Japan's geography and climate come race and prehistory, patterns of the earliest recorded Japanese societies, and evidences of early cultural diffusion from Korea, China, the Amur region, and Oceania.

To indicate the use of local cultural features to lead the student through their wider Asian ramifications, I shall dwell here in some detail on a typical class presentation of the Japanese language. Undergraduate ideas about languages are limited almost exclusively to European languages. Students often are surprised to learn that nearly all European languages may be regarded as dialects of a single Indo-European stock. The idea that other linguistic stocks may exhibit incommensurable items of vocabulary, grammar, and implicit logic has a disturbing impact. Phonetic differences raise few issues; Japanese phonetics is simple and correct pronunciation is easily learned. The near identity of phonetics in Japanese and Polynesian languages invites comment, despite the scant evidence of historical contacts.

A new dimension in student thinking about languages emerges with the discovery that thoughts can be communicated in the absence of familiar categories of gender, number, definite and indefinite articles, and relative words, phrases, or clauses. All too rarely a thoughtful student suddenly asks, "Well, then, do *we* really need gender? Or number?" Absence of fixed stress accent in words, with shifting of accent to other syllables according to context; the syllabic concept of phonetic units; absence of meaningful voice inflection (as in question versus declaration); the general irrelevance of word order (in contrast to English or Chinese); postpositions instead of prepositions; the proliferation of homophones consequent upon adoption of thousands of Chinese loanwords divested of the tones that differentiate the originals in Chinese —all provide further contrasts with more familiar languages. Even uniformity of vowel pronunciation surprises American students. New concepts of social relations accompany the realization that Japanese verbs must be conjugated according to relative social status of speaker and addressee. At this point, the ubiquitous Japanese calling card acquires meaning as enabling newly introduced persons to use appropriate courtesy forms. The fact that until recently personal pronouns were avoided in conversation and their function performed by courtesy conjugation is almost shocking to an American who tries to imagine communication without the first person singular.

Habitually, students have dismissed ideographic writing as obsolete primitive "picture writing." Slowly, they grasp the distinction between semantic and phonetic writing systems—not without surprise that ideographs save time in note-taking. The question, "Does our own writing system include non-phonetic semantic symbols?" elicits puzzled incredulity until someone remembers Arabic numerals and mathematical notation—to say nothing of punctuation, italics, capital letters, the ampersand, and proofreader's marks. The feeling that no one could remember so many characters is countered by ironic comment on English spelling among college students. But what about dictionaries? With no alphabet, can the Japanese really make and use dictionaries? Physical presentation of a Japanese dictionary answers that question. Fifteen minutes of explanation teaches no ideographs, but it makes their classification plausible and meaningful.

Consideration of ideographic writing leads to China. The Japanese faced real difficulties in adapting the ideographs to their language, which differs in almost every way from Chinese. Japanese is polysyllabic and highly inflected, while Chinese is largely monosyllabic and uninflected, with emphasis on word order and grammatical particles. Each ideograph symbolizes a meaning, rarely influences pronunciation, and allows no suffixes, prefixes, infixes, or other incorporation of grammatical guideposts. The root portion of a Japanese word can be symbolized by an ideograph, but the inflections remain beyond the scope of ideographs divorced from Chinese grammatical devices. The Korean scribes who introduced ideographs to Japan gave up the struggle to adapt and used ideographs phonetically in defiance of their semantic role. Moreover, they used their own mispronunciation of Chinese and mispronounced

Japanese as well. The ensuing confusion is the despair of students of early Japanese documents.

The solution was typically Japanese. Perhaps Japan is unique among historic nations in avid importation of alien cultural features; the tradition that good ideas may be found abroad characterizes much of Japanese history. Whether or not they like foreigners, they have typically sought out and adapted foreign ideas without waiting for some allegedly benevolent foreign power to enlighten "underdeveloped" Japan. The Japanese are the first to regard themselves as "underdeveloped" and invariably they do their own developing. When recorded Japanese history begins, individuals are already going to China to study Sui and T'ang civilization and bring back whatever they find useful. Such men were not content with a year or two at the Chinese capital. Many of them stayed for decades until they had mastered the learning which they sought.

Since the art, literature, and architecture of T'ang China were deeply Buddhist, not a few of these expatriate scholars learned Pali and Sanskrit, and thus encountered the phonetic alphabet. Once exposed to the idea of phonetic writing, they found it useful in dealing with the problem of Japanese suffixes and particles. They did not renounce the Chinese model and abandon the ideograph. Ideographic writing carried too much prestige, plus the advantage of symbolizing specific meanings while leaving any people free to use their own pronunciation. Some scholar acquainted with Pali or Sanskrit devised a phonetic system of writing Japanese syllables —allegedly, this was the work of Kōbō Daishi, founder of the Shingon sect of Buddhism in Japan. Thenceforth, the Chinese ideographs were used as intended: as purely semantic symbols for the root elements of Japanese words. The phonetic syllabary (*kana*) served to indicate suffixes, prefixes, and grammatical particles without Chinese equivalents. Its inventor did not adopt any of the Indian alphabetic symbols; he accepted the phonetic idea and contrived new phonetic symbols by using fragments of Chinese ideographs. The late A. L. Kroeber would have called this "stimulus diffusion." This system is still used in modern Japanese.

Such a discussion of the Japanese language can, if necessary, be condensed into one class session. The student learns none of the language as such, but he may arrive at a major revision of his ideas about languages and writing systems in that one hour. Other aspects of the language are considered in relation to subsequent topics: for example, skill in using the ink-brush introduces the discussion of painting; the magical function of ideographs naturally fits into the discussion of magic, divination, and shamanism. At the very least, he is prepared for thoughtful consideration of other languages and writing systems beyond the familiar patterns of Indo-European dialects.

The selection and order of other topics of class presentation differ each time the course is offered. Franz Boas used to complain that in order to write the first chapter of an ethnography, it is necessary to have written all of the other chapters. There can be no final or universal logic in the order of presentation of any human way of living. One may start with livelihood and run the gamut of religion, family patterns, technology, rites de passage, mythology, architecture, shamanism, and end with poetry. But with equal cogency these topics may be handled in reverse order, or in any other sequence that illuminates a tribal or national way of living. The objective remains constant: to convey the reality and vital quality of a culture alien to the student's familiar world in such a way that he emotionally apprehends the validity of that culture for those who live thereby.

Always, I find it fruitful to provide some indication of the poverty, monotonous toil, and insecurity of many millions of Asia's people. American students are so far removed from grinding poverty and daily hunger that one easily recalls the historic tragedy of "Let them eat cake!" Japan's relatively high standard of living—so enormously improved during the forty-odd years of my acquaintance with that country—does not convey an adequate notion of the privations of most other Asian peoples. In the Ryūkyū Islands, a scarcity economy is more obvious, as it still is in remoter mountain villages of Japan proper. I find that the details of rice cultivation, even with vast improvements due to modern invention and hybrid seed, afford a measure of insight into the toilsome hand labor by which Asians struggle to survive. My own movies were taken with this theme in mind; I tried to pace them to the monotonous rhythm of peasant toil, in mud and rain and burning sun, with fatigue and backache from the urgency of speed to keep pace with nature's readiness, alleviated by song and close human contacts. A former Hollywood director found these movies tedious and boresome; for good or ill, this was what I wanted—it symbolizes reality. If students feel their back muscles tighten as they watch a peasant stand erect for a moment's stretch during the rush of rice planting, if their own boredom be translated as a bare hint of the monotony of peasant existence, the contrast with Hollywood's pace is worthwhile.[3] The bare statement—that all of the rice for all the millions of rice-consuming Asiatics is transplanted by hand, plant by plant, weeded, cut, and threshed by hand with tender preservation of the straw that has so many uses—takes on meaning if pictures are handled rightly.

Wet rice cultivation, incidentally, directs attention to Malaya, Indonesia, South China, and India. How it reached Japan is arguable, but the ancient basic technique is diffused throughout the area. Modern Japanese scientific methods enormously increase yields by dint of chemical fertilizers, hybrid seeds, and careful adjustment of the variety of rice to the local climate and soil. Dry rice cultivation by slash and burn methods also occurs in Japan and can hardly be discussed apart from its predominance elsewhere in allegedly "underdeveloped areas." Japanese achievements in scientific

[3] One widely circulated, superbly photographed color movie of Japanese peasant life misses the point entirely; it has been speeded up by 50 percent in order to dub in sound.

agriculture hold out great promise for other Asian countries—if, as in Japan, they can be coupled with population control. Both the old and the new techniques merit analysis.

Almost any Japanese handicraft invites comparison with its parallels elsewhere in Asia. In the Ryūkyū Islands, at least, the people are quite aware of the diverse sources of their culture. In Amami Ōshima, I found it necessary to study a complex *ikat* dyeing and weaving technique—perhaps the most intricate of its kind to be found anywhere. *Ikat* dyeing is familiar to anyone who knows Indonesia—or India, for that matter. My ignorance of weaving was profound, and I studied such materials as I could acquire in the field. Comparing looms, I proudly deduced that the Ryūkyū loom was based on the Malayan loom and announced my discovery to a peasant weaver. In essence, she replied, "Of course, our forefathers found that loom somewhere around Singapore five centuries ago and we have improved it!" The Ryūkyūans are deservedly famous as smugglers—an activity that they denote by the term, "international trade." Their pride in a seafaring past is manifest in considerable folklore—much of it verifiable—concerning innovations learned abroad and brought home by specific ancestors whom they describe by name and approximate date. Not only handicrafts, but other cultural items are acknowledged importations—often combining features derived from many sources. A local shaman in Amami Ōshima volunteered information as to the sources of his paraphernalia: "This is derived from Chinese Taoism, that from Tibetan Buddhism, another object from the Amur region . . ." His description of the process of acquiring familiar spirits reminded me vividly of conversations with the late Waldemar Bogoras, who wrote so clearly on Siberian shamanism. The ubiquitous banyan trees of the Ryūkyūs, which serve as defense against typhoons but also are feared as abodes of malicious spirits, are described as importations from India, via Malaya. Although in Japan proper I did not encounter this kind of folk awareness of the sources of plants, customs, and artifacts, written history links almost anything Japanese with some other part of Asia. There remains also the mute evidence of idioms, phrases, house and shrine architecture, courtesy conjugations, and other details to turn one's speculations toward Oceania; compare, for example, Japanese peasant homes and shrines with the photographs of their counterparts in W. Caudern's *Ethnographical Studies in Celebes.*

Japanese family patterns are best understood by comparison with those of China—both resemblances and differences exemplify the traditional Japanese habit of adopting, and then adapting, foreign ideas. Confucian doctrine has shaped Japanese social organization, government, and family life—not indirectly, but with conscious effort and much reading of Confucian and Neo-Confucian writings. Ruth Benedict's *The Chrysanthemum and the Sword* elicited admiration from readers of the Japanese translation; they marveled that one who had not visited Japan should understand their moral codes so well. She noted the Confucian origin of such concepts as *on* and *giri;* she also noted that, as usual, the Japanese picked and chose what they wished. In this case, they rejected the Confucian idea of *jen* ("benevolence"?), even as they rejected the civil service examination system, because the Japanese Emperor, and to a lesser degree, the nobility, were regarded as *kami* (i.e., having *mana* or supernatural virtue) and hence above the law. Confucius and Mencius justified revolution against an emperor who lacked *jen* (righteousness?). Influence from China does not explain the "divinity" of the Japanese Emperor; Polynesia, however, provides illuminating parallels. There, the chieftains are so charged with *mana* (supernatural power) that whatever they touch becomes dangerous to commoners. Divinity, as in ancient Japan, is conveyed by a sacred drink made by chewing a vegetable product and fermenting the resulting fluid; ancient Japanese writings refer to guilds of food chewers in Imperial service. The king in ancient India—and as late as the present century, in Thailand—was transformed from a human prince into a god by a priestly ritual. In the last analysis, the presence of priests who could make a man into a god assured the priestly caste of supreme status. In China, the Emperor performed rituals that had power over the seasons, the fertility of man and beast, and even over the gods—but thanks to Confucius and Mencius, he never acquired divinity. Polynesians and Japanese, however, conceived of divine power as transmitted by birth; genealogy became all-important, but no priestly caste stood above the ruler. The sanctity of the Japanese Emperor, so recently asserted in war and renounced in defeat, leads the inquisitive student to Oceania and thence to India for historical insight.

Pervasive distinctions between *uchi* (inner, domestic) and *soto* (outer, foreign) are characteristic of all Japanese social organization from families to empire and are derived directly from China. In the absence of insight into this distinction, the relations of husband and wife are misinterpreted naïvely in Occidental terms, as female inferiority. In China as in Japan, however, a husband's responsibilities are *soto,* i.e., the relations of the household to the external world; the wife is in charge of *uchi,* i.e., internal affairs. Superficial interpretation in terms of superior-subordinate misses the real point.

Our literature on Japanese religions has suffered from inadequate attention to actual behavior of participants, whether routine or extraordinary. In Occidental discussions of Japan as of other Asian countries, doctrine and organizational history often have outweighed observation of people in action. Our own students understandably envision the religious activities of alien peoples in terms of customs and rites with which they are familiar, such as congregational assembly, preaching, sacraments, and church-affiliated social groups. The circumstance that the Judaic, Christian, and Moslem faiths are oriented to sacred books has inspired Occidental scholars to discover and translate so-called "sacred books" of other religions. In consequence, Occidental scholars are better acquainted with Buddhist and Hindu philosophical-religious works than are many active priests and members of Asian religious orders. I suggest that Occidentals tend to overestimate the role of the voluminous writings that we indiscriminately term "sacred" and to devote relatively less attention to the daily practices, rituals, and attitudes of Asian peoples. Too readily, we use such terms as "believers" or "members" to denote Asians who inherit a specific religious tradition, without asking whether these concepts are pertinent. Admittedly, some Asian sects do define membership and regard belief as a criterion of affiliation. Far more often, however, the ordinary Asian individual is a "believer" only in the sense that an American carpenter or factory hand is a "believer" in capitalism. Asian religions, like economic systems other than communism, are simply part of a traditional cultural milieu—not foci of devotion. Ethnographic studies are beginning to fill these gaps in our perspective on Asian religions; at last there are available excellent descriptions of ritual, worship, and daily behavior of participants in Buddhist, Shinto, and other Japanese religious systems.[4]

Since Occidental religious bodies insist upon exclusive allegiance, and since simultaneous practice of two or more distinct faiths is almost unthinkable to them, American students have difficulty in grasping the general tolerance and lack of absolutist claims of a majority of Buddhist sects. Still more baffling are the facts of simultaneous acceptance of contrasting religions by individual Japanese. This latter practice explains some of the published statistics of religious affiliation in Japan. There are tables that give the alleged numbers of Buddhist, Shinto, Christian—and even of Confucian! —"adherents"; the totals exceed considerably the population of Japan. Japanese who accept Confucian teachings do not regard themselves as affiliated with "Confucianism"; and a probable majority of the people worship at Shinto shrines or have some interest in a modern Shinto sect without the slightest feeling of incongruity in depending upon Buddhist temples, priests or nuns for important public and private rituals. I am convinced that multitudes of Japanese would regard themselves also as Christians were it not for the

[4] For many years, the only teachable description of Japanese Buddhist ritual and practice that I could find was Armstrong's *Buddhism and Buddhists in Japan* (New York, Macmillan, 1927), Chapter III. Recent valuable ethnographic and sociological studies include works by Embree, Norbeck, Beardsley and associates, Dore, and others.

insistence of missionaries upon exclusive affiliation with their churches. There are indeed some indigenous cults of Buddhism and Shinto that officially denounce all other faiths; recent ethnographic studies, however, indicate that many of their lay members are less bigoted in practice. Conflicting theologies trouble the average Japanese very little; in such matters, he is more pragmatic than dogmatic. I recall an educated gentleman who often sneered at religion as "superstition." Once, however, I caught him praying at a fox shrine; shamefacedly, he remarked, "You never know. There might be something in any of these religions—and also, business is bad right now!"

The basically atheistic outlook of Buddhism presents a considerable emotional obstacle to American college students. Naïve definitions of religion as "belief in God" persist in many English dictionaries, to say nothing of books about theology and "comparative religion"—and college classrooms. Such definitions are culturebound—valid enough among Moslems, Jews, and Christians—and some of them are intended to rule out of consideration the alleged heathen. No wonder that the notion of an atheistic religion shocks a majority of those who have been reared in the Euro-American tradition. Any inductive study of the range and diversity of human cultures, however, requires redefinition of religion in non-theistic terms. One need not accept that controversial task in order to teach about Japanese religious behavior; he need only quote Buddhists of all times and places, from Theravada to Zen. Moreover, it is easy to remind the disturbed student that religious people of any faith, confronted with a culture divergent from their own, unerringly select certain activities of the alien people and regard them as religious. I never have met a Christian missionary who did not refer to Buddhism as a religion, although he might stigmatize it as a "false religion." Nor have I encountered a Shintoist or Buddhist who questioned the status of Christianity as a religion—even if he deemed it a subversive doctrine. To an ethnographer studying an exotic culture, questions of truth or falsity of observed beliefs are irrelevant; his goal is accurate description of what the people do and say. Japanese Buddhist sects stress diverse doctrines. Some of them are frankly atheistic; others, such as Jōdō and Shinshū, may be regarded as theistic for all practical purposes. A student who becomes informed respecting the diverse cults and practices of the Japanese may be well-prepared to understand whatever religions he may encounter elsewhere in Asia.

The significance of Buddhism as a gateway from Japan to Chinese and Indian culture in no way diminishes the importance of specifically Japanese religious history and practice. Stress upon alleged historic parallels in countries that differ culturally always risks superficial misinterpretations; there may be enlargement of perspective, however, as students learn that the Jōdō and Shinshū sects effected a religious reformation in Japan that not only antedated Europe's Protestant Reformation by nearly four centuries, but also anticipated some of its doctrines—such as salvation by grace and justification by faith. Again, the thirteenth-century charismatic Buddhist reformer Nichiren, basing his doctrine upon the apocalyptic Lotus Sutra, founded a vigorous sect that still claims exclusive status as the only true faith. A facetiously inclined foreign observer may view the modern Nichirenites as a blend of fundamentalists, Nicholas Chauvin, the Salvation Army, a nursery of assassins, and a number of scholarly intellectuals. Such comparisons probably are superficial and misleading; Nichiren's fanatical followers, however, for centuries have sparked the emphasis upon loyalty to the emperor and the doctrine of Japan's world mission, and their enthusiasm continues worthy of careful attention.

Shinto is inseparable from much of Japan's history, for its varied practices antedate the coming of Buddhism. Unlike Buddhism, its literary tradition is slight (prior to the Shinto Revival), and a wealth of folk rituals and festivals is disclosed in numerous excellent studies, both ethnographic and historical.[5] In recent times, State Shinto provided the major vehicle of nationalist indoctrina-

---

[5] For example, the historical and ethnographic works of D. C. Holtom.

tion, especially in the schools. The postwar eclipse of the state cult has stimulated the rise of syncretistic cults that combine Shinto traditions with universal goals of a common humanity, faith healing, and evangelism. Tenri Kyō, currently Japan's most active sect, claims millions of converts. At its Nara headquarters, substantial modern dormitories accommodate thousands of pilgrims, and a library of half a million volumes provides for much scholarly study of the whole range of Oriental and Occidental theology. Like Christian Science, Tenri Kyō was founded by a woman and denies the reality of illness, suffering, and death. Chronologically, Tenri antedates Christian Science, for the visions of its foundress began in 1838. I vividly realized the number and zeal of Tenri missionaries in 1951 when I was studying the Amami Archipelago in the Ryūkyū Islands. Some 300 missionaries were then at work among the local population of a quarter-million. Tenri, however, is only the most conspicuous of many recent Shinto-inspired cults.

Japanese culture does not lack for original, indigenous achievements. A persistent, almost indefinable core of stubborn continuity modifies whatever comes from abroad. Because the outward aspects of Japanese ways of living change almost overnight as new ideas arrive, careless generalizations have characterized the Japanese as imitators. Barely a century ago, however, Europeans were calling the Yankees imitators—and Yankees are no less proud of their originality than are the Japanese. After all, nowhere does the behavior repertory of an individual include more than a tiny fraction of self-produced ideas and habits. Japan's combination of stubborn identity with eager acceptance of foreign cultural features provides a fertile topic for teachers of Asian civilization. Whether one investigates land tenure, the rise of money economy, the rise and eclipse of *hōken shakai* (too loosely translated "feudal society"), the modification of Confucian and neo-Confucian philosophy, the adoption of Occidental music, or native fine arts and literature, the study of Japan contributes richly to general education, however conceived.

What of contemporary Japan—the Japan of subways, steel and concrete, political parties, movies and juvenile delinquency, the Japan that in many respects is closer to the United States than are the nations of Europe? Here, I revert to my philosophy of approaching the world of Asia by way of a single nation. All Asians are busily adopting Occidental culture, be it labeled capitalist or communist. In either case, the adopted elements stand out clearly if one has a reasonable knowledge of the indigenous culture of the adopting people. So I leave it to my students to explore the contemporary borrowings and rejections of Euro-American culture by the Japanese. Once familiar with the outlines of Japanese tradition —or with traditions of some other Asian country—a normally alert student easily recognizes adopted elements in the contemporary culture. Moreover, given moderate understanding of the pre-European background, he can evaluate the difficulties in "modernization" and bring to the daily news insights that the reporters have not provided.

Perhaps, the accidents of living that placed me in Japan in 1917 provided an advantage that might have been less easily exploited had I found myself in some other Asian country. Japanese culture is unusual in that it leads so surely into the major cultures of eastern and southern Asia, even as it leads to Europe and the Americas in these latter days. There is good reason to suspect that someone who had been immersed in Chinese culture would have found far less reason to follow its outward flow toward Japan, Southeastern Asia, or the central Asian deserts. Such a student of China would be directed to Indian culture even as the Japanese were guided in that direction by Buddhism. Study of the ancient Chinese trade routes also directs attention outward—in this case, to Western Asia, which hardly comes within the scope of the student of Japan. China's Mongol interlude offers leads to every part of Asia and some parts of Europe; but after the Mongols came the anti-foreign reaction of Ming.

From the cultural point of view, India, like China, exported heavily. The probing of Indian antiquity reveals strong and protracted contacts with Western Asia, the Nile valley, and the Mediterranean. A glance at the tides of emigration from India takes the student to Indonesia, Southeastern Asia, and East Africa. The diffusion of much of Indian civilization by Buddhist missionaries is one of history's great epics. If a teacher, or student, approaches Asia by way of Indonesia or any country of Southeastern Asia, he occupies a vantage point comparable to that afforded by Japan; here, also, cultural influences have entered from China, India, and early Malayan tribes, plus strong Moslem influence in the last half millennium.

On the whole, my original thesis stands: he who would introduce students to the vast diversification that is Asia may well start by concentrating on whatever Asian country he knows best. As the cultural history and external contacts of the chosen region are unraveled, Asia will be discovered up to the capacity of teacher and students.

I wish to make clear the fact that such an approach in no way implies that knowing one Asian culture automatically equips one to understand any other Asian culture. I contend only that any Asian culture, studied in some detail, points to many and diverse sources. Each of these sources has its unique civilization that must be studied for its own sake in order to be understood. I think, however, that students may gain more by knowing some one people well than by a survey of the whole vast continent, valuable as a general survey can be in competent hands. Certainly I do not present my pattern of operations as a model to be copied. The procedure of working from a fairly well understood area to other regions from which or to which cultural diffusion has occurred is practical, feasible for one of limited experience, and adapted to the normal sequences of human learning. Usually, all of us first master the immediate and thence proceed further and further afield; failing to do so, one may be ensnared in a fabric of reified abstractions.

As an anthropologist, I venture a final caveat with respect to excessive reliance on native documentary sources. Living in a society in which literacy is a monopoly of an elite fosters a suspicion that, however profound the literary products of that elite, writers of books often inhabit a rarefied sphere remote from the daily life of the mass of people. I think that our habitual dependence on written sources and implicit downgrading of the illiterate have distorted Occidental concepts of Asian peoples. Thanks to acquaintance with non-literate peripheral tribes, an ethnographer knows from experience that people innocent of books often manifest cultural achievements rich in dignity and intrinsic worth. Much that has escaped inclusion in "classical" writings may be reassessed to the enrichment of human understanding. To say this does not approve imposition of an alien dichotomy of literate-illiterate upon the "Great Tradition" of Japan or any other Asian nation—to borrow Redfield's fruitful concept. If students of Asia have erred at times in overstressing literary traditions, the current interest in ethnographic and sociological study of peasants and fisher-folk, factory workers and laborers may aid perspective. If I could relive my years in Japan, I would not sacrifice a single contact with the rickshaw pullers, peasants, craftsmen, longshoremen, and shopkeepers who unwittingly taught me.[6]

[6] That in modern Japan such people are literate does not imply their familiarity with the writings that foreign scholars study. When I first encountered Japan, however, the wayside booths of professional scribes were everywhere, and I knew many wise older people who could not read. The last two centuries have witnessed a proliferation of books (and since the restoration, magazines) designed in Tokugawa times for the *chōnin,* and currently for the masses. Such materials are of very great value in studying popular ideas and practices.

Comment: On Behalf of Comparative Civilizations Through Intellectual Cooperation Between Disciplines

FRANCIS L. K. HSU

Professor of Anthropology, Northwestern University

Professor Douglas Haring has presented a number of interesting ideas in his paper, of which the most striking to me are the two following points:

A. In order to teach about a large cultural area, it is necessary to concentrate first on one small area, give it a thorough coverage, and then extend from there. In teaching a course on Asia, he would begin with Japan, which he knows well by first hand experience, and which has derived her institutional and cultural origin in diverse ways primarily from China and secondarily from the South Seas. In this way, after the students have acquired thorough acquaintance with Japan, they are imperceptibly led by the thread of diffusion into China and the rest of Asia.

B. In trying to understand any civilization, especially a large civilization, it is necessary to give equal attention to literate and non-literate traditions or forces of civilization, which affect each other.

However, although Professor Haring's two points provide us with an excellent beginning in the study of a large cultural area such as Asia, they do not, in my view, hold the promise of a deeper understanding of cultural Asia unless we go beyond such phenomena as the threads of diffusion between Japan and China, or between

Japan and the South Seas. It is perfectly true that many of the basic institutions and ideas in Japanese culture have a Chinese origin. But, in spite of such historical connections, many characteristics of the Japanese culture and psychology are extremely different from those of the Chinese. For example, why were the Japanese people so enterprising and so aggressively successful in dealing with the impact of the West while the Chinese showed such prolonged inaptitude under it? How would tracing Japanese institutional forms and ideas to those of ancient China help our understanding of this difference? We can, of course, say that the differences between the Japanese and Chinese responses to the impact of the West are only a matter of degree. We can say that the Japanese succeeded in modernizing themselves within less than 75 years, but that the Chinese are aggressively doing it now under the Communists. But this does not give us the true picture. The obvious thing is that Japan has succeeded in meeting the challenge of the West without serious change in her basic social and political system, but the most recent developments in China threaten to destroy all or most of her ancient institutions.

Furthermore, if we examine the histories of specific organizations of enterprise in Japan and in China, we will not fail to see the drastic differences between Chinese and Japanese behavior. For example, the Chinese National Merchant Navigation Company was organized sometime before the start of the Japanese Nippon Yusen Kaisa. But, up to the 1930s, the Japanese concern had ships sailing all the four seas and held the blue ribbon record for the United States to Far East run, while the Chinese corporation had only some steamships plying the Yangtze River and only a few other miserable boats begging for no more than a small portion of the Chinese coastal trade.

Then, it is also well-known that there was a tremendous amount of corruption in Chinese officialdom; there is still a tremendous amount of corruption in Chinese officialdom under the Nationalist government. This is an old Chinese culture pattern whereby the officials get the major part of the income due their position through extra-legal but customary means. In contrast to this Chinese situation, it is not often noted that there is almost complete lack of such corruption in Japanese officialdom, except where Japanese officials went into China after the Japanese invasion and occupation of a major part of China since 1937. If categorical statements make some of my audience unhappy, I am willing to modify the above by saying that, at any rate, there was a relative lack of corruption in Japanese officialdom just as there was a relative abundance of it in Chinese bureaucracy. How would the tracing of Japanese institutional forms and ideas to China help us to understand this basic great difference?

It seems that in aiming at scientific understanding of civilizations, whether in teaching or in reasearch, there are at least two other lines of approach besides those expounded so eloquently by Professor Haring. First, we must resort to explicit comparison. In Asian studies, there should be two kinds of comparison, both equally important: (1) for American researchers and teachers, comparison between Japan and the United States, China and the United States, Indonesia and the United States, and the like; and (2) for researchers and teachers in all countries, between Japan and China; Hindu India and Japan; etc.

These comparisons are necessary for the following reasons: Any student of culture or civilization will make implicit comparisons between the culture he studies and his own culture, whether such a research worker or teacher consciously wishes to do so or not. Since the researcher or the teacher is, like all human beings, a product of his own culture, with its own particular values, assumptions, and prejudices, it seems imperative that such comparisons be made on the conscious rather than the unconscious level. In this regard, I cannot agree with Professor Theodore de Bary,[1] when he said, during a panel discussion at this conference, that it is better to allow implicit comparison rather than explicit comparison.

[1] See footnote 6 in Professor de Bary's Preface.

In my view, implicit comparison is far more dangerous than explicit comparison. In explicit comparison, the student at least puts himself on record, so that he himself can rationally examine the result of his comparison, and others can judge the factual or logical bases of his comparison as well as the merits or the demerits of his comparison.

Besides the danger of implicit comparison and therefore of hidden bias, it is necessary to make explicit comparisons in the study of cultures because human affairs cannot as a rule be described or evaluated in absolute terms. For example, how do we measure despotism? How despotic is despotic? How do we measure oppression? How bad must the conditions of a prison be when we can really call them bad or oppressive?

What the students of human culture might do to get out of the dilemma and be more accurate is to make comparative statements in the evaluation of the conditions of any one society. Making explicit comparisons between the conditions of different societies, he will be entitled to state that the oppression of this society would seem to be greater than that which exists in that society; or that the prosperity of this society would seem to have reached a higher level than that of that society, etc. He can make these explicit comparisons either on a point by point basis (e.g., Chinese educational practices versus Japanese educational practices; American parent-child relationship with parent-child relationship in Thailand, and others), or on a whole with whole basis (e.g., Japanese cultural orientation compared with its Korean counterpart, and the others).

The pitfalls of comparison are, of course, numerous, but in my view none of them presents any insurmountable barrier. In this regard, I find myself in strong disagreement with Professor Arthur Wright, whose negative view concerning comparison was eloquently aired in his paper. He maintained that when he wanted his students to compare, for example, Confucian ideas with those of Hobbes or those of Christ in the Bible, his students did not know

Hobbes even if their graduation depended upon it, and the scantiness of their knowledge of the Bible was truly extraordinary. Therefore, Professor Wright argued, there was no use in attempting any comparison because the students lacked intellectual basis for such comparison. I think Professor Wright's negativism is unnecessary. If some American students in Oriental or Indian culture studies do not happen to know about Hobbes or the Bible, it is high time for them to do something about it. In fact, they should not even go through a short-cut by looking up some encyclopedia but by studying the originals in earnest. On the other hand, I have found that whenever I pointed out to my students the necessity of comparison and confronted them with the poverty of their knowledge about the significant thoughts, theological details, and historical events in their heritage, a majority of them could be galvanized into seriously doing something about it, by shame if not by more lofty motives.

Another possible pitfall with comparison is the commonly heard plea that the different cultures or societies are not comparable. Many scholars of the Orient have the peculiar view that the societies under their scrutiny are unique or are totally dissimilar to anything that is known in the West. My comment on such a view is that, if we seek differences, no two individuals are ever identical, but two individuals who are not identical can be compared for their similarities just as much as for their differences. An attempt to compare different phenomena for the common principles and common factors which govern them does not mean the negation of the particular characteristics and unique features which distinguish any one of them. The fire generated on a match is certainly different from the fire radiated from the sun. These two phenomena can nevertheless be compared, and must be compared, at some point of our research on heat.

A third possible pitfall in explicit comparison is not connected with scientific considerations but is connected with a danger, consciously or unconsciously felt, by some American students of Oriental or Indian civilization. As a result of explicit comparison, such students may be forced to draw adverse conclusions about some aspects of their own culture. Such students are often most eloquent in defense of the view that the civilization which they are studying is really unique. Occasionally, by a curious psychological twist, one of these students is likely to be "converted" to the civilization he has researched on all his life. Such a student will then develop a new ethnocentrism under which the society and people of his "adoption" can do no wrong.

No scientific view of civilization can come about as a result of either of these attitudes. If each civilization were unique, then we could learn nothing from history or ethnography, and we will be forced to throw the sciences of man into the river. The data in all sciences, whether physical or social, must be comparative. Without comparative data, we cannot have science. A defensive and protective attitude is detrimental to all scientific endeavors whether it is applied to the civilization of the student's own or of his subjects of study, as much as religious premises or political interests will surely curtail the accuracy of good research.

Beside the importance of explicit comparison between cultures, we must seriously address ourselves to the problem of interdisciplinary research.

Up to this point, most of the efforts on behalf of interdisciplinary research have been made more by students in the social sciences rather than by those in history. I am especially delighted to see and participate in this interdisciplinary conference in which the leadership is assumed by historians. In my view, history needs, as much as, if not more than, the social sciences, the breadth of vision provided by an interdisciplinary approach. Historians are in the first instance trained to look at particulars, either the particulars of individual personalities or the particulars of an area, or the particulars of a given society. There are some historians who have been able to look at the particulars in the perspective of the general, but such historians are often branded by other historians as being pseudo-historians, popularizers, or philosophers rather than historians. This is an old trick among scholars. If I do not like the work of a fellow anthropologist, one polite way to express my disapproval is to describe his work as non-anthropological.

However, not only history but all branches of the social sciences need each other as well. It is by pooling the resources and the insights derived from psychology, sociology, anthropology, psychiatry and wherever such resources and insights are available, that we can interpret often otherwise unintelligible material at hand, move beyond mere description and recording toward understanding of its guiding principles and prediction. But such understanding and prediction are not possible without two of the most crucial elements in science—hypothesization and quantification. Anthropology, for example, has proceeded for many years purely on a descriptive level, with no efforts at hypothesization or quantification. It is under the pressure of the other branches of the behavioral sciences such as psychology and sociology that some anthropological scholars are beginning to become more sophisticated in hypothesis formation and more enthusiastic about the need for quantified research. Admittedly from the point of view of many an anthropologist, some of the current psychological and sociological researches are exact exercises in triviality. But, from the point of view of many psychologists and sociologists, the results of some of the anthropological researches are often global, vague, and impossible to verify. It is only when the different disciplines dealing with human affairs can see their way clear to not only cooperating but also borrowing from each other in viewpoint, insights, methods, and results that we can hope to achieve a greater and truer understanding of man himself.

Here again, as in the case of explicit comparison, there are many misconceptions about interdisciplinary research. I regret that I have to argue with Professor Arthur Wright again, this time with his defeatist attitude. The word "defeatist" was Professor Wright's, and I think that such an attitude on the part of a Chinese historian of his reputation is not calculated to open up new frontiers of research. One of the reasons for his defeatist attitude is that, as he saw it, interdisciplinary research usually led to tensions. I do not deny that interdisciplinary research often generates tensions. In fact, I think all joint efforts are inherently tension producers. There are, therefore, plenty of tensions in the operation of the United Nations. There is also plenty of tension among different religious denominations. For anyone who cares to see, there is no absence of tensions, even within the organization of any united fund or community chest, between those who want more for cancer and those who want more for the Red Cross, between those who favor the YMCA and those who go all out for multiple sclerosis.

We must realize, first, that interdisciplinary cooperation is hard work. It is not a tea party. It is arduous. Second, I would also underline the fact that for any interdisciplinary cooperation to bear any kind of fruit, the personalities of the scholars involved in it must not clash to begin with. No matter how brilliant the scholars involved, they cannot come to any common intellectual good if they get on each other's nerves in the first place. Third, I would like, therefore, to underscore the fact that any interdisciplinary cooperation must take time. It cannot be accomplished by just a conference of a few days, a few weeks, or even a few months. It involves hard plowing of the field by the different scholars involved for years.

Ten years ago, interdisciplinary cooperation was mainly at the level of the three-day conference. I took a minor part in that type of activity when, in 1951, during Northwestern University's centennial celebration, I convened an interdisciplinary Conference on Culture and Personality under the generous sponsorship of the Wenner-Gren Foundation for Anthropological Research of New York. In this conference, I brought together for three entire days a group of distinguished anthropologists, sociologists, psychologists, psychoanalysts, and psychiatrists. We had prepared papers and discussions. We recorded other impromptu utterances during the con-

ference. As we looked over the results, we could not help lamenting
the fact that our conference did not really bring the participants
intellectually together to any great extent.[1]

If we judge interdisciplinary cooperation only by the results of
this sort, we should have been very pessimistic. The reality is far
brighter as we persevered. Today, we have a number of much
more truly long-term as well as short-term interdisciplinary efforts
which are beginning to bear fruit. The older interdisciplinary departments such as the Department of Social Relations at Harvard
seem to weather the difficulties well, after several modifications
of their initial designs and policies. There are other similar efforts
in the University of North Carolina, the University of Chicago,
Cornell University, and elsewhere. At Northwestern University,
we have recently set up a Group for Intersocietal Studies. Its most
important interdisciplinary activities consist of faculty seminars from
several different disciplines which design and carry out researches
according to social science and comparative approaches to area
studies. As to published results in interdisciplinary cooperation, two
very successful ones have recently seen print.[2]

I must warn, though, that when I talk about interdisciplinary
cooperation, I do not mean that historians should become anthropologists or sociologists should become psychiatrists. What I do
mean is that, through the process of interdisciplinary cooperation
or stimulation, participants from each of the disciplines will be
intellectually enriched by the others. Today, we have established
disciplines such as astrophysics, biochemistry, ethnomusicology, psy-
chosomatic medicine. When these compound disciplines were first
coming into being, there were many fights and many resistances
and many prophesies of doom. But, today, no harm has come to
any of the individual disciplines. In fact, while a whole lot of com-

[1] Francis L. K. Hsu, ed., *Aspects of Culture and Personality* (New York, Abelard-
Schuman, 1954).

[2] Bert Kaplan, ed., *Studying Personality Cross-Culturally* (Evanston, Ill., Row, Peter-
son and Co., 1961); and Francis L. K. Hsu, ed., *Psychological Anthropology: Approaches to Culture and Personality* (Homewood, Ill., Dorsey Press, 1961).

pound disciplines have been born, the individual disciplines have all been enriched rather than depleted. Scholars and scientists maintain their position and enjoy their privileges only if they can maintain their curiosity and are constantly in search of new frontiers, but not if they shut their eyes to new frontiers and simply gloat in the security of their self-imposed Chinese Great Wall.

In conclusion, I ask leave to say a few words about teaching Asia to American students. There is always the problem of limitation of time. In one quarter, semester, or even a year, it is difficult to cover the subject of Asian culture or history adequately, especially for students who have never had any experience with Asia or who have only extremely limited prior reading on the subject. Professor Haring's idea of intensive analysis of one community or one area, leading from there into the wider geographical and cultural space, is indeed a good one. His counsel that both the literate and the non-literate traditions are of equal importance is beyond dispute. But I would suggest that, even if it is a one-quarter or semester course, the instructor should at least make some explicit comparisons of the Asian society in question with the society and culture of America if not comparisons with another Asian culture.

With reference to the problem of interdisciplinary approach, it would be quite difficult for the instructor in any field to do it in a quarter or semester or year course, if he is not already himself somewhat steeped in interdisciplinary research. If the instructor himself has carried out or been interested in interdisciplinary research and has done some integration in his own approach, this will be the best. I think the best way to introduce any interdisciplinary point of view is through the discussion of problems centering around problems rather than the study of society and tradition as they are. One of the problems that engage the attention of many social scientists today is the problem of social and economic and political transformation of many of the traditional societies.

In the last analysis, however, I personally am of the opinion that teaching is a highly individualistic matter. In this I am impressed by the distinction made in old China between a true teacher and a teaching technician. A teaching technician is a person who can only teach the students the elements of knowledge or at best to reproduce that which he himself had learned before according to a certain blueprint. But a true teacher is one who will not only give the students what he himself has learned, but must also integrate the diverse elements of the knowledge that he has learned with new insights of his own or new creative combinations of his own. Within a broad scientific framework, each teacher must do research, keep up with research, and creatively find his own combination of approaches.

May I be permitted to offer something personal? My introduction to my students in almost any class includes at least the following. I tell the students that, if they take this course from me, or any other course from me, they are going to get a lot of me whether the course be Chinese culture, Hindu caste system, primitive religion, or psychological anthropology. This does not mean that we have absolutely no basis for comparison between the contents that different instructors teach students. But, with the most detailed framework, the last thing that a university teacher should look for is uniformity of content. The university is a place for intellectual exercise and in any intellectual exercise the most important thing is to keep the minds both of the instructor and the student open.

Basic Problems in the Contemporary Transformation of Traditional Societies[1]

DANIEL LERNER

Professor of Sociology, Massachusetts Institute of Technology

I have been asked to discuss basic problems in the contemporary transformation of traditional societies. I have been asked, further, to focus this discussion with reference to "the education of the undergraduate who may never become a specialist himself and yet should acquire, before he leaves college, some basic familiarity with how Oriental peoples have lived and what they have lived for." Within the severe limits of my competence, I shall seek to respond to this challenging invitation, for the objective it defines seems to me as worthy as it is difficult to attain.

My discipline is sociology, more specifically social psychology. The only "Oriental civilization" with which I have had direct and sustained contact are the diversified societies based upon, or partially derived from, the Arab-Muslim psychocultural syndrome. In considering "how these peoples have lived and what they have lived for," diversity is the keynote. The Turks and Persians have differed greatly from each other and from the Arabs. The Arab peoples have differed greatly from each other—Shia from Sunni sects, northern from southern regions, nomadic tribes from settled communities. Any accurate landscape of the Middle East must depict the ties that bind in pale pastels over a distant horizon; the bold primary colors in the foreground will represent multiplicity and diversity.

---

[1] This paper has been adapted from the author's book, *The Passing of the Traditional Society* (Glencoe, Ill., Free Press, 1958).

The unifying element in the Middle East is not its past but its future. The historic "sharing" of Muslim religion, Shariya law, Arabic language has shown itself to be a weak link. Far more compelling is the common challenge brought home to every Middle Eastern country by the process of modernization. As a world conference of leading Islamists patly stated the case:

The disorder and poverty which rage in the Middle East . . . seem incapable of being remedied except by a greater solidarity among Islamic countries and by a general modernization of these countries. But though modernization is a tangible fact, only the pace of which might require control and acceleration, Muslim solidarity is only a fleeting, variable, uncertain supposition.

Modernization, then, is the unifying principle of action in the Middle East today. This is the "contemporary transformation of traditional societies" to which our attention has been invited. Our studies at M.I.T.'s Center for International Studies have shown that the process of modernization is at work throughout the underdeveloped world, that its impact is global in scope. Our understanding of the modernization process goes beyond the Middle East to include each and all of the great and small Oriental civilizations. It is this understanding that seems worth conveying to an undergraduate who will not be a "specialist," for we are concerned with a historic process whose personal consequences are being felt acutely by many hundreds of millions of people outside of the diminutive Western world and will continue to be felt by their children's children. What do we have in mind?

BASIC TRANSFORMATION:
MOBILITY AS A SOCIAL SYSTEM

What the Oriental civilizations face in the process of "contemporary transformation" is a fundamental revision of lifeways that must touch directly every man, woman, and child now living, and yet to be born for generations ahead, in those regions of the world.

It is the shift from a traditional society to a "modern" society. The principal feature of a traditional society is *stability*. This means that the daily round of life that will be followed by each person is fixed by his birth. He is his father's son. This is his identity, this is the meaning of his existence, this defines the scope and limits of his behavior. He will till the same field, using the same seed and the same tools, as his father did. He will stoop, having learned this following his father in his youth, as his father stooped. He will know every person in the village as the "son of"—or, if he is important sociologically, the wife, daughter, or cousin of—the patriarchal head of a family. His universe is known—in its physical, social, and psychic dimensions—and it remains stable. He does not expect change, is not trained to cope with change, ignores change.

This is a somewhat idealized epitome of what traditional societies have been like on all continents and in all times. What makes them traditional societies is that, over the course of centuries, they have succeeded in evolving behavior patterns that "fit" the needs of the vast majority of their population. Through the powerful oral network of parent to child, each person knows his identity at birth and learns his daily round of life by simply being alive. When this oral network—which corresponds to the "chain of command" by which social control is exercised—no longer fulfills its functions effectively, then traditional society is passing. The transition to "modern" society is under way.

Modern societies are just as diversified as traditional societies. We have indicated that any serious student of the Middle East will represent its multiplicity and diversity in the foreground of his landscape. What they have in common is a traditional social order—a social system based on stability from generation to generation. In just the same way, there is great diversity among the modern societies. The nations of the so-called "modern West" are more striking to the detailed observer by reason of their differences than their similarities. One can hardly think of the nations grouped as Western Europe and North America—ranging from Denmark, Germany,

France through England to Canada and the United States—without promptly conjuring up images of "national differences." What they have in common, however, what cements their political, military, economic, and even ideological sense of community is that they share the principal feature of modern society, namely, a social order based upon *mobility*. They have lived through the deep and dramatic transformation of lifeways from a traditional and stable social order to a modern and mobile social order.

Western men need only reflect on the titanic struggles whereby, over the course of centuries, medieval lifeways were supplanted by modernity. Hindsight now summarizes these struggles as The Age of Exploration, The Renaissance, The Reformation, The Counter-Reformation, The Industrial Revolution. But well we know that this historical sequence worked itself out through millions of individual lives; that many suffered, others prospered, while their world was being reshaped in the modern image. In the end—and the end is not yet—all men of the West had acquired a new style of life.

What deeply complicates the "contemporary transformation" of the Oriental societies is their sense of urgency, and hence the erratic tempo of their policy planning, generated by their desire to "overtake and surpass" the modern West. For these "societies-in-a-hurry" have little patience with the historical *pace* of Western development; what happened in the West over centuries, some Orientals now seek to accomplish in years. Moreover, they want to do it their "own way." A complication of Oriental modernization is its own ethnocentrism—expressed politically in extreme nationalism and psychologically in passionate xenophobia. The hatred sown by anti-colonialism is harvested in the rejection of every appearance of foreign tutelage. Wanted are modern institutions but not modern ideologies, modern power but not modern purposes, modern wealth but not modern wisdom, modern commodities but not modern cant. It is not clear, however, that modern ways and words can be so easily and so totally sundered. Underlying the variant ideological forms which modernization took in Europe, America, and Russia, there have been certain behavioral and institutional compulsions common to all. Some Oriental leaders now seek to obviate these historical regularities, trying instead new routes and risky by-passes. We alert ourselves to the novelty of these efforts by recapitulating briefly some essential elements in the modernization of the West.

COMPONENTS OF MOBILITY:

DYNAMICS OF MODERNIZATION

The components of mobility are physical, social, and psychological. Physical mobility liberates a man from his native soil, by conferring upon him the right and means to move about the surface of the earth. Social mobility liberates a man from his native rank, by giving him the right and means to change his place in the social order. Psychic mobility liberates a man from his native *self*, by giving him the right and means to shape for himself a different personality than that with which he was born. When all three components coexist in a society, shaping the daily round of activities and expectations among its people, then we have a social order based upon the rule of change as normal.

People in the Western culture have become habituated to the sense of change and attuned to its various rhythms. Many generations ago, in the West, ordinary men found themselves unbound from their native soil and relatively free to move. Once they actually moved in large numbers, from farms to flats and from fields to factories, they became intimate with the idea of change by direct experience. This bore little resemblance to the migrant or crusading hordes of yore, driven by war or famine. This was movement by individuals, each having made a personal choice to seek elsewhere his own version of a better life.

Physical mobility so experienced naturally entrained social mobility, and gradually there grew institutions appropriate to the process. Those who gained heavily by changing their address soon wanted a convenient bank in the neighborhood to secure their treasure; also a law-and-police force to guard the neighborhood against disorder and devaluation; also a voice in prescribing standards of behavior for others. So came into operation a "system" of bourgeois values that embraced social change as normal. Rules of the game had to be worked out for adjudicating conflicts over the direction and rate of change. Who was to gain, how, and how much? As the profits to be gained from mobility became evident to all, conflicts over access to the channels of opportunity became sharper. The process can be traced through the evolution of Western property and tax laws, whose major tendency is to protect the "haves" without disqualifying the "have-nots." It was by protecting every man's opportunity to gain that the modern West turned decisively in the direction of social mobility.

Social institutions founded on voluntary participation by mobile individuals required a new array of skills and a new test of merit. Every person, according to the new democratic theory, was equally entitled to acquire the skills needed for shaping his own "future" in the great society. The vigorous controversy over public education that agitated the eighteenth century produced a net affirmation of equal opportunity. In every Western country, the verdict was pronounced that education should be freely available to all who wanted it, and in some countries whether they wanted it or not. Thus, the idea spread that personal mobility is itself a first-order value; the sense grew that social morality is essentially the ethics of social change. A man is what he may become; a society is its potential. These notions passed out of the realm of debate into the Western law and mores.

A mobile society has to encourage rationality, for the calculus of choice shapes individual behavior and conditions its rewards. People come to see the social future as manipulable rather than ordained and their personal prospects in terms of achievement rather than heritage. Rationality is purposive: ways of thinking and acting are instruments of intention (not articles of faith); men succeed or fail by the test of what they accomplish (not what they worship). So, whereas traditional man tended to reject innovation by saying, "It has never been thus," the contemporary Westerner is more likely to ask, "Does it work?" and try the new way without further ado.

The psychic gap between these two postures is vast. It took much interweaving through time, between ways of doing and ways of thinking, before men could work out a style of daily living with change that felt consistent and seamless. The experience of mobility through successive generations gradually evolved participant lifeways which feel "normal" today. Indeed, while past centuries established the public practices of the mobile society, it has been the work of the twentieth century to diffuse widely a *mobile sensibility* so adaptive to change that rearrangement of the self-system is its distinctive mode.

Empathy is the inner mechanism which enables newly mobile persons to *operate efficiently* in a changing world. Empathy, to simplify the matter, is the capacity to see oneself in the other fellow's situation. This is an indispensable skill for people moving out of traditional settings. Ability to empathize may make all the difference, for example, when the newly mobile persons are villagers who grew up knowing all the extant individuals, roles, and relationships in their environment. Outside his village or tribe, each must meet new individuals, recognize new roles, and learn new relationships involving himself. A rich literature of humor and pathos once dealt with the adventures of the country bumpkin in the big city, the bewildered immigrant in a strange land. They had to learn their way in these new settings. Learn, in swelling numbers, they did. The story of the nineteenth-century West includes this learning, which now enters the story of the twentieth-century East. Accordingly, we are interested in the mobile personality mainly as a social phenomenon with a history. Our concern is with the large historical movement, now becoming visible in the Orient, of which an enlarged capacity for empathy is the distinctive psychic component. Our interest is to clarify the process whereby the high empathizer tends to become also the cash customer, the radio listener, the voter.

It is a major hypothesis of this study that high empathic capacity is the predominant personal style only in modern society, which is distinctively industrial, urban, literate and *participant*. Traditional society is nonparticipant—it deploys people by kinship into communities isolated from each other and from a center; without an urban-rural division of labor, it develops few needs requiring economic interdependence; lacking the bonds of interdependence, people's horizons are limited by locale and their decisions involve only other *known* people in *known* situations. Hence, there is no need for a transpersonal common doctrine formulated in terms of shared secondary symbols—a national "ideology" which enables persons unknown to each other to engage in political controversy or achieve "consensus" by comparing their opinions. Modern society is participant in that it functions by "consensus"—individuals making personal decisions on public issues must concur often enough with other individuals they do not know to make possible a stable common governance. Among the marks of this historic achievement in social organization, which we call participant society, are that most people go through school, read newspapers, receive cash payments in jobs they are legally free to change, buy goods for cash in an open market, vote in elections which actually decide among competing candidates, and express opinions on many matters which are not their personal business.

For, in any society, only when the accepted model of behavior is emulated by the population at large does it become the predominant personal style. The model of behavior developed by modern society is characterized by empathy, a high capacity for rearranging the self-system on short notice. Whereas the isolate communities of traditional society functioned well on the basis of a highly constrictive personality, the interdependent sectors of modern society require widespread participation. This in turn requires an expansive and adaptive self-system, ready to incorporate new roles and to identify personal values with public issues. This is why modernization of any society has involved the great characterological transformation we call psychic mobility. The latent statistical assertion involved here is this: in modern society, *more* individuals exhibit *higher* empathic capacity than in any previous society.

The historic increase of psychic mobility begins with the expansion of physical travel. Historians conventionally date the modern era from the Age of Exploration. Every Western schoolboy knows the names of Cabot, Columbus, Cortez and is dimly aware that they "opened new worlds." This was an initial phase in the modern expansion of human communication. Gradually the technical means of transporting live bodies improved and physical displacement became an experience lived through by millions of plain folk earlier bounden to some ancestral spot. Geographical mobility became, in this phase, the usual vehicle of social mobility. It remained for a later time to make vivid that each mobile soma of the earlier epoch housed a psyche. We accent the contemporaneity of the psychic dimension, because the moral injunction to "look shining at new styles of architecture" is something new in the world.

The expansion of psychic mobility means that more people now command greater skill in imagining themselves as strange persons in strange situations, places, and times than did people in any previous historical epoch. In our time, indeed, the spread of empathy around the world is accelerating. The earlier increase of physical experience through transportation has been multiplied by the spread of *mediated* experience through mass communication. A generation before Columbus sailed to the New World, Gutenberg activated his printing press. Radio, film, and television climax the evolution set into motion by Gutenberg. The mass media opened to the large masses of mankind the infinite *vicarious* universe. Many more millions of persons in the world were to be affected directly, and perhaps more profoundly, by the communication media than by the transportation agencies. By obviating the physical displacement of travel, the media accented the psychic displacement of vicarious experience.

The mass media have been great teachers of interior manipulation. They disciplined Western man in those empathic skills which spell modernity. They also portrayed for him the roles he might confront and elucidated the opinions he might need. Their continuing spread in our century is performing a similar function on a world scale. The Middle East shows the marks of this historic encounter. As a young bureaucrat in Iran put it, "The movies are like a teacher to us, who tells us what to do and what not." The global network of mass media has already recruited enough new participants in all corners of the earth to make "the opinions of mankind" a real factor instead of a fine phrase in the arena of world politics. There now exists, and its scope accelerates at an extraordinary pace, a genuine "world public opinion." This has happened because millions of people, who never left their native heath, now are learning to imagine how life is organized in different lands and under different codes than their own. That this signifies a net increase in human imaginativeness, so construed, is the proposition under consideration.

A second proposition of this large historical order derives from the observation that modern media systems have flourished only in societies that are modern by other tests. That is, the media spread psychic mobility most efficiently among peoples who have achieved in some measure the antecedent conditions of geographic and social mobility. The converse of this proposition is also true; no modern society functions efficiently without a developed system of mass media. Our historic forays indicate that the conditions which define modernity form an interlocking "system." They grow conjointly, in the normal situation, or they become stunted severally.

It seems clear that people who live together in a common polity will develop patterned ways of distributing *information* along with other commodities. It is less obvious that these information flows will interact with the distribution of power, wealth, status at so many points as to form a system—and, moreover, a system so tightly interwoven that institutional variation in one sector will be accompanied by regular and determinate variation in the other sectors.

Yet, just this degree of interaction between communication and social systems is what our historical exploration suggests.

THE SYSTEM OF MODERNITY

The sociologist is solicited by the idea of a social system. When he can specify the necessary and sufficient components that explain the operation of a society, he is able to distinguish what is sociologically essential from those features of life in a given time and place that may be interesting and important but not indispensable. To cope with a historical process, which introduced common sociological results in many different places at different times, he is likely to seek stages or phases that enable him to identify the key variables and the sequence of interaction between these variables which made them into a "sociological system." This is the procedure we followed in dealing with modernization as a social system that evolved historically.

The secular evolution of a participant society appears to involve a regular sequence of three phases. Urbanization comes first, for cities alone have developed the complex of skills and resources which characterize the modern industrial economy. Within this urban matrix develop both of the attributes which distinguish the next two phases—literacy and media growth. There is a close reciprocal relationship between these, for the literate develop the media which in turn spread literacy. But, historically, literacy performs the key function in the second phase. The capacity to read, at first acquired by relatively few people, equips them to perform the varied tasks required in the modernizing society. Not until the third phase, when the elaborate technology of industrial development is fairly well advanced, does a society begin to produce newspapers, radio networks, and motion pictures on a massive scale. This, in turn, accelerates the spread of literacy. Out of this interaction develop those institutions of participation (e.g., voting) which we find in all advanced modern societies. For countries in transition today, these high correlations suggest that literacy and media participation may be considered as a supply-and-demand reciprocal in a communication market whose locus, at least in its historical inception, can only be urban.

Later, we shall examine the idea that a common psychological mechanism underlies these phases—that it is the more empathic individuals who respond, in the first place, to the lure of cities, schools, media. Urban residence, schooling, and media exposure then train and reinforce the empathic predisposition that was already present. On this view, the modern "style of life" can nowadays be acquired as a whole by individuals living in modernizing societies. This interpretation is quite plausible, but it does not clarify what happens to empathic individuals who are ready and able to modernize more rapidly and completely than their society permits. A large and important class of Middle Easterners are in this position today. Our data on 73 countries, distributed over all the continents of the earth, indicate that many millions of individuals everywhere are in the same position. This further suggests that the model of modernization follows an autonomous historical logic— that each phase tends to generate the next phase by some mechanism which operates independently of cultural or doctrinal variations. To understand the position of those millions who may be caught in some historical lag today, we look more closely at our three phases.

The first phase, then, is *urbanization*. It is the transfer of population from scattered hinterlands to urban centers that stimulates the needs and provides the conditions needed for "take-off" toward widespread participation. Only cities require a largely literate population to function properly—for the organization of urban life assumes enough literacy to read labels, sign checks, ride subways. A population of illiterates might learn that they are not to smoke and spit in the subway, or that express trains run on the local tracks between 5 and 7 A.M.; but trial-and-error can be a wasteful societal procedure. The primitive social function of literacy, as of all skills, is to reduce waste of human effort. Its higher function is to train the skilled labor force with which cities develop the industrial complex that produces commodities for cash customers, including newspapers, radios, and movies for media consumers. Cities produce the machine tools of modernization. Accordingly, increases of urbanization tend to multiply national increases in literacy and media participation in every society. By drawing people from their rural communities, cities create the demand for impersonal communication. By promoting literacy and media, cities supply this demand. Once the basic industrial plant is in operation, the development of a participant society passes into a subsequent phase. When voluntary urbanization exceeds 25 percent, thereby assuring the conditions of modern production, further urbanization no longer automatically guarantees equivalent increases in consumption. The need then shifts to modernizing the conditions which govern consumption.

Of this second phase, *literacy* is both the index and agent. To spread consumption of urban products beyond the city limits, literacy is an efficient instrument. The great symbol of this phase is the Sears-Roebuck catalogue. The mail-order house replaces the peddler only when enough people can read catalogues and write letters. In this sense literacy is also the basic skill required for operation of a media system. Only the literate produce the media contents which mainly the literate consume. Hence, once societies are about 25 percent urbanized, the highest correlation of media consumption is with literacy. We shall soon describe more fully how literacy operates as the pivotal agent in the transition to a fully participant society. Here, we wish to suggest that by the time this second phase gets well under way, a different social system is in operation than that which governed behavior in a society that was under 10 percent urban and under 40 percent (roughly, less than half) literate. For, when most people in a society have become literate, they tend to generate all sorts of new desires and to develop the means of satisfying them.

It is this interplay of new desires and satisfactions which characterizes the third phase of modernization, namely *media participation*.

Once people are equipped to handle the new experiences produced by mobility (via their move to the city) and to handle the new experiences conveyed by media (via their literacy), they now seek the satisfactions which integrate these skills. They discover the tingle of wondering "what will happen next"—the tingle which sounds the knell of traditional society, of routinized lifeways in which everyone *knew* what would happen next because it had to follow what came before. To satisfy this new desire requires the personal skill of empathy which, when spread among large numbers of persons, makes possible the social institution of media participation. This was the phase in which the West developed the "penny press," early symbol of the accelerating supply and demand for media products, which continues today with the pocket radio and the portable TV. It is characteristic of this phase, as the production, consumption reciprocal of media participation develops, that economists come to find production of radio sets a useful index of growth in total industrial production.

For rising media participation tends to raise participation in all sectors of the social system. In accelerating the spread of empathy, it also diffuses those other modern demands to which participant institutions have responded: in the consumer's economy via cash (and credit), in the public forum via opinion, in the representative polity via voting. Other studies had already shown high pairwise correlations between our indices and economic participation—e.g., around the world, literacy correlated at .84 with per capita income and at .87 with industrialization. Accordingly, we undertook to establish their connection with political participation, in such fashion as to determine whether the interdependence between these four participant sectors was genuinely "systemic."

We did this by multiple correlations of the four indices already described. This procedure enabled us to rotate each index in the matrix, thereby obtaining the simultaneous degree of correlation between it and all three of the other indices. Based on 54 countries (those reporting data on all four indices), the coefficients obtained in turn for each dependent variable are reported below:

Dependent Variable	Multiple Correlation Coefficient
Urbanization	.61
Literacy [a]	.91
Media participation	.84
Political participation	.82

[a] A notable feature of all literacy correlations was their stability, regardless of sample size. The correlation of .82 with media participation was for N = 54 countries; for N = 73 countries it was .84 (standard deviation was 31.4). UNESCO literacy data come grouped in five categories, each covering 20 percentage points. All other data were ungrouped.

The size of these coefficients demonstrates that the relationship between the four sectors *is* systemic. These independent tests of the participant style of life do in fact "go together" in 54 extant societies. Beyond this, their ascending order appears to support the historical phasing that has been sketched.

That the urbanization coefficient should be lowest is as expected. Our earlier data indicated that about 10 percent of the population must be urbanized before the "take-off" occurs. At this point, it becomes "economical" to develop literacy and media; hence urbanization and other modernizing trends grow together for a period. But, after a certain degree of urbanization exists, then further growth of cities no longer affects other factors in the same degree. Our analysis locates this "critical optimum" at 25 percent, after which urbanization ceases to play a determinant role because enough people have been relocated in cities to assure the personnel requirements of modern production. As many countries in our sample long ago passed this urbanizing optimum, and since have turned to other factors to maintain self-sustaining growth, urbanization naturally yields the lowest (though still high) coefficient of correlation.

That the literacy coefficient is highest also supports our analysis.

Literacy is the basic personal skill that underlies the whole modernizing sequence. With literacy people acquire more than the simple skill of reading. Professor Becker concludes that the written word first equipped men with a "transpersonal memory"; Professor Innis writes that, historically, "man's activities and powers were roughly extended in proportion to the increased use of written records." The very act of achieving distance and control over a formal language gives people access to the world of vicarious experience and trains them to use the complicated mechanism of empathy which is needed to cope with this world. It supplies media consumers, who stimulate media production, thereby activating the reciprocal relationship whose consequences for modernization we have noted. This is why media participation, in every country we have studied, exhibits a centripetal tendency. Those who read newspapers also tend to be the heaviest consumers of movies, broadcasts, and all other media products. Throughout the Middle East, illiterate respondents said of their literate compatriots: "They live in another world." Thus, literacy becomes the sociological pivot in the activation of psychic mobility, the publicly shared skill which binds modern man's varied daily round into a consistent participant lifestyle.

We come, then, to political participation. Democratic governance comes late, historically, and typically appears as a crowning institution of the participant society. That the voting coefficient is so high indicates that these 54 countries have achieved stable growth at a high level of modernity. In these countries, the urban literate tends to be also a newspaper reader, a cash customer, and a voter. The modern system of self-sustaining growth operates across the land in these 54 countries—as their cities sprouted suburbs and their urban districts grew into "urban regions," their national increase of literacy and participation kept pace. This capacity to incorporate continuing social change within the existing framework of institutions has become a distinctive structural feature of the developed modern societies. In a century that has reinstated revolution as a method of social change, they have managed to adapt their own accelerated growth mainly by non-violent procedures.

THE MODEL OF TRANSITION

Our historical model provided suitable terms for describing the degree of modernization present in a given society at a given time. The indices of urbanization, literacy, media and political participation discriminated efficiently the relative positions in 1950 of very many countries on all the continents of the world. But the model was static to this point. A dynamic component was needed to show how a country *moved* from one phase to the next, why an urban person regularly *became* a literate and a radio-listener and a voter. Such a dynamic component must connect institutional changes with alterations in the prevailing personal style.

We have already identified the characterological transformation that accompanied modernization as psychic mobility, with empathy as its mechanism. The questions now were: how can empathy be tested? How can the results of such testing be collated with the indices of participant behavior? What we needed to learn was whether a person who shows high empathy also exhibits the other attributes, and vice versa. Since empathy is an autonomous personality variable, it is not revealed by any census data, but must be elicited through psychological testing of individuals. At this point the Middle East survey supplied the missing link. The interviews contained a set of nine "projective questions" which we used to test each respondent's empathic capacity:

(1) If you were made editor of a newspaper, what kind of a paper would you run?

(2) What do you think you miss by not knowing what the newspapers have to say?

(3) How do you think people who go to the movies differ from those who don't?

(4) If you were put in charge of a radio station, what kinds of programs would you like to put on?

(5) If for some reason you could not live in our country, what other country would you choose to live in?

(6) Suppose that I could tell you anything you wanted to know about (this country): What two questions would you be most interested in asking?

(7) What is the biggest problem that people in the same circumstances as yourself face in life?

(8) What do you think people in the same circumstances as yourself can do to help solve this problem?

(9) Suppose that you were made head of the government. What are some of the things you would do?

What these questions have in common is that they ask the respondent to imagine himself in a situation other than his real one. They are "role-playing" questions that require, for responsiveness, some capacity to empathize—to imagine what it must be like to be head of a government, editor of a newspaper, manager of a radio station, or even "people like yourself." The strenuousness of such demands upon persons untutored in empathic skills was underlined by the many respondents, in every country, who thought of suicide rather than imagine themselves in these exalted ranks. "My God! How can you say such a thing?" gasped a shepherd in Turkey when such questions were put to him.

The historical course of empathy was underscored for me, while working on these interviews, by an advertisement that came through the mail one morning. Printed across the envelope, in bold red letters, was the query: "Suppose you were the editor of *Time*. . . ." The circular letter inside described the typical workday of a *Time* editor. An American mass-circulation magazine mails such an item to millions of names, assembled from a variety of "lists," confident that the "teaser question" on the envelope will be comprehensible, interesting, and entertaining. In the Middle East, for many millions, such questions are baffling, disturbing, and even impious: "It has never been thus!"

Our task was to devise a method to determine the degree of association between empathy, as tested by these questions, and the life-ways of modernity. The solution of this problem provided our theory of modernization with the dynamic component needed to analyze ongoing changes in the Middle East today. Our solution was to show, empirically, that persons who are urban, literate, participant, and empathic *differ* from persons who lack any of these attributes—and differ on a significant personal trait which is distinctive of the modern style. Such a trait is "having opinions" on public matters. Traditional man has habitually regarded public matters as none of his business. For the modern men in a participant society, on the contrary, such matters are fraught with interest and importance. A broad range of opinions on public questions can be taken as a distinctive mark of modernity. Accordingly, the central schema of this study can be represented in the basic typology of modernization in Table 1.

Table 1. The Basic Typology of Modernization

Type		*Literacy*	*Urbanism*	*Media Participation*	*Empathy*	*Opinion Range*
Modern		+	+	+	+	1
Transitional						
	A	—	+	+	+	2
	B	—	—	+	+	3
	C	—	—	—	+	4
Traditional		—	—	—	—	5

If modernization is the transition to participant society, then the direction of change in public communication is toward a constantly expanding opinion arena. The significant mode of participation, in any network of human communication, is by sharing a common interest in the message it transmits—i.e., by having opinions about the matters which concern other participants (nonparticipation, conversely, consists of neither knowing nor caring about the messages relayed through a given network). In a large public network, such as that of a nation, perfect participation is impossible—and perhaps undesirable. A network should hardly be manageable in which all citizens attended to all messages and expressed opinions on all public questions. There are determinate limits—maximal as well as minimal —to the degree of participation appropriate for particular networks. The modernizing tendency is toward networks that can handle maximum participation and concurrently to develop the participants needed to man these networks.

A person becomes a participant by learning to "have opinions"— further, the more numerous and varied the matters on which he has opinions, the more participant he is. To rank each respondent as a participant in the Middle Eastern opinion arena, we counted the number and variety of items in the questionnaire on which he expressed *some* opinion (i.e., did *not* say "I don't know" or "I have no opinion"). This enabled us to find a number for each respondent which determined his rank-order in the column headed "Opinion Range." Those in rank 1 had the most opinions, those in rank 2 somewhat fewer opinions, and so on down to those in rank 5 with the fewest (or no) opinions.

We then sought to determine whether, as hypothesized, the higher a person's opinion range, the more likely he was to score high on all indices of modernity. And so, as the scale patterns show, it turned out. The top opinion-holders (rank 1) typically were literate, urban, media participants, and high empathizers. Among illiterates, those living in cities tended to have more opinions (rank 2) than rurals. Among illiterate rurals, those with a significant measure of media exposure scored higher (rank 3) than those without such exposure. This left a group which—in terms of literacy, residence, media exposure—should have been homogenous in the opinion range but, in fact, was not. Some of these individuals had significantly more opinions than the others. The only satisfactory way to account for this divergence was by our personality variable—empathy. For what distinguished these illiterate, rural, nonparticipant individuals (rank 4) from their peers (rank 5) was a keener interest in impersonal matters, a deeper desire to become participants of the opinion arena. They were marked less by their manifest ways than by their latent wants.

Once this was clear, our data fell into place. For the true transitional is defined, dynamically, by what he wants to become. What differentiates him from his traditional peers is a different *latent structure* of aptitudes and attitudes. The aptitude is *empathy*—he "sees" things the others do not see, "lives" in a world populated by imaginings alien to the constrictive world of the others. The attitude is *desire*—he wants *really* to see the things he has hitherto "seen" only in his mind's eye, *really* to live in the world he has "lived" in only vicariously. These are the sources of his deviant ways. When many individuals show deviation in this direction, then a transition is under way in their society. This transition is at work in every Middle Eastern country, with results that spell the passing of traditional society from that area of the world.

There is reason to believe that this model helps to account for the "contemporary transformation" now at work in many Oriental societies. There is also reason to believe that this model, because it derives from a historic sense of how the Western people have lived and what they have lived for, may be an illuminating way of teaching the undergraduate how Oriental peoples have lived, what they have lived for, and what they are now in process of becoming.

Comment: Comparativists and Uniquists

RICHARD D. LAMBERT

Professor of Sociology, University of Pennsylvania

Daniel Lerner has given us a very good paper. There can be so little question about its competence and it is presented with such clarity that I am going to touch upon the content of it only tangentially. For the purposes of this conference, I am going to consider this paper as representative of a developing trend in scholarly work dealing with Asia which, for want of a better term, might be called *comparativist*. I mean to exclude from this term those scholars who compare total cultures or institutions within those cultures in order to emphasize and illuminate the differences and the special characteristics of each—*contrastists,* if I may ignore grammar and make a parallel set of endings. Rather, I have in mind scholars who examine a number of societies with a limited number of variables in mind to determine whether there are any uniformities or regularities in the distribution of the variables. Studies in the latter vein are usually undertaken with at least the trappings of scientific method. It is not uncommon for them to find a remarkable similarity among countries, or that different countries represent stages in a single transformation (one-way or cyclical), or that one or a few variables are the keys to understanding the apparent great diversity among societies. The present paper argues all three of these positions at once. Most of the people at this conference are not comparativists in the sense I have just indicated, but are what might be called *uniquists*. This term implies something more than the fact that each of us tends to be working on only one area, it implies the belief that the culture we are studying is in many ways unique. Light is to be shed upon one aspect of the culture by probing more deeply into its unique setting. In contrast to the comparativist realm where the grand system builder is king, in the ranks of the uniquist, the man with the greatest depth of erudition in the smallest fragment of a single culture reigns supreme.

One should not infer that the division into comparativists and uniquists is just another of those clusterings of pendants which are as ephemeral as they are trivial. Unfortunately, the division bids well to become a battle line with all of the closing of ranks among allies and mutual denigration of enemies so often found in tribal warfare. The current overlap of the two categories in which members of each group now dabble a little in the other camp's province is likely to be discouraged. Just as the interdisciplinary wars have some permanence, and just as the area specialist is genuinely juxtaposed against the disciplinary specialist in some disciplines, so the inherent logic and internal ordering of the camps of the comparativists and the uniquists moves them to engage in a continuing dialectic that has already begun to take on ritual aspects. For instance, I have in mind the typical cross-national comparative symposium, which proceeds somewhat as follows. One or more comparativists call a conference in which a concept or a variable—such as, industrialization, feudalism, labor commitment, attitudes toward wealth, acculturation, and the like—are to be examined by scholars who are to write on the application of that concept or variable to the geographic region on which they specialize. To stimulate the individual participants and to give the various papers some centralization of focus, a conceptual and theoretical paper is written first, generally skimpy in substantive content. At this point, the uniquists tend to write papers which find the conceptual and theoretical framework either incorrect or irrelevant to their area. Before the whole affair is put between hard covers and published, the comparativists normally write a summary article pointing out how the uniquists either misquoted or misunderstood what was said in the original paper.

This type of published symposium is merely a tangible form of a continuing dialogue between comparativists and uniquists. It dramatizes the type of problem involved in the topic central to the present conference: how best to teach undergraduate courses in Asian civilization. Most of the suggestions I have heard here for the structuring of such courses stress the uniquist approach; that is that the contrast of a non-Western with their own culture will lift the student out of his own cultural bind, that one should study at least one other culture than his own thoroughly, that the student will enhance his ability to universally empathize. It is a moot point as to whether these goals require or in what ways they can be served by the comparativist materials. At the same time in some of the social science disciplines, some of the best of the research scholars will not be bound by the uniquist approach to a single area and the pressure upon the uniquists to use comparativist findings will steadily mount.

The resistance to the use of comparativist writings is not based upon trivial academic jealousies but involves genuine intellectual reservations concerning their soundness. Perhaps I can dramatize this situation by taking the present paper and subjecting it to a brief exercise in the "yes but" or "what about" technique which typically accompanies a uniquist's reading of a comparativist's work. As a uniquist, I would try to see whether the statements fitted the case of South Asian societies, and secondly, whether the variables specified by Mr. Lerner would be those which would most effectively organize and illuminate events in South Asia. In the one case, my criterion is validity, in the other, strategy. For instance, if one takes Mr. Lerner's indices of modernization, the increase in number of literates has been great, in certain areas of the sub-continent, even spectacular, but to lay a modernization continuum along side of the qantitative increase in literacy would not be very helpful. Certainly, irregularities in the demand side of education reflected in the frequency of lapses into illiteracy and the growing number of educated unemployed must be considered, and the qualitative aspects of content and style in education must be considered to make literacy a meaningful index of modernity. Similarly, urbanization is not the same as urbanity. Except perhaps for the first stage of severing conservative peasant ties, increasing urbanization implies little more than its literal meaning, more people in the cities, particularly in what Sjoberg calls the pre-industrial city. Lerner's key factor in modernization—increasing empathy—also leaves me a bit puzzled. One immediately asks empathy with whom, or is this solely a unidimensional quantitative variable? If so, it seems to make little sense for much of India. The argument on mass media seems to derive more from its implications of a higher technological level rather than elaborateness of the communications network. The latter may be extensive indeed for certain kinds of messages in pre-industrial societies. In any event, I suspect this a particularity of the Near East. The implications of the transformation of peasant societies from tranquil, stable equilibria to rapidly changing, unsettled modern societies exaggerates a bit the earlier lack of change in many regions in countries. In essence, Lerner's conception is one of two alternative social evolutionary concepts, the one that holds that olden times were idyllic, bucolic, certain, and non-individuated until the twin demons of the city and industry despoiled the landscape. The other alternative, perhaps best associated with such phrases as *Pax Britannica,* holds that chaos is gradually surrendering to some semblance of order. The juxtaposition of these two alternate theories of history makes one wonder a bit about the extent of the difference between olden times and now. Perhaps the most serious "yes but" to Lerner's paper concerns the treatment of all individuals and all responses as if they were of roughly equal weight, a procedure implicit in many attitude polling techniques. If there were ever societies in which the opinions and characteristics of strategic influentials should be given more weight in arriving at national indices, it is the societies of South Asia. In Mr. Lerner's larger work on which this is based, attention to such matters is surely paid, but the specificity of the weightings to each country supports the uniquist position rather than the comparativists.

But I have no desire to engage in a long critique of this paper which, as I said at the outset, is a very good one. My intent is only to show that dozens of substantitive and methodical questions immediately occur to a uniquist in reading any comparativist paper and to inquire into the implications of the reservations for the future collaboration of the two types of scholarship. So far, the responses of the comparativists to the types of criticism given above are fairly clear. At the beginning of most comparative work is an apologetic, self-abasing paragraph which confesses to the author's lack of expertise on each of the countries covered. Most likely, this is an exaggeration—the comparativist is at home in at least one culture other than his own and he tends to use this for his illustrative materials. Thus, the apologia is never so strong as it sounds. Second, the comparativist readily admits the crudity of his indices and the roughness of fit in individual cases, but argues that the uniquists are certainly not generating any better ones and a start must be made at comparison or all of the separate little studies will have little cumulative effect. Third, he waits patiently for the scholars on non-Western areas to become sufficiently numerous and skilled that they will develop some of their own integrating superstructures so that he need not deal with primary or heavily detailed secondary works in order to be authoritative.

But this conference is not really concerned with the woes of the comparativists. Our problem is the reverse: how to prevent the threatening divide from cutting uniquists off from the very valuable services of the comparativists, or more specifically at this time, how to utilize their materials in our essentially uniquist courses. There is, of course, no one major venture which will solve these problems, and, at any event, the friction is likely to be with us for sometime to come. It is unlikely that uniquists will adopt any one comparativist's model of a society or a transformation. For one thing, like many religions, such models tend to be mutually exclusive and they lay claim to total loyalty. For another, the fit with each of the countries we are teaching is too loose to satisfy our scholarly tastes.

We can, however, use comparativists' schema and terminology as sensitizers to order and select from among the almost infinite number of facts about another culture we could conceivably want to convey to our students. In particular, comparativists' concepts can be extremely useful as organizing principles for students' reading, even if their lack of exact fit to the culture being studied must be pointed out by the instructor. I have heard several scholars lecturing on different countries usefully employ the concept of feudalism as a clarifying device while they were busily describing and decrying its inapplicability to the case in hand. Another major use which uniquists might find for comparativists' studies is as a very fruitful source of hypothesis for their own and their students' research. Such studies can at least help us to look for the things that "should" have happened but didn't and make us wonder whether the theory is wrong or needs some limitations upon its domain. They can also help us to begin the painful process of asking questions and writing up our results in a fashion that the accumulation of knowledge to some level above the first-stage processing of raw materials may be accomplished by the uniquists themselves.

Most important of all, I hope that we will self-consciously inhibit the development of the threatened comparativist versus uniquist warfare.

Comment: Choosing a Position

RICHARD K. BEARDSLEY

Professor of Anthropology, University of Michigan

Contrasts in the viewpoints ably expressed by Douglas G. Haring and Daniel Lerner certainly merit the attention of anyone debating what to teach students about Oriental cultures and how to express it. One cannot teach everything or serve every purpose; a commitment to one goal may be irreconcilable with the path to another goal. Together, these two papers neatly illuminate contrary positions in a situation where either extreme may be more rewarding than a midpoint compromise.

Should one teach about the "cultures-under-transformation" of the present day, as Professor Lerner recommends, or select the more traditional or classic aspects of Oriental cultures which by their very strangeness, Professor Haring argues, pique the students into reexamining their assumptions about culture in general? Should one present the rich, interwoven details of whatever Oriental society one knows best and merely reach outward for frequent comparison elsewhere, as Haring does; or begin with many societies (or their recurrent features) built into a model and discuss any given Asian society as an instructive but not unique test for this model? Haring tends to point out contrasts with the students' own culture, whereas Lerner reveals similarities. Which method takes us farther in our teaching —or, viewed in another way, which engages the student more quickly?

My own impression is that these choices are not to be resolved either by snap judgments or by lining up teachers into partisan camps to defend one or another alternative and then counting noses to discover the winner. The alternatives have to be considered carefully, for they tend to produce students with quite different outlook on many subjects. Yet, each one of us, as a teacher, finds it possible to turn in either direction, and must constantly make these or similar choices within himself. Our advantage in having these papers is that they help us to perceive quite clearly some consequences of each alternative approach as it is voiced against the other in unpremeditated counterpoint.

It occurs to me that the choice of alternative has to do with the temperament of the teacher as well as with the subject matter or the goal to be attained. It is clear that Haring, along with many other anthropologists, is rather "thing-minded," while Lerner is more strictly "concept-minded." Haring snares the interest of students with an object—be it a tangible thing such as a dictionary or a bit of weaving, or a less literally material thing such as a particular religious activity or bit of familial behavior—and then reveals the sociocultural network that produced the object; whereas Lerner first alerts the student to a concept and then proceeds to test it against observed fact, intriguing the student by his gamble that the concept will not shatter against fact. His game is played primarily with abstract counters, whereas Haring's opening gambit, at least, may involve quite visible and tangible elements. Now, this sort of choice is partly a matter of temperament and training; a teacher's method must seem natural for him to succeed, though he may train himself ideally to handle "things" as well as "concepts."

Viewed another way, Haring's approach is something of an art, depending on contrast, timing, and the instructor's intuition as to what specific subject matter is most appropriate at what moment. Lerner's approach is the stricter in scientific terms, being controlled by rules and conditions he makes clear beforehand. The abovementioned analogy to game-playing is not frivolous. As his discussant, Professor Richard Lambert, observes, Lerner must call his shots before he makes his move, not afterward; he predicts that conditions required by his hypothesis will, in fact, exist in the societies examined. While this is game-playing, it is also scientific use of the comparative method; whereas Haring's comparisons, though perhaps equally telling, are not predicted beforehand.

Now, inasmuch as comparisons—whether implicit or explicit, preplanned or ad hoc—reveal both regularities and variances running across societies, there is some room for either approach, the one that stresses general, widely shared features or the one that stresses particular, distinctive features. Social scientists are deeply concerned with inculcating in their students a respect for orderly, systematic thinking, which in their own research they recognize to be difficult and, as yet, only barely adequate for certain problems in the study of alien cultures. This very concern suggests that, as Lambert says, in due time the concept-manipulators, the systematic comparativists, the persons most interested in common processes of organization and change will grow in numbers and strength as against the thing-minded, particularizing persons most interested in studying Oriental societies in their own terms. Strong pressures in the scientific direction are evident. Yet, we must note that difficulties arise even when teaching about foreign cultures gets most scientific.

The systematists may deprecate Haring's approach in several aspects. It is partial and selective on an intuitive rather than precontrolled basis; however well-rounded the presentation of one culture (Japan), few if any others are given similar treatment. His usual comparisons are historical, not structural or functional, and may encourage students to make wild comparisons by analogy in the absence of a formal-functional test of similarity. And so on. Yet, attempting to view the Lerner approach with equally skeptical criteria, one wonders whether it does not suffer the usual disadvantages of a closed system, which cannot be enriched from new data but must be broken down and rebuilt. Convincing as the co-variant indices are for urbanism, literacy, mass-media participation, and empathy, as long as one perceives society as unitary, how does one introduce new elements as one perceives their importance? Suppose we come to perceive two sorts of mass media, one developed by and for the state in its own interest, the other evolving in the individual interests of its citizens? Chinese and Egyptian sponsorship of mass media for propaganda in the state interest, in contrast to the history of mass media as a vehicle for popular expression in Europe, suggests that one may have to perceive (1) the people vis-à-vis (2) the state as separate though interlocked entities. That is, one must go outside the particular comparative system Professor Lerner offers. Again, the figures show that these factors of urbanism, literacy, mass media, political participation, and empathy have strong indicial value; they measure a process that occurs over and over again. But are they more than measures? Can one judge that factor X, preceding factor Y, in fact influences or causes the latter, rather than look for an unnamed independent variable outside the system as the sufficient cause, for both factors? Does not market-production or the industrial process, diversifying society, somehow make city life different in the last three centuries from the preceding several millennia during which cities existed? Whether this suggestion be accepted or not, my point is that the decision as to causal relations seems to require historical, qualitative, and partly intuitional judgments not unlike those made by Haring.

In raising such queries about these papers, however, I verge all too near uttering a "Yeah, but . . ." to their authors. Neither approach merits an attack on its content at this point, for each constructively meets a challenge that is not quite answered in the other paper. Rather than seek a middle ground of reconciliation, I recommend both to the reader as able and persuasive statements of opposing extremes along an axis where true compromise is difficult, but where each of us, as a teacher, must choose a position, preferably with a clear view of the consequences. At the same time, I recommend a careful review of the discussion, particularly Professor Lambert's lucid rephrasing of the opposition I allude to here, and Professor Hsu's defense of the relativist position implicit in Professor Haring's paper.

Part Five: General

The Integration of Asian Studies into the Undergraduate Curriculum

MERIBETH CAMERON

Academic Dean and Professor of History, Mount Holyoke College

My only claim to appear in a symposium of this sort is professional longevity, a claim which however should appeal to students of cultures in which age has been a source of honor. Ever since 1928, I have been concerned with the teaching of Far Eastern history to undergraduates in American colleges. Whether in this third of a century I have achieved the integration of Asian studies into any of the many curricula with which I have been involved I am not sure; I am sure that in the process I have suffered disintegration, so that I now am a split personality—part teacher, part administrator.

Our topic is "The Integration of Asian Studies into the Undergraduate Curriculum." The American undergraduate college, the institution with which this conference is concerned, wears two faces. On the one hand, it is the prime agency for liberal, general, non-professional education. But it is also a pre-professional institution, preparing students for the professional education of the graduate schools. These two aspects of our undergraduate program are represented by the two divisions into which nearly all American curricula fall—the general education program and the "major." Every college faculty member is aware of the pull of these two purposes. Is one's chief responsibility to serve the unwashed who are going no further in one's particular discipline than the basic course will take them, or is it to foster the special interest of those who intend to or may be persuaded to major in the field?

Asiatic studies belong in both parts of the curriculum—they have an essential role in general education and in specialization. Why this is so, I do not need to say. We have been hearing moving and well put arguments for the saving grace which can flow from study of Asia by American undergraduates; anything I might say now would only be preaching to the already converted. The question is not whether Americans should study Asia, but how—the question of procedures, methods, tactics.

Let me, at the outset, propose an amendment of our topic. There is no such thing as *the* American undergraduate curriculum; one must use the noun in the plural. American higher education confounds, confuses, and occasionally edifies foreign students by its diversity and variety. Colleges and universities in this country come in all shapes, sizes, and previous conditions of servitude. Each has its own academic climate, its own curricular tradition. This being the case, Asian studies must be presented in each college in a way which harmonizes with the curriculum of that college. There are institutions in which the general education program consists of a set of broad interdisciplinary courses, courses constructed in brave defiance of the growing complexity and range of knowledge and in hope of distilling and conveying to undergraduates the essence of the human experience. In such curricula, it is natural to construct introductory courses in Asian studies along interdisciplinary lines, since here are faculty members experienced in developing and conducting courses of this sort. In this environment may emerge interdisciplinary courses, often taught by teams of instructors, which purpose to integrate all aspects of a single Asian culture or even to integrate all Asian cultures. Perhaps because I have tried to do this sort of thing and have not done it well, I have come to regard it as extremely difficult to do. It calls for remarkable teachers in effective cooperation, excellent teaching materials, and relatively mature, sophisticated students. Without these ingredients, it may degenerate into a process of poking predigested generalizations into the beaks of little birds. Observing some of the especially ambitious and comprehensive introductory courses in the Asian field, I have wondered whether they may not be unconscious reactions of our uneasy American academic conscience; we have in the past almost completely omitted the rest of the world from our curricula. Are we now tempted to repair our past sins of omission by administering the whole thing in one comprehensive dose, even at the risk of inducing acute cultural indigestion? An introductory course dealing with the history and cultural characteristics of Asia from Constantinople to Tokyo and from the Stone Age to Mao Tse-tung moves me to awe and dismay, but in most cases to more dismay than awe. I do not say it cannot be done—I have great respect for some of the people who are trying to do it—but I do feel that the odds are against it. My own inclination is to place such interdisciplinary, comprehensive courses relatively near the end of the college course, so that students can come to them as participants, not merely as recipients. In short, interdisciplinary, broadly paced courses in the Asian field flourish best in curricula where "interdisciplinarianism" is prevalent, and even there are apt to be more successful relatively near the end of the college course.

I myself am more accustomed to a more conservative, if you like "old-fashioned" curriculum—the kind which combines predestination and free will by requiring the student to undergo experience in certain broad areas of the curriculum but allowing him some choice of the particular experience. There is a requirement in the social studies, but it may be met by a course in economics, sociology, or political science. In this situation, the general education program is made up of a group of symptomatic rather than comprehensive experiences. Perhaps as the result of years spent in this sort of academic atmosphere, also perhaps because of the growing skepticism of age, I have come to feel that no single sort of course is the only or even the best introduction to Asian studies, suitable to be adopted by all colleges everywhere. In institutions with a relatively flexible and permissive curriculum allowing of student choice, various departments can develop courses to which students can have easy access at a relatively early stage, say the sophomore year, and which will give an effective introduction to another culture in terms of a particular discipline. Departments of art, philosophy, religion, sociology, anthropology, geography, political science, economics, and most particularly history may be the staging grounds of such courses if their personnel and general pattern of department offerings permit. After all of the discussion which we have had, "single-discipline" courses may sound pedestrian and unimaginative. It is my proposition that Asian studies can not be saved by interdisciplinary courses alone, and that a departmental course in one aspect of an Asian culture can set up great reverberations in the minds of a student and serve as a representative, initiatory experience which may lead him to the sort of self-scrutiny through knowledge of another culture which is perhaps the primary purpose of Asian studies in liberal education. Each college searches for a "tao," for a curriculum which will embody its ideal of liberal education. Students of Asian cultures, too, seek a "tao," a way by which Asian studies can become a living and significant part of American educational experience. I suspect that neither all colleges nor all Asianists will ever agree on the same way, but I see nothing wrong with this. The study of Asian culture is an immense, many-faceted enterprise and allows for many sorts of procedures and efforts.

Administratively, one thing is clear, whatever the nature of the particular curriculum of the institution involved, the introduction of Asiatic studies in any form, like the introduction of any other "new" subject, necessitates a review by the college as a whole and by many of its departments of its whole educational program. Such a review is imperative both for financial and for intellectual reasons. A new field of study means more books in the library, more members of the faculty—in short, more money. Even if a foundation launches the project with a grant, the grant runs out in three or five years and the college budget has to take over. Today, colleges are up against it financially; many are caught up in a process of raising money, expanding enrollments, increasing fees, practicing economies. In pushing their field today, Asianists are competing for dollars at a time when colleges are watching and counting dollars with special concern. Proposals to introduce or expand Asian studies raise formidable intellectual questions as well as financial ones. American college curricula tend to proliferate as new, worthy, beautiful, and true subjects come forward and are added to the existing already over-abundant repertory. Old courses never die; even when they are not given for several years, they lie in the catalogue dressed in brackets, awaiting resurrection. This won't do. Students spend only four years in undergraduate institutions, they "take" only so many of the "course-credit" packages in which we organize knowledge. Not only administrators but, even more, faculty members should set their faces against this sort of open door policy as well. If new things are to come in, something should go. Indeed, a highly beneficial by-product of the expansion of Asian studies in American colleges may well be an "agonizing reappraisal" by "Westernerists" of the habitual ways in which the college has been organizing and conducting the study of Western culture, which has in the past been almost the exclusive object of contemplation in American college curricula. Put more crudely, Asianists are or ought to be inviting Westernists to commit murder for their sake, by killing off some of their courses to make room for Asian studies. This may seem an unlikely sacrifice, contravening the fundamental human impulse of self-preservation. Nevertheless, I have become an optimist on this point. I have lived to see the faculty of a liberal arts college vote unanimous support for the development of Asian studies and to see appropriate departments survey their offerings and implement this vote by a reorganization of their course offerings. American academic attitudes toward the East are, like the East itself, not unchanging.

Whether Asianists should lobby for a college requirement in Asian studies is a delicate question, to which there may be answers varying with the curricular theories and structure of different institutions. In any case, one can always work for the inclusion in existing courses, wherever it is appropriate, of greater attention to Asian problems and materials. I am convinced that, at the present moment, Asian studies do not need required status to insure their development; they can make their way in the academic world under the free enterprise competitive system. Today, American undergraduates are certainly not intellectual isolationists; quite the contrary, they are almost too responsive to anything which is foreign, exotic, or international. They flock into courses on other cultures, other areas, other peoples. The reasons for the popularity of "Non-Western Studies" may not all be the right reasons, but, whatever the reasons, we are certainly experiencing a boom in Asiatic studies. Thirty years ago the standard reaction to my admission that I was teaching Chinese history was an expression compounded of surprise and pity and the question, "But does anyone want to study that?" Now, attitudes of college students, faculty members, administrators, and Americans in general toward the study of other cultures have become relatively warm and receptive; the climate has changed and Asian studies can hope to flourish. Asianists have lived through lean years; now come fat years, when the virtue which we shall most need to cultivate may well be humility.

Most of what I have had to say so far has been related to the role of Asiatic studies in liberal education in the large. How can it best function in the other pre-professional phase of American undergraduate education—the preliminary stage in the training of future specialists, of the people who will go on to graduate school in some aspect of Asian studies? Should there be an undergraduate major in, say, "Far Eastern Civilization"? My answer is a strong negative. Such majors almost inevitably are vague, diffuse, and paper thin, not to mention the problem of language competency in the areas with which we are concerned. Turn the proposition inside out and see how it looks. What value as a central, disciplinary experience would you put on a major in Western civilization in an Asiatic institution? It seems better that the student carry on a major program in one of the established disciplines, while bringing together as a "minor" a range of courses dealing with a single Asiatic culture from various points of view.

In the end, one must bring all of these discussions of the ideal things to do down to earth, to the hard question of who is going to do them. The arrangers of this conference have shown a sharp realization of this problem is bringing together Asianists and non-Asianists who would be willing to be part-time Asianists. American colleges are facing a shortage of qualified faculty members all across the board; this shortage is especially acute in the Asian field. American liberal arts colleges have had and will continue to have great difficulty in securing and keeping on their faculties high-powered specialists in Asian studies. After all, the members of the faculty of a liberal arts college are called on constantly to demonstrate the liberality of their education by being men or maids of all work within the discipline which they profess. I once coped with a teaching schedule which embraced (without too much enthusiasm) courses in general European history, Russian history, world history (for prospective high school teachers), historiography—and the history of Eastern Asia. Foundations and universities are now organizing special programs to help college teachers who have not been trained as Asian specialists to acquire the wherewithal for the giving of general undergraduate courses in this field. Short conferences of this sort, special summer institutes, and full years of study at major universities are available; better teaching materials are being provided. Are there other methods that can be used to increase the teaching force in the Asian field?

I am shy to mention local and personal experience; conferences of this character should not become testimonial meetings in which one person after another tells "how we do it in our college." Nevertheless, I believe that the four-college cooperative program in what we are rather infelicitously calling "Non-Western Studies" for lack of a more positive term may provide, in its general outlines at least, a useful model for other colleges similarly situated. The four institutions are Smith College, Amherst College, the University of Massachusetts, and Mount Holyoke College. They are within a radius of five and half miles of each other. In the past, each of them has had some interest in and had some courses in cultures other than our own. In 1959, they received a foundation grant (it is Ford whom we remember in our orisons) to develop studies in four areas— Eastern Asia, South and Southeast Asia, the Middle East, and Africa. Each institution provides at least one introductory course at the "200" or sophomore level in each of these areas, but not according to a standard formula agreed to by all four. Whether these courses are interdepartmental or departmental, whether in history, sociology, or art depends on the general character of its curriculum, the nature of the particular culture concerned, and the interests, skills, and time of its faculty members. Advanced courses in the four areas are open to students from all four institutions. We are now in the transportation business, having bought buses to move students around the circuit. The libraries of the four institutions are being expanded in these areas and more specialized materials are being bought for the four-college library, the so-called Hampshire Inter-Library Center. Faculty members are encouraged to use summers and leaves of absence in ways which will make them useful in this program. In making appointments, we are watching for relevant experiences and competences. Each year, we plan to import either a single visiting scholar or a team of experts to give a senior course and to confer with the members of the local faculties; last year, members of the Harvard Middle Eastern Center gave such a course; in 1961–62 we anticipate a senior course on the emerging nations of South and Southeast Asia given by a team from M.I.T. None of these four institutions offers "area majors"; we favor departmental majors with area minors. In cooperative programs, we see an answer not only to the problem of expanding Asiatic studies but also to other characteristic problems of liberal arts colleges. By cooperation, we can each enrich our curriculum without duplication and can "stretch" the usefulness of our faculty, with desirable results both financially and intellectually. Isolated small colleges cannot experiment with intercollegiate cooperation. But, for such colleges, the chief answer to the question of how to expand Asiatic studies may lie in the "retooling" of faculty members, so that the specialist in American history can also undertake a course in the history of the modern Far East and the political scientist can broaden his course in comparative government to include consideration of Asiatic political systems. The present and potential importance of Asiatic studies in American liberal education is tremendous; the present and future number of specialists, small; and Asianists welcome as valuable and trusted auxiliaries those specialists in other fields who, out of their interest and belief in the significance of Asian studies, are willing to prepare themselves to give introductory courses in the Asian field.

Soviet Approaches to Oriental Civilizations

GEORGE A. LENSEN

Professor of History, Florida State University;
spent spring semester of 1961 in the U.S.S.R.

In the Soviet Union as in the United States, the pace of Asian and African studies has quickened in recent years. But although Russian interest in the Far East antedates the founding of the United States and Russia has the advantage of a long line of distinguished Orientalists, the United States is ahead of the Soviet Union in the study of Oriental civilization.

The reasons are various:

Soviet universities are more exclusively centers of instruction than their American counterparts. Professors do write articles and books, but the bulk of research is carried on at "off-campus" institutes, such as the Institute of the Peoples of Asia, with the result that Soviet research is less directly related to the needs of the classroom teacher.

Soviet thinking in the social sciences is atrophied by the one and only permissible Marxist methodology, a new scholasticism which exercises logic to prove preconceived beliefs. Not only are events fitted into the scheme to the detriment of fact but also the stimulus of different approaches—the excitement and discoveries of the inquiring mind—are lost. The common American view that Soviet scholars merely pay lip-service in citations of Marx and Lenin is wishful thinking. Although some Soviet historians will admit privately that they "had to" make certain interpretations in print, more often than not Soviet authors, like their American colleagues, write what they sincerely believe to be true.

The best of Soviet scholarship is relegated to areas on the outer fringes of the Marxist "discipline," notably to philology, where the more original and independent minds seek shelter. In this respect, Asian studies are in a better position than the more tradition-bound and relatively fully explored European studies. There is need for the translation of Oriental sources, the compilation of bibliographies, and the like; and Soviet scholars excel where they can avoid historical interpretations. Significantly, seven out of the eleven departments which compose the Faculty or School of Asian Studies of Leningrad State University are philological (the departments of Chinese, Korean, Japanese, Mongolian, Turkic, Indian, Arabian, and Iranian philology); one is integrated (the department of African studies), and only three are history-centered (the departments of the history of the cultures of the Far East, the Near East, and the Ancient East). Of a total of seventy-eight faculty members listed for the School of Asian Studies in 1960, thirty-seven are classified as linguists, two as philologists, seventeen as specialists in literature, one as both a linguist and a specialist in literature, and only twenty-one as historians.

The systematic rewriting of history and the limited availability of non-Communist, not to mention anti-Communist, sources, give faculty and students an inadequate foundation for serious work. Even Soviet source material is not easily located in Soviet libraries. Generally, only the subject catalogues are open to the public. More extensive than their American equivalents, they are still quite incomplete. Alphabetical catalogues are closed to the public except for books published in recent years and even then the listing is selective. The extent to which the Soviet reader is conditioned at every step may be seen from this subject heading in the card catalogue of the celebrated Lenin Public Library in Moscow: "The American Policy of Aggression and World Domination. Preparation of a New World War." (It should be noted parenthetically that Soviet Orientalists, both professors and students, are friendly, if restrained, in their personal contact with foreign scholars. Obstacles to research are encountered on a non-academic administrative level, officials in Moscow ignoring requests for admission to archives.) The search for truth is not the primary object of Soviet research. All forms of endeavor are viewed as weapons in the class struggle.

Access to state archives is difficult even for Soviet citizens. All research, as indeed all forms of endeavor in the Soviet Union, are slowed down by endless red tape in securing authorization to see, use, copy, and publish various material. "To Whom It May Concern" letters are not in fashion. For every step of every process, letters of recommendation and approval must be obtained laboriously. It takes months to accomplish in the Soviet Union what can be completed in England or the United States in weeks, if not days.

Soviet students in the social sciences and humanities, generally speaking, lack the dedication and intellectual alertness popularly ascribed to them in the United States. They compare favorably with the average student at the average American university, but not with the Ivy League and institutions of similar caliber. It may be that the cream of the student body is skimmed by the physical sciences. It may be that the Marxist methodology is uninspiring. Whatever the causes may be, the ostentatious lack of attention paid by Soviet students in the classroom is remarkable.

The nature of Soviet Oriental studies is best described by the Russians themselves:

After the October revolution the character and direction of Oriental studies changes radically. The Soviet school of Oriental studies differs basically from bourgeois Oriental studies in its approach to subject matter, methodological foundations, political content and ideological level.

Soviet Oriental studies examine all historical events in the light of analysis of the relationship between classes and the struggle of the oppressed peoples for their social and national liberation. In their work Soviet Orientalists are guided by the Marxist-Leninist methodology and by the policy of the Communist Party of the Soviet Union in the national-colonial question. Soviet Oriental studies lean also on the numerous special analyses of the classical writers of Marxism-Leninism, which are devoted to the history of the countries of the peoples of the East, to the specific problems of their economics and politics. Soviet Oriental studies decisively put an end to the contrasting of West and East.

"For us there does not exist," S. F. Oldenburg wrote, "a division of countries into East and West, which are opposite to each other and are to be studied differently: the East entered our Union having equal rights with the West, and we study it with the same Marxist methodology with which we study the West. The class struggle took place and goes on in the East just as it does in the West. The history of the East gave the same structures as the history of the West." [1]

Contrast this with the steady search for new and better approaches and interpretations, the dynamics of learning, in American universities. While every Soviet student is worked into a prefabricated mind-shelter of Marxist dogma, general education programs in the United States confront American students with rival philosophies and theories to develop his critical thinking. To be sure, not all introductory courses, be they part of general education or not, are of equal merit; nor do all American students rise to the challenge. But, on the whole, American undergraduates receive a better intellectual preparation for advanced work on Asia and with it a deeper understanding of Oriental civilizations than do their counterparts in the Soviet Union.

The one advantage the Soviets have in the Oriental field lies not in training but in placement. Fairly assured of a job in their specialty, be it as interpreters, translators, members of a diplomatic or economic mission abroad, or as researchers or teachers, students are attracted even to "minor" Asian languages. Communist success in the world arena cannot be ascribed to the superiority of Soviet universities. It is due in part to the fuller employment of specialists at all levels in the foreign service.

[1] A. N. Kononov, "Vostochnyi fakul'tet Leningradskogo universiteta" (The Oriental Faculty of Leningrad University) in *Vostokovedenie v Leningradskom Universitete* (Oriental Studies in Leningrad University), No. 296 of the Scientific Papers of the Leningrad State University (issue No. 13 of the Series of Oriental Studies) (Leningrad, 1960), pp. 23–24.

Asian Studies in a
Canadian Undergraduate Program

W. A. C. H. DOBSON

Professor of Chinese, University of Toronto

I thought it might be a useful contribution to our discussion, if I take as my cue the remarks of Dean Cameron, and sketch for you a simple factual account of just how, and the extent to which Asian studies *have* been integrated into the undergraduate program of an institution with which I am familiar. For, however much we as scholars and, I hope, enthusiasts for our subject might indulge in the luxury of speculating on the place and extent, on the purpose and method of Asian studies in undergraduate education, we are confronted, as practical men, by concepts of education and with administrative structures already extant. It is within this framework that we must devise *possible* ways and means for integrating Asian studies. There is an infinite variety and a wide divergence of both aim and structure in our institutions; this has been illustrated frequently in our recent discussions. Clearly, we must content ourselves as often as not with the art of the possible rather than the achievement of the ideal. My illustration comes from a university in which Asian studies are comparatively new, in fact, have only been introduced in any serious way during the last ten years. Personally, I have had a hand in their introduction. In doing so, I have had to keep Mencius' remark constantly in mind. "On entering another state the Master first enquired of the prohibitions in force there, for without doing so, he would not presume to proceed further."

In the University of Toronto, undergraduate education in the Faculty of Arts and Science proceeds upon two levels. That of the General Course in which a student selects groups of subjects from several departments, and obtains a B.A. degree in three years. And that of the Honors Courses in which a student remains largely within one department, and takes an Honors B.A. in 4 years. These two routes march in parallel but are quite separate. The entrance requirements for each are different. Since entrance to either requires the completion of a Grade 13 or its equivalent, which in turn usually demands at least two foreign languages, we do not encounter some of the difficulties that were discussed earlier. I should say here that teaching is organized on a departmental basis, drawn along conventional disciplinary lines, and staff is recruited by one of the eighteen departments of the Faculty of Arts and Science. The primary emphasis is upon undergraduate education. Postgraduate work, though very extensive, is administered by committees drawn from the teaching personnel of these undergraduate departments.

Administratively speaking, Asian studies are represented in the University by two departments of the Faculty of Arts and Science: the Department of East Asiatic Studies and the Department of Islamic Studies. In devising the curricula of these two departments, three types of program have to be devised. First, a four year Honors course, taken largely within the department which has to correspond, in discipline and extent, with other Honors courses. Second, courses offered in the General Course, which correspond with the aims and objects of the General Course. And thirdly, postgraduate programs for the M.A. and Ph.D. which satisfy the requirements of the Graduate School. At all stages, these programs are subject to scrutiny and sanction by committees, which are not primarily composed of Asian specialists. In very broad terms, the Honors Course prescription must provide, largely within itself, a locally well-understood ideal of a liberal arts education, for which a single academic discipline must carry the main burden. The General Course, as its name implies, is in intention, closer in theory to that of general education which we have heard discussed at this symposium.

In the Department of East Asian Studies, the Honors Course, follows most closely the tried and true formula of the Department of Classics, that is to say, the primary emphasis is upon the reading, in the original classical Chinese, of set texts, in the exposition of which (classes being very small) a very wide variety of topics—philosophical, historical, literary, etc.—are dealt with. In the first year, the set texts are taken from the classical philosophers *Mencius, Micius,* and *Chuang-tzu;* in the second year, from the classical historians the *Tso Chuan,* the *Shih Chi, Han-Shu,* and *San Kuo Chih;* in the third year, from the poets Ts'ao Chih, Pao Chao, T'ao Yuan-ming, Tu Fu, Po Chu-yi, Li Po, and Su T'ung Po; and in the fourth year, from classical novels, modern novelists, essayists, and dramatists. This intensive reading is accompanied by more general courses on history, philosophy, religion, and literature. And, here, I should like to interpolate a more personal word. It is always, to me, a matter of very grave responsibility, when I am confronted with a pupil for whose education (and not just professional training) I am in so great measure responsible. And I take the pupil-tutor relationship very seriously, indeed. Always bearing in mind that after four years, it is as much my responsibility to see to his general education, as to ensure his professional efficiency. Here, I am reminded, of the matter raised so frequently during this conference, of the importance of the *person* of the teacher, no less than that of the content of the course.

In the general course, we offer introductory courses in the Religion and Philosophy of East Asia, the History of East Asia, and the Civilization of East Asia. The content and purpose of which are, I imagine, very close to the course in many American colleges. How far in all this are Asian studies integrated in the undergraduate program? As far as the Honors Course is concerned Asian studies are represented and can be chosen by students. As far as the general course is concerned, courses are available to students at large. I should say that they are as well-integrated as any other studies and as integrated as the system permits.

But Asian and African Studies are represented at a different level also. Recently, a Presidential Committee has been examining the possibility of including Asian and African studies within other departments, such as, history, anthropology, philosophy, and political economy. Some headway has already been made. Here such departments can, by making appointments of specialists within their discipline, include special studies in Asian and African subjects in the fourth year of their Honors Course. We hope thus to side-step the question of whether an area approach or a disciplinary approach is preferable, since we hope to have the best of both.

Finally, "Oriental studies," as they are conventionally conceived, should, in this program be ultimately self-liquidating. In the very long term, "Asian and African" will be subsumed within the general spectrum of the humanistic and social sciences. The Department of East Asiatic studies will then become a department of Language and Literature. We hope to see what Jacques Barzun calls the "object of contemplation" universal man in all his civilizatory complexity, and not just Western man as a projection of Universal Man. The *literae humaniores* of the twentieth century must be concerned with the whole of man, be he Western or Asian, and not preoccupied with that half-object of nineteenth-century humanism, Western man.

Part Six: Comments: The Organization
of Courses

The Self-Image Approach

KARL POTTER

Professor of Philosophy, University of Minnesota

I should like to propose a method of organizing an introductory course in Indian (or Chinese or Japanese) studies which avoids some of the difficulties which have been raised in these papers. The method may be characterized as the "self-image" approach to a civilization. Essentially, it involves an effort to see how the people of a given culture view themselves and their surroundings, rather than using the categories of any one discipline or of Western values in studying an Asian civilization.

It seems to me this kind of approach has a number of advantages. Here are a few that occur to me.

It encourages students to read materials written by members of the civilizations concerned in a sympathetic manner, with a feeling for what matters to the writer. A course dominated by the methodology of one or more disciplines of the usual academic variety tends to discount the assessment of the members of the culture being studied in favor of an assessment engendered by the particular perspective of the discipline or disciplines. It seems to me as important to understand how Asians think about things as to understand the political, economic, or historical patterns of their civilization.

It avoids undue emphasis on a particular discipline or disciplines without being interdisciplinary, multi-disciplinary, or undisciplined. The disciplinary categories which are taken for granted in the West do not always apply in Asia. For example, the distinction between philosophy and religion does not seem fruitful in the case of India;

again, an undue emphasis on industrial expansion, natural to economics, may result in distortion of the Asian picture (as Stephen Hay pointed out in discussing Lockwood's paper).

This approach can be used to illuminate, without duplicating, factual text materials prepared by Western scholars. Thus, for instance, in using A. L. Basham's *The Wonder That Was India,* a teacher may have his students read the text for the facts and use his lectures to attempt to characterize the Indian attitudes toward the events and processes discussed.

Lest it should be supposed that I am urging another Northropian overgeneralizing kind of approach, let me insist that an important part of the method I am suggesting consists in the teacher's emphasizing the differences among the people which he is discussing. Thus, in teaching on India, one would want to characterize not only the Brahman's point of view but that of the other classes as well; not only the point of view in modern times of the city-dweller but also that of the villager; not only the point of view of the Hindu but likewise that of the Moslem; and the like. In this way, the important cleavages within the society can be illuminated from the inside, by making the student understand what emphases and interests each sub-cultural group has.

The approach comprehends both static and diachronic accounts of a civilization. One can study the Indians' attitudes toward their contemporary events, as well as to those in their past and those in the future. For example, it is productive of great insight to study the traditional Indian idea of the degeneration of the cosmos; this is not, of course, the way a Western historian thinks about history, but it is no less relevant to understanding India for all that.

The disadvantages of this approach lie mainly in the undeniable fact that the student does not learn to *explain* the processes and events which he is learning about and does not learn to explain them, that is, according to the concepts of explanation assumed by the various disciplines. I do not believe this is a defect in an introductory course, since, if the approach I advocate is attractively done, it will lead students to take further work in disciplines concerned to explain Asian history, sociology, politics, and the like, where specialists can have their day. Nor is the type of course I envisage undisciplined (though, it is "no-disciplinary"), since rigorous care in accurately characterizing the viewpoints of the various classes of Asians being studied is necessary if the job is to be done well. The teacher will, to be sure, have to be up on the latest literature concerning his area— the present approach certainly does not condone laziness on his part. Nevertheless, the portion of the material which he will utilize in his lectures and discussions will not be tied to any discipline, though its origin in his awareness may be due to his study of some or several disciplinary approaches to his area.

It may be said that my approach stresses rationalizations at the expense of the truth. But, as long as the teacher teaches the truth about the Asians' rationalizations, the cause of truth will be served; what the critic really has in mind is that a no-disciplinary approach serves no purpose in terms of long-range reforms and values. But it is precisely because I doubt that we can assume that the long-range purposes and values of our academic disciplines necessarily match those of the Asians that I believe it is folly to try to understand them first in disciplinary terms.

One of the delegates to the present conference, an Asian himself, complained during discussion that there were too few facts and too much theory in what was going on. I suspect what he meant was that the representatives of the disciplines (history, economics, political science, etc.) were much more interested in their theories as applied to Asia than in Asia itself. I agree with the complaint.

Specialization for Teacher and Student

WILLIS D. WEATHERFORD

Professor of Economics, Swarthmore College

We have been asked to comment on the conference proceedings from the viewpoint of actual and practical teaching of Asian studies to undergraduates. I wish to present three simple but specific thoughts.

First, I would make the plea that every Asian studies curriculum offer an interdisciplinary course as an introduction to the Asian cultures included in the undergraduate program. Although I believe advanced work on Asia should be approached from within a single discipline, it seems to me that we should offer students an *introductory* course that cuts across the whole, or most of a culture, and is not wedded to the approach of a single discipline. Among our speakers this view was reflected in the remarks of Mr. Crane and Mr. Feis, and is implicit in the Columbia general education program.

I state this view for the following reasons. (1) It is important for as many undergraduates as possible to understand something of a culture outside their own. The average student has a difficult time equipping himself to comprehend the many facets of Western culture, and can spare the time for only one or two courses on other cultures. He simply will not take separate courses on Indian philosophy, literature, history and political institutions. I believe the best use of the limited opportunity to reach such a student is through an interdisciplinary approach to the many aspects of the culture in question. (2) The second reason for this view is that this interdisciplinary approach, at the introductory level, has a greater impact, and is more likely to arouse an interest for further knowledge.

At the large university, this approach is likely to involve a team of specialists in a coordinated effort as at Columbia. In the liberal arts college with fewer facilities, this may be done by one man who naturally stands primarily within one discipline, but has the interest and flexibility to stretch into at least some fields outside his own. I believe this is the pattern suggested by Mr. Wright. For example, in teaching an Introduction to India I find myself able, with some success, to grapple with problems of history, social structure, religion, political institutions, and economic development, but, through lack of competence, must omit completely the development of art and literature. Unlike Mr. Feis, I believe the course loses by this omission. Mr. Crane's paper has been most helpful by showing several alternative approaches to the study of Indian history.

A second problem involves the training of faculty to teach the rapidly expanding courses in the Asian field. My opinion is that this should be left to the graduate centers. As a stop-gap measure a number of colleges here represented have instituted on-campus and in-service training programs to quickly increase the available teachers with some knowledge of Asia. I speak from experience since I have been in one such program on China this past year.

A wisely guided program of faculty study on one-third released time is perhaps sufficient to enable faculty members to introduce appropriate illustrative material from some Asian culture *in already existing courses.* Although such a released time in-service training program is good, it is not enough. We found that continuing teaching duties usurped part of the time we should have put upon our own study of China. We felt that our time, and the Ford Foundation's money, would have been more profitably spent in releasing faculty full time for a more intensive study of Asian matters at a graduate center. The latter arrangement gives greater benefit for the time and money spent, since it is more flexible, and each person can pursue a program best suited to his own needs, rather than be forced to follow the same program with his colleagues from several disciplines.

The third matter about which I wish to comment relates to those students who wish to specialize in Asian studies, although they have not been the focus of our interest at this conference. At what stage should the study of Asian languages be introduced? Should it be left entirely to the graduate centers as in the past? Russian has crept into the curriculum of many colleges since the War and enrollment is rapidly growing. I venture that in a few decades Chinese will be in the place Russian occupies today. In this, probably educators will be led by events rather than being the initiators.

I certainly have no final answer, but would propose that while the study of the more exotic languages should be left to the graduate centers, it is time that a few liberal arts colleges introduce language (but not literature) instruction in a few of the more important languages such as Chinese, Hindi, and Arabic. One or more of these might be offered to upperclassmen who wish to specialize in those cultures.

Compromising on Coverage

ELLSWORTH C. CARLSON

Professor of History, Oberlin College

Despite the fact that we represent different disciplines and area interests, this meeting has seen, it seems to me, a rather surprising agreement on what the main issues are in thinking about the undergraduate, general education course on Asia. Again and again, the discussion has come back to a number of main foci: the question of course coverage; the value of the comparative method; the merits and limitations of interdisciplinary courses; the usefulness of emphasizing what have been variously called "regularities," "models," or "constructs"; the adequacy or inadequacy of the preparation of students for a worthwhile Asian course.

Discussion of these issues has been very stimulating and, I am sure, highly worthwhile. At the same time, I have had the uneasy feeling that sometimes we were talking about what we would do in a perfect world, or, at least, a large university world. In the situations in which many of us do our teaching, I suspect that many of the *either or* questions, that we have been talking about, have to be answered in *both and* terms. As we go about our teaching, our decisions are compromises between what we would like to do and the limiting circumstances in which we find ourselves. What I am saying is especially true, I think, for the teacher of the Asian course in a liberal arts college. I would like to develop my point with relation to several of the central issues that have taken much of the attention of this conference.

The question of coverage of the Asian course in a liberal arts college is one that has to be settled by compromise. It happens to be my own conviction that it is better to do a somewhat limited job with some thoroughness and depth than to do a broader one more superficially. My competence and interests, which make for teaching effectiveness, would lead me to want to offer a course on Chinese history very much like what Mr. Wright has proposed. But my decisions about what I should do have to take into account the fact that I do not have colleagues prepared to give courses on other areas of Asia. At Oberlin, we have students who come to college with rather strong interests in various parts of Asia, some of them with plans for future graduate study of these areas. There is, therefore, considerable pressure for me to enlarge the coverage of my Asian offering, and what I do represents a necessary compromise between what I believe I could do best and what the situation seems to demand. I emphasize the Chinese material but extend the coverage to other parts of Asia.

The question of relevance of the Asian course to contemporary problems is another that tends to be settled by compromise. This compromise is especially difficult for the historian, whose main interest and competence have to do with the recreation and understanding of the past. Even though he believes that a knowledge of the past contributes to understanding the present, as a historian, he must be on guard lest preoccupation with the present distorts his view of the past. In an ideal world most historians would probably choose to concentrate on the past—to deal with relationships within the past rather than on relationships between the past and present. But there are pressures to make the past relevant to the present, not just as a by-product but as a substantial aim of study. These pressures are several. It has been my experience that the desire to obtain an understanding of contemporary problems is an important factor bringing students into the Asian course, and there is pedagogical reason for exploiting this student motivation instead of frustrating it. And there is, of course, the fact that we do face very serious problems in Asia, and the teacher of the Asian course cannot escape concern that we prepare to solve them, no matter how much he would like to be able to advocate knowledge for knowledge's sake. My own particular compromise is as follows. At the beginning of my course I do survey some of our contemporary Asian problems, and I stress the importance of seeing them in historical perspective and of getting acquainted with the various elements of these problems by learning their history. But I go on to make the point that the contribution of history to our understanding of current problems will be enhanced, in the long run, if during the larger part of the course, we prepare to bring history to the present instead of letting the problems of the present dominate our view of Asian history. I believe very strongly that the introductory course on Asian history should come down to the present. I ordinarily devote about three weeks to post-World War II developments.

The question of the relative merits of disciplinary and interdisciplinary courses on Asia is, it seems to me, an example of a question which is almost inevitably answered in *both and,* rather than *either or,* terms. At Oberlin I have sole responsibility at present for our offerings on Asia, and my courses are offered within the history curriculum. I am convinced that the teacher of the Asian course must be competent in a discipline. I am, nevertheless, impressed with the extent to which it is desirable and possible for a teacher whose training is primarily within one discipline to make use, in the introductory Asian course, of the concepts and contributions of scholars in other disciplines. This is especially true, in my own experience, in the part of my course which deals with relatively recent developments in Asian history. What is primarily a history course becomes more interdisciplinary as the course reaches contemporary issues. When I think of the "interdisciplinary approach" in abstract terms, the difficulties seem frightening and almost insuperable. But in dealing with a particular subject matter—say, for example, the transformation of India under British influence—the barriers to interdisciplinary cooperation seem to disappear. I was quite startled recently to discover the similarity between the read-

ing list on modern India, which I give to my *history* students, and
the syllabus of a course on the "Social Structure of India" taught
by a sociologist in another institution.

Having said that the teacher of the Asian course in a liberal arts
college may have more difficult compromises to make than his more
fortunate colleagues in the university, I should, perhaps, add that in
some respects the liberal arts college teacher may also have some
advantages, and that he can turn some of his difficulties to advantage.

I suspect that it may be more possible in the small college, than
in the larger university, to control the extent to which students are
prepared to take the course on Asia. At Oberlin, the Asian course,
which is offered in the history department, can be elected only by
students who have had the introductory course on the history of
medieval and modern Europe; and it usually works out that by
the time the student has this history prerequisite, he has also had
courses in two of the social sciences. My own feeling is that there
are definite advantages to limiting admission to the Asian course in
this way. It is possible, for example, to contrast "Oriental Society"
and European feudalism with some assurance that "feudalism" is a
familiar concept. Students who have had introductory sociology and
economics courses are better prepared to discuss the Chinese family
system or Communist China's economic development than students
without such background. The obvious disadvantage of enforcing
a prerequisite is that it limits the enrollment in the Asian course,
but I prefer acceptance of this reduction of the number of souls to
be saved to foregoing the advantages of better preparation for the
course.

The likelihood that the teacher of the Asian course in a liberal
arts college will be called upon to teach non-Asian courses within
his discipline may be used as an example of a disadvantage which
can be turned to an advantage. For several years, I had to teach
sections of our introductory European history course. While this
was a handicap, in terms of possibilities for specialized scholarly
achievement in Asian history, it was not an unmixed disadvantage.

My acquaintance with the European course that my students have had prior to the Asian course has facilitated use of the comparative method. I am convinced that use of the comparative method need not degenerate into a listing of superficial similarities. Perhaps, its main value lies in bringing out the uniqueness of each of the things being compared. I believe that students do find it worthwhile to think about similarities and differences between the Confucian ideal of the "gentleman," or "complete man," and the Renaissance ideal of the "well rounded individual." I believe that it is instructive to consider the reasons why the outcome of the Cheng Ho maritime expeditions was so different from that of the Portuguese explorations begun by Prince Henry. In studying the failure of the Chinese republic, established after the 1911 revolution, it is helpful, I believe, to consider the differences between traditional European and Chinese institutions and the values which help to account for the difficulty of the Chinese in introducing Western democracy.

The Problem of Objectives

JACKSON H. BAILEY

Associate Professor of History, Earlham College

It would be nice to neatly tie up everything that has been said here and go away in a glow of sentimental satisfaction. Unfortunately, instead, I have to go back to my own institution to try and convey specific knowledge and appreciation of Chinese civilization to a group of undergraduate students. I can't say that I have solved the problems which I face; on the other hand I have been stimulated to rethink my approach and have received new ideas and been exposed to new interpretations which will be helpful to me as I go back. No doubt many of you, as I have, have said to yourselves, as we listened to one or more of the papers that have been given, "that's all very well, but my situation is different." Yet, we do have points of convergence and common problems with which to deal, and I think it can be helpful to have serious intellectual exchange on the methods and content of our approach. I have reacted to many of the statements of fact and opinion; but, rather than catalogue these reactions, I should like to speak briefly to three problems which I believe are crucial to all of us. These three problem areas as I see them are:

(1) The problem of objectives. We need to think clearly about what we want to accomplish with a specific course, and we need to be prepared to rethink periodically what our objectives are; because it is conceivable that they will change. We need to continue to question ourselves and each other about these objectives. I think this has been one of the values of our conference.

(2) I believe we have opened up a problem area in escalation. We need to have the courage of our convictions that we can produce growth in the students with whom we are dealing; that this growth can occur during the course, and we need to look for ways to elicit a response and to promote this growth.

(3) I think we have exposed a problem area in the interrelations and the interactions in the community of higher education as it deals with non-Western studies. I should like to say a few words about each of these problems and to ask that we think together what can we do to understand them better and to help each other in solving them. Perhaps, what I am saying is that we need to increase communication on these common problems. First, I am going to deal with the problem area of objectives. I am going to have the temerity to ask some questions and to suggest some possible responses to these questions. Why should we have Asian studies in the undergraduate curriculum? Let us be clear and as precise as possible, and let us be as individual as we need. Perhaps, each institution will have a slightly different answer or at least a different emphasis in this. I would suggest that we need to try to distinguish between primary objectives and secondary objectives. If I understand both graduate schools and colleges correctly, I believe that they do not want Asian specialists produced as undergraduates. This means that the primary objective that we are trying to define is non-Western studies in a liberal education. This must include attention to the intrinsic values of the non-Western traditions, the art, the literature, the philosophy. It is related to the comment that has been made a number of times that we need to stimulate students to know themselves and that one way to do this is to help them to understand an alien tradition, that, through the making of meaningful comparisons, they can achieve some understanding of their own culture. In addition to giving attention to intrinsic values, we are also, as a primary focus, attempting to produce educated citizens with a concern for the world beyond their own nation. This is a distinctive goal and a primary goal in liberal education.

To turn then to secondary goals, and I think we should say that these are not at all less important nor in any way illegitimate concerns, we find wide divergence. These will depend for their emphasis upon the particular institution. Among the possible secondary goals there are, for instance, a desire to train political science majors who can move on to have a specific influence in the development of American foreign policy. There are schools which want to provide pre-professional training in art, music, the social sciences, and area studies. In a particular institution, any one of these or a number of them may be an important objective, but it will, I think, remain secondary. It seems to me that primary and secondary objectives should be supplemental and reinforcing to each other and they should be a stimulant to further growth.

To turn now to the second problem area, that of escalation, I would like to say again, I believe we need the courage of our convictions. Our operation as teachers is not a one-way street in which we give out and the student absorbs. If it is effective, it elicits a response and this response should lead to growth on the part of the student. We have, at Earlham and Antioch, been striving to awaken our whole campus communities to an awareness of problems beyond Europe. If this effort is successful, then we shall be able to start with our students in any specific course from a higher base of general information. We can begin to assume some background knowledge of other parts of the world. We should expect and assume that this is going to happen and prepare to adjust our presentation of material to this growth. On the other hand, we have to take students as they are, as they come to us; therefore, we may need to make a start at a very elementary level. But we should, I think, push them as rapidly as possible toward sophistication, understanding, and appreciation at a level far above that of the introductory. Students may come to us mouthing such phrases as Asiatic hordes but surely they will leave us understanding that this is not a meaningful term, understanding even perhaps that the split between North and South in China is a very important cultural divergence and that one cannot talk even of Chinese society as a monolithic thing. Similarly, in dealing with Japan, a student may come knowing only the words geisha and being aware only of cherry blossoms as stereotypes to characterize Japan. But, surely, we can expect growth which will include an understanding of the sophistication and complexity of Japanese industry as represented in such a giant industrial complex as the Yawata Steelworks. And we can expect and push toward understanding and appreciation of Japanese poetry, Haiku for example, as an exquisite form of human artistic expression. As we are able to accomplish this process of growth, students will be forced to return to their own civilization to find out about Hobbes, Marxism, and William Blake, and in fact, we ourselves, will be stimulated to return to the study of our own culture and to begin to make comparative references. Much can be accomplished. Let us have the courage of our convictions.

Now to turn to the third problem area which I have suggested, that of interrelations and interaction within the academic community. Here, perhaps, I am treading on thin ice, but I believe we need to face frankly at least two facts, or I believe them to be facts. The first is that the big university centers tend and perhaps rightfully so to mistrust the spread of Asian studies into the undergraduate college and to fear the suggestion of devolvement of their introductory responsibilities upon the small college. Contrarily, the small colleges fear the commitment of the resources, time, and interest which may be required if they are even to start at the introductory level in non-Western studies. Moreover, they feel isolated and inadequate to deal effectively with these matters. Having faced these two situations, I think we must then light a candle. There must be communication and exchange, both formal and informal. The university programs which have brought faculty from small colleges for summer institutes and year-long study in non-Western areas (such as the Columbia-Harvard-Michigan-Indiana University programs) have made an important beginning in this exchange. I believe that conferences such as this one can also make a contribution. In addition, we need to have visits between people at the university centers and people in the undergraduate institutions and perhaps summer contacts as well. A start has been made in this. I believe we must push forward carefully and thoughtfully, remembering that familiarity can breed contempt and not respect for each other, but this is not necessary. So I suggest that we need to explore more thoroughly the problem of interrelation and interaction and relate this to our objectives. How can a small institution do an adequate, scholarly job on non-Western studies within the liberal arts context? I would say that a partial answer is that it cannot without help and advice from the large institutions; advice in the form of consultation, access to materials, information about on-going research, and debate in a friendly spirit between the two groups. If we can explore and open up avenues of communication, then perhaps we can reduce the fears of the big institutions regarding the possible debasement of the academic coin. Second, we can reduce the isolation of the small institution and its consequent feeling of inadequacy. Third, we can reduce to a manageable size the commitment necessary for the undergraduate institution. Fourth, we can reduce the sense of competition which may inhibit the development of non-Western studies. The devolvement of the role of presenting introductory material to the undergraduate level would allow the big center to do one of its real jobs to train specialists at the graduate level, to train linguists, to provide more monographic materials, and to provide bibliography. I suspect that until we push down to the high school level the sampling process and to the undergraduate level the introductory process, we shall not begin to meet the need for special training that only the graduate program can provide.

I believe that we need to address ourselves even more strenuously than we have to these three problem areas: the area of defining clearly and precisely our objectives, the area of meeting the rising student level of expectation and ability, and the area of the interrelation and interaction of the academic community.

Courses and Conferences

JOHN MESKILL

Assistant Professor of Chinese and Japanese, Barnard College

Convinced though the teacher of Asian subjects may be that the glory of education lies in the dialogue between him and his disciples searching for uncompromised truth, more often than not he probably comes to his course informed of the wishes of the committee on the curriculum and the attitudes of the chairman of his department, and he knows that he is less than free. In himself, poor thing, he is limited. He cannot really do justice to all the major civilizations of Asia—their histories, economic changes, psychological and social responses to the West, institutional eccentricities and correspondences, and spiritual centers—primarily not because it is impossible to do so but because he hardly knows Asia. He has been trained in knowledge of one civilization, one country, or one aspect of civilization which interests him and which he thinks he can teach. With luck, he also has a fair grasp of the development and characteristics of his own Western world. All these imperfections notwithstanding, however, he is a well-meaning man and wants to do the best he can. This is where I think a conference like the present one helps.

It is appropriate that a conference like ours that begins with questions should end with the same questions, for, in a rough way, they are, like scientific theories, aimed at suggesting policies more than final truths. No firm answers are possible or expected; the value of asking the questions lies in the exploring of them, not in answering them. Here, the analogy to science ends, however. Theoretical policies in the natural sciences may command a broad consensus, but the policies we can suggest compel only individuals. What emerges from our conference is not agreement but individual discovery. For myself, the discovery was what others interested in different disciplines and regions thought to be important questions in the study of Asian civilizations, impelling me to ask whether the same questions applied to my region. The opportunity to be educated in such matters is rare, it seems to me, and therefore precious. For many, I suspect, the fact that the conference asked what knowledge of Asian civilizations should be considered essential for any educated man was of itself a stimulation to the vocation of teaching. At least, one courteous guest remarked to me that in all his years as an economist he had never attended a conference centered upon the importance of teaching his subject. Most satisfying of all, the conference sought statements describing human experiences over great time and space, which might embrace much of the nature of civilization itself, and from study of which might come the wisdom we wish for our students.

Conference on
Oriental Civilizations
in General Education

COLUMBIA UNIVERSITY, SEPTEMBER 13 AND 14, 1961

First Session, Wednesday, September 13
CHAIRMAN: Wm. Theodore de Bary, Columbia University
"Chinese History in a Proper Perspective for Under-
graduates"
Arthur F. Wright, Yale University
Discussant: Albert Craig, Harvard University
"Indian History in a Proper Perspective for Under-
graduates"
Robert I. Crane, Duke University
Discussant: James T. C. Liu, Stanford University
"Some Problems in the Teaching of Oriental Civiliza-
tions"
(Special reference to Islamic History)
Charles Issawi, Columbia University
General Discussant: Hellmut Wilhelm, University of
Washington

Second Session, Wednesday, September 13
CHAIRMAN: President W. G. Cole, Lake Forest College
"The Spiritual Form of Oriental Civilizations"
Thomas Berry, St. John's University
Discussant: Charles O. Hucker, Oakland University
(Michigan)
"Ideas and the Power Structure"
Karl A. Wittfogel, University of Washington
Discussant: Ainslie T. Embree, Columbia University

Dinner Session, Wednesday, September 13
"The Integration of Asian Studies into the Undergraduate Curriculum"
Dean John G. Palfrey, Columbia College; Dean Meribeth Cameron, Mount Holyoke College; W. A. C. H. Dobson, University of Toronto; George A. Lensen, Florida State University

Fourth Session, Thursday, September 14
CHAIRMAN: Ardath Burks, Rutgers University
"Modern Far East and the Undergraduate"
Herbert Feis
Discussant: Vera M. Dean, New York University
"Asia's Significance for World Politics"
Harold D. Lasswell, Yale University
Discussant: J. C. Hurewitz, Columbia University

Fifth Session, Thursday, September 14 (Two Groups)
Group One
CHAIRMAN: George B. Cressy, Syracuse University
"Basic Economic Factors in the Study of Asian Civilizations"
William W. Lockwood, Princeton University
Discussant: Stephen N. Hay, University of Chicago
"Some Basic Geographical Factors in the Study of Asian Civilizations"
Theodore Herman, Colgate University
Discussant: John E. Brush, Rutgers University

Group Two
CHAIRMAN: R. K. Beardsley, University of Michigan
"Aspects of Japanese Society of Special Importance for an Oriental Civilizations Course"
Douglas G. Haring, Syracuse University
Discussant: Francis Hsu, Northwestern University
"Basic Problems in the Contemporary Transformation of Traditional Societies"
Daniel Lerner, Massachusetts Institute of Technology

Discussant: Richard D. Lambert, University of Pennsylvania

Dinner Session, Thursday, September 14
   Evaluation
CHAIRMAN: John Meskill, Barnard College
DISCUSSANTS: Ellsworth Carlson, Oberlin College; Jackson Bailey, Earlham College; Willis Weatherford, Swarthmore College; Stanley Spector, University of Washington

DATE DUE

MR 21 '85			